ALAN PATON

KNOCKING ON
THE DOOR

SHORTER WRITINGS

SELECTED AND EDITED BY

COLIN GARDNER

CHARLES SCRIBNER'S SONS / _NEW YORK_

To my wife, Anne,
and to David and Jonathan

Library of Congress Catalog Card Number 75-39502
ISBN 0-684-14429-8

Contents

Titles of poems, short stories and short play are in italics

iv

Introduction

This volume consists of pieces – poems, short stories, articles, speeches – which have not previously been collected into a volume. About a third of the items are published here for the first time; most of the remainder, having appeared in small journals or newspapers, had become almost inaccessible.

The pieces are arranged in chronological order (though it has not been possible in every case to specify an exact date), and they are divided into four sections to correspond with the four periods into which Alan Paton's life seems naturally to fall. Each section is preceded by a brief introduction which contains a biographical sketch and a list of the books upon which the author was working at the time.

This arrangement of the material enables the reader to get some sense of Alan Paton's development – as a writer, as a speaker, and as a thinker and sensitive observer in a number of different fields. It is interesting and valuable, for example, to recognise that the passionate concerns that have helped to make *Cry, the Beloved Country* famous grew to some extent from the professional and scientific interest in juvenile delinquency which is given eloquent expression in the last two articles in Part One. It is fascinating, to take another example, to compare the early piece on Roy Campbell with the recent one on the same subject. Every item has been included because of its intrinsic worth, but a few of those in Part One are perhaps even more valuable for what they point forward to than for what they are in themselves.

There is, however, another way in which the material in this volume may be viewed. In the Table of Contents the titles of articles, speeches and autobiographical pieces are printed in roman type, while the titles of poems, short stories and the short play are given in italics. The distinction between these two kinds of writing is clearly a crucial one: imaginative writing is less wedded to the temporal than what one might call 'discourse'; it is apt to be the expression of a richer, more intense awareness, and it evokes a somewhat fuller and more complex response – though, needless to say, the volume contains very many passages of 'discourse' which are of deep and lasting value. The distinction and at the same time the interplay between 'discourse' and imaginative writing are especially important and poignant in the case of Alan Paton's work. For more than a quarter of a century he has attempted, on and off, to move

vii

away from the world of action and discourse and to devote himself wholly to writing of an imaginative nature, but he has been pulled back again and again by his immediate concern for the society around him (and of course in South African society there are always very many things to be validly concerned about). Indeed, as I have already suggested, it was partly his direct involvement with a major social problem – during his years as principal of Diepkloof Reformatory – which created the moral, psychological and imaginative pressure out of which came the first full flowering of his powers in *Cry, the Beloved Country*. Moreover many of the themes of the 'discursive' pieces reappear, in a transmuted form, in the poems and short stories. Alan Paton discusses this tension within himself and within his writing in some of the autobiographical passages in this volume and, more indirectly, in several of the poems.

I make no attempt to offer an appreciation nor an evaluation of Alan Paton's writing. It is all deeply pondered and deeply felt, but at the same time it is direct and powerful: let it speak for itself.

Finally, two practical points. Where a poem or a short story first appeared in an anthology, the name of the anthology has not been given. At the end of the volume there is a Glossary of names and words likely to be unfamiliar to readers living outside South Africa.

COLIN GARDNER

Pietermaritzburg

PART ONE

1903-1948

Alan Paton was born in Pietermaritzburg and attended both school and university in that town. After graduating and paying a brief visit to England, he was for eleven years a science teacher in white high schools, first in Ixopo then in Pietermaritzburg. In 1935 he became principal of Diepkloof Reformatory (on the outskirts of Johannesburg), an institution for young Africans, aged 7 to 21. His experience at Diepkloof – where he introduced daring reforms – made him profoundly aware of the social and political problems of South Africa.

When the Second World War broke out, Alan Paton was refused permission to enlist. This permission was refused again at the time of the fall of Tobruk. Partly because of this frustration, and partly because he wished to strengthen his candidature for the South African Directorship of Prisons, he undertook a tour of prisons in Sweden, Britain, the United States and Canada. The two articles at the end of Part One resulted from that tour and his experiences at Diepkloof Reformatory. In 1946 and 1947, while on this study tour, he wrote the novel *Cry, the Beloved Country*, which appeared in 1948. In that year he resigned from Diepkloof Reformatory in order to devote his time to writing.

The reformatory was eventually closed down by Dr. H. F. Verwoerd in 1953 after he became Minister of Native Affairs. This was partly on ideological grounds, because the reformatory contained black boys of different races, and this was contrary to Dr. Verwoerd's theories of separate racial development. Dr. Verwoerd also had a strong animus against the modern reformatory methods introduced by the principal. He called the methods *'vertroeteling'* (cosseting, mollycoddling), and described the reformatory as a place where one said 'please and thank you to the black misters'.

[Pietermaritzburg, 22.9.1923. *Natal University College Magazine*, October 1923.]

Old Til

Olgan am I, first-born and noblest son of Til,
Emperor of far dominion sea to sea.
Olgan am I, praying that I may be
Father as kingly as mine own to me.
Olgan of the Blind Eyes, given by the gods
So that my vision might be kingly, and my will.

Othan am I, second and fairest son of Til,
Othan the Limbless, and so born to be,
For the all-seeing gods, then fearing me
Lest I should injure Olgan, that could see,
Gave me no limbs to injure; yea, ye gods,
I reck not, yet pray for my sire – he sorrows still.

Borsad am I, youngest and saddest son of Til,
Sad and made desolate beyond my years.
Borsad the Dumb, Borsad of the Maimed Ears,
Fit but for woman's sorrowing and tears.
Who made me thus? ah, I could tell, but dumb
Is tongue and heart and soul of me; all still.

Old Til am I, emperor from sea to sea,
Brother of that great king whom men called Til,
Which is my secret and my secret still.
For I was like to him, and he to me
That none knew us apart save only one,
His eldest Olgan, Olgan of the Blind Eyes,
Blind that he might not know the foul deed done.
But Til swore dying that his second son
Would venge him, but I tore him limb from limb,
Othan the Limbless, I am safe from him.

But when the infant Borsad waxed and grew
There waxed and grew some knowledge in his eyes,
Some inborn knowledge, some god-sent surmise,
So frighted me, that I whom men call wise,
Made Borsad dumb, Borsad of the Maimed Ears.
These thinking these god-given, thank the gods
And spend in praying all their empty years
While Old Til rules their empire sea to sea.

[*Natal University College Magazine*, May 1931.]

Roy Campbell

South Africa's poetic achievement is not considerable; and to say that Mr. Campbell's contribution is outstanding would not be to pay him a great compliment. But it is certain that his work is recognised outside our boundaries, and by more knowledgeable critics than our own. It is often his pleasure to ridicule our customs, and to pour uncouth and uncultured contempt on our traditions, but that may well be overlooked in the light of what he has achieved. We may pride ourselves that the South African influence is not lacking in his work, but he is not a national poet in the sense that many of his Dutch contemporaries are national poets. It is because of his very freedom from the taints of narrow nationalism that we are most justified in acclaiming him the first of African poets.

His vitality and his vividness are (till now) his outstanding characteristics; the criticism that his work overshadows the bagatelles of modern poets, that one of his lines contains more fire than many volumes of his contemporaries, exaggerates and therefore emphasises an undeniable truth. When he writes, in his fifth published line, of Earth, 'Her vast barbaric haunches, furred with trees', he gives us a foretaste of his mastery of simile. It might be said, and with caution, that no English poet has ever surpassed him in that particular art. Take two passages from *The Flaming Terrapin*:

> Slithering like quicksilver, pouring their black
> And liquid coils before his pounding feet.

and again:

> And gleaming serpents, shot with gold and pearl,
> Poured out, as softly as a smoke might curl,
> Their stealthy coils into that spectral light.

There is genius in the choice of words, a genius that is not conspicious in modern verse; in his stanzas 'To a Pet Cobra' one finds the same mastery. One does not read Mr. Campbell for peace and quiet; his own restlessness awakens restlessness in us, his similes explode in line after line, a series of startling detonations to which we cannot accustom ourselves. That I think is rightly regarded (till now) as his unique virtue. His love of the terms of electrical science is significant, his own 'coils are volted with electric power'. We are subjected to a succession of shocks, shaken out of our composure. It is no mean genius who can write a poem of the length of 'The Albatross', and throughout the whole maintain the violence of the hurricane, the splendour of the lightning that

> Crested the turrets of the storm, and plied
> His crackling whip with forkèd lash to scar
> Red weals across the gloom.

What Goddess of Aptness stirred him to write that the

> . . . top, whipped into frantic pain,
> Scribbles the dust . . . ?

Mr. Campbell is the most quotable poet alive, yet quotations are so often the picked fruit that make the uppermost layer, that to quote him in that spirit were to insult him. When one quotes from Mr. Campbell one offers a fragment of a mosaic that must be seen whole or not at all.

This in itself is not enough. Granted that his vividness is unique, we must yet remember that vividness is not the prime essential of poetry. But we should be doing Mr. Campbell an injustice were we to forget that vividness for him is not an end in itself. The simple truth is that he cannot write without being vivid. What as an end would be weakness is as a means his strength. His 'Theology of Bongwi' is vivid, but it is also perfection; it is a picture in which nothing has been left out, because there is nothing we can think of to put in. One does not wish of Mr. Campbell that he had written this in one way, and that in another; one accepts what he has written, and accepts it very often as perfection. 'The Serf' is perfect. 'The Zulu Girl' is perfect. We cannot criticise them, because they leave us room for no emotion other than that of admiration.

Mr. Campbell has a tendency to repetition; it is inevitable that one who has consciously or unconsciously so explored the possibilities of the English language should do so. But it might become a fault; we might grow sleepy over his somnambulists, drowse unconcerned through his voltages, fail to grasp the true import of his sometimes obscure hosannas. Yet that would not be to deny that he has given these words a richer meaning. Our modern poets have written of slums, cheap tin trays, and other common realities of life, and because it was a departure from the Victorian tradition we have often, probably half-heartedly and not too sure of our ground, disapproved. But Mr. Campbell has taken the words out of their mouths, and by his daring 'bracketed [their] purpose with the sun's'; he has given to words like 'bullets', 'wheels', 'squibs', a universal application. All life is grist to his mill – the cordite which he perhaps ate unawares at the Durban High School, the bore of a gun, the rotting whales at the Bluff. In his mouth they are more than the common realities of life; he spews them out over the universe, so that they return to him with a majesty not their own. Add to his vividness this truest characteristic of poetry, and understand why he was so instantly acclaimed.

One must note then that Mr. Campbell is concerned with the world of men only when he can turn its content to a universal purpose. With men and women themselves he has little traffic; if this is to be a permanent feature in his work, he will never join the ranks of what we might call the philosophic poets. But then we can well imagine Mr. Campbell turning up his nose at the philosophic poets, claiming that poetry is poetry and not philosophy. And he certainly is the man to make such a claim. It is significant that the town of Durban and the people of Durban have left little impress on his true poetry; it is doubly significant when we remember that Mr. Campbell's boyhood was spent there, and that Durban is for many people a town of romance. Nor have the people of South Africa left much impress upon his true poetry. It is at this point that we must take notice of what he *has* written about the people of Durban and South Africa, and some of it is venomous stuff. His picture of Smuts the philosopher, who undoes the trousers of the universe, must wring a smile from the most ardent S.A.P. man, but when Mr. Campbell writes of the vultures of Bull Hoek, he is below notice. His appended fragments to *Adamastor*, with the brilliant exception 'On Some South African Novelists', are so much waste paper. One could hardly imagine his writing a stirring ballad about Dick King's ride, a very seemly ambition for a Natal poet; he probably regards Dick King as several kinds of a fool for expending such an undue amount of energy on such an unworthy cause. But the ride itself would grip Mr. Campbell, not as a deed of derring-do, but as an opportunity of letting fly upon the world a fearsome nightmare of volted crocodiles and high-tension puff-adders. And Mr. Campbell would do it well, were it not for the necessity of ending such an electric adventure in the mundane aridness of Grahamstown. When Mr. Campbell refers to South Africa (in his true poetry), it is to a South Africa independent of the impudent intrusions of a Dutch East India Company or a few undesirable traders at the Point. He writes, for example, that

> . . . the grey sharks move,
> And the long lines of fire their fins would groove,

Seemed each a ghost that followed in its sleep
Those long phantasmal coffins of the deep.

None other than a Durban poet, accustomed to the Durban soil, would write that the serf grooves 'crimson furrows', or that 'in the sun the hot red acres smoulder'. But he is no provincial; he shows his nationality in his attachment to the desert and semi-desert outside his parish-pump. When he writes of South African things he is inspired with a fire that this country has never before known. When he writes of African people and their traditions (with the exception of its natives), he spits forth the venom of the snakes with whom he so often allies himself:

I too can hiss the hair of men erect
Because my lips are venomous with truth.

Under the influence of this evil spirit he often is unworthy of his name, and yet at times he can write:

The wind with foetid muzzle sniffed its feast,
The carrion town, that lulled its crowd to rest
Like the sprawled carcass of some giant beast
That hives the rustling larvae in its breast.

There is no danger – for us – that Mr. Campbell may lose that characteristically South African note; there is a danger – for him – that he may become confirmed in his rebellion, that, blinded by his superlative egoism, he may narrow his work to a venomous spitting of truth that leaves us unmoved. Mr. Campbell's development will be watched by many of his fellow South Africans, and it will be all the more interesting in that his future is an unknown quantity. One feels that his wild spirit may leave this wandering through the universe, and come to earth, though not to flute a leaky bagpipe with his nose. One hopes that he may overcome his unreasonable hatred of the traditions of the South African soil; he has proved himself universal and runs no risk in now becoming national. Yet if he writes nothing more, he will have made a contribution to English poetry that is unique.

[*Natal University College Magazine*, May 1931.]

The Hermit

I have barred the doors
Of the place where I bide,
I am old and afraid
Of the world outside.

How the poor souls cry
In the cold and the rain,
I have blocked my ears,
They shall call me in vain.

If I peer through the cracks
Hardly daring draw breath,
They are waiting there still
Patient as death.

The maimed and the sick
The tortured of soul,
Arms outstretched as if
I could help them be whole.

No shaft of the sun
My hiding shall find,
Go tell them outside
I am deaf, I am blind.

Who will drive them away,
Who will ease me my dread,
Who will shout to the fools
'He is dead! he is dead!'?

Sometimes they knock
At the place where I hide,
I am old, and afraid
Of the world outside.

Do they think, do they dream
I will open the door?
Let the world in
And know peace no more?

[Pietermaritzburg, 27.9.1931. Not previously published.]

Faith

I see with passing of the tragic years
Children made fatherless, mothers forgot
By those whose liberty was bought with theirs,
What time the Author of the shining spheres
Stands leagues aloof from their unhappy lot
Till He sends Death upon them unawares.

I see the tott'ring of man's house of faith.
They flee for refuge to their man-made law
Unwitting of its birth of their own lust.
A vain security that's but a wraith
Hiding a moment the red tooth and claw
That makes us beasts and chains us to the dust.

I hear the welling warmth of chants and creeds
Fashioned by men and hallowed by belief.
I hear the welling deepness of the notes
Of some cathedral organ. Wind in reeds,
The same our pagan sires on some wild reef
Heard and held captive in their pagan throats.

I hear the poignant valour of their hymns
To unknown Gods within their hallowed place,
Songs of despair sung on a darkling shore.
A torch of faith that spurts and wanes and dims
Casting its paleness on each wasted face
Leaving the darkness darker than before.

There comes to me a vision of the end
Distorted in the chaos of my mind
Fouling my sleep and catching at my breath.

Burn out my eyes, but pity will not send
That my imagination be as blind.
No hand can still it but the hand of death.

The suns glow redly in the universe,
And in the gloom the earth's miscegenates
Learn at their mothers' knees in nameless fright
How once before the coming of the Curse
The days were glitt'ring jewellery, and spates
Of yellow stars adorned the pall of night.

Legend is all that lives of peace and wars,
Men crash their murd'rous way for human food
Like carnivores through jungles of the past.
And ruined cities silent on the shores
Of dying seas, hive in their sewers the brood
Of man-faced rodents, Evolution's last.

I marvel in the foul faeces of Doom
That some kill not nor eat the flesh of man,
A dwindling brotherhood bound by their vow.
Whose children in this horror-pit of gloom
Reach manhood safely, even to the span
Of three and thirty years, man's measure now.

A dwindling brotherhood that men call Christ's,
Who travel unafraid the streets, and with
Curses and yells are murdered as they go.
And keep in some old ruin faithful trysts
Talking with shining faces of some myth
Someone who died a million years ago.

[Pietermaritzburg, 3.4.1932. Not previously published.]

Trilemma

I dreamt three students walked a road,
Nobly degreed and capped and gowned;
A humble labourer in a field
Close on the roadside tilled the ground.

One student wrapped in lofty thought
Passed by with neither sight nor sign.
I saw his face beneath the hood
And gaped bewildered – it was mine!

One student smelt the honest sweat,
Screwed up his nose in cold disdain.
I saw his face beneath the hood,
Gaped more bewildered – mine again!

One student leapt the roadside hedge
And tilled the ground without a word
Beside his mate – I saw his face,
This dream was growing more absurd!

But most absurd of all was me,
The real me, not the other three,
Going from hood to hood to see
Which of the three was really me!

[*Natal University College Magazine*, October 1934.]

Sonnet

There's no way carved yet, no applauding crowd
To watch my lonely figure in the mist,
Scaling the peaks I longed for. No clenched fist
Has struck the table of the world and cowed
Rapacious men. But head's a little bowed
And mind from dreams a little does desist,
And soul in prayer a little does persist,
And voice in argument's but half as loud.
Yet free my mind from dreams and soul from prayer
And I'd be rather dead than so alive
To find within myself so little there.
I'll yield the peaks if it be mine to strive
To reach some gentle summit amply trod
And stand more humbly in the sight of God.

[*Natal University College Magazine*, October 1934.]

Translation

From the Hindustani

Life was bitter, be that said,
So I prayed my God for a small knife.
For thus I reasoned, if I be dead,
What matter how bitter be life?

God was bitter, be that said,
For He sent me never a small knife.
He sent me a woman, a woman instead,
So what matter how bitter be life?

The woman was bitter, be that said,
So I prayed my God for a small knife.
For thus I reasoned, if she be dead,
What matter how bitter be life?

God was bitter, be that said,
For He sent me a knife, a small knife.
And now I'll hang till I be dead,
So what matter how bitter be life?

[An address delivered to the National Social Welfare Conference in September 1944. Penal Reform Series No. 2, S.A. Institute of Race Relations, 1945. (In the 1940s the words 'non-European' and 'Native' were not considered offensive, as they now are.)]

The Non-European Offender

You will have noted, Mr. Chairman, that both chairmen and speakers at this conference were reminded in black and white of the importance of bearing in mind the whole theme of the conference, which is the post-war planning of welfare work in South Africa. Addresses should, we were told, be blueprints for welfare work for the next decade or so. And indeed, there could be no better time for them; for there has never been such interest in and such concern about non-European delinquency and crime. This is partly the result of propaganda and education, partly the result of the effect of such crime on our own property and personal safety.

I am fortunate today in having received an offer of over £4 million to carry out the plans of this blueprint. This came from the second speaker at this discussion, Mr. Julius Lewin. It might be called a spiritual gift, for in the flesh he is quite incapable of producing such an amount. He chooses the figure of £4 million because it is the annual expenditure on police, courts and prisons, although he does not for one moment suggest that it is the non-European offender alone who makes this expenditure necessary. Nor does he suggest that the spending of £4 million on carrying out the blueprint will do away with the necessity of spending money on police, courts and prisons.

How are we to spend this £4 million which has so fortunately come to hand? We shall be able to answer more clearly if we first analyse briefly the causes of crime. The diagram [on page 16] will help.

It is right that the family should be in the centre of the diagram, because the family is the heart of the nation. But it is possible to draw superficial and dangerous conclusions from this. If a child is troublesome, and the family and its environment bad, it is easy to conclude that the mere removal of the child is the correct solution. This solution takes the form of (1) deportation, (2) transplantation, and (3) apprenticeship. If the child is a Zulu from Zululand, and is giving trouble in Durban, send him back to Zululand. Or again, send him right out of harm's way, say to the Bapedi country in the Northern Transvaal. (This is a hypothetical case and the

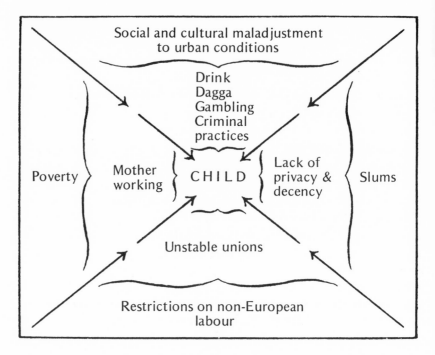

authorities in Durban are the least likely to use this method. But it is often used elsewhere.) Or lastly, apprentice him to a master. It is distressing to me that though these methods have proved almost invariably unsuccessful in the past, they are still cherished and practised by some of those who have the authority to do so. At Diepkloof Reformatory we are compelled in a small percentage of cases to use these methods, because the area which raised the delinquent refuses to have him back again. The resultant success is as near to nothing as matters. I say without hesitation that this solution should be discarded for ever; it is cruel, if not deliberately cruel, and wasteful beyond words. If the authorities who use these methods were to keep the scantiest records, they would not use them again. A bad home is not good, but it is better than no home at all. A Zulu child with Durban in his blood will not stay in Zululand; much less will he stay in the land of the Bapedi, and if he goes to a master, he may or may not go to a good one, but he almost never goes to one with whom he will stay. The result is in almost all cases abscondence and further offences.

It is not hard after a study of the diagram to see what a large number of families must inevitably produce delinquent children, nor to see how a non-delinquent child may still grow into a criminal under these conditions. And these are the conditions under which many non-European families produce children, and under which these children grow up. (This is of course equally true of many European families and their children.) I note in passing that not even a good home and a good family are exempt from the operation of these influences. A good home may produce, to its shame, bewilderment and grief, a delinquent child under these conditions.

Now the outer square contains the more profound causes of crime, and the inner square the less profound, though not in any way less important. I have omitted the most immediate causes, such as temptation and opportunity, passion, drunkenness and the like, because, for one thing, a diagram cannot do everything, and for another, temptation is more firmly met, passion more efficiently controlled and drunkenness less frequently resorted to, when the child or the man has clearer ideals, greater knowledge, a more secure existence, and an upbringing at the back of him.

I think that the diagram will make much clearer the reasons for the proposed allocations of the windfall of £4 million. Allocations have been made for three types of measures – the indirect preventive, the direct preventive and the direct curative.

INDIRECT PREVENTIVE £

Education	1,000,000	(To all this add: removal
Family allowances	1,000,000	of some of the restrictions
Housing	1,000,000	on non-European labour,
Community centres, with provision for boys' and girls' clubs, Pathfinders and Wayfarers, playgrounds, swimming baths, etc.		with consequent higher wages and expanded markets)
25 centres at £30,000 (two-thirds chargeable to the State)	500,000	
5 local courts	200,000	

DIRECT PREVENTIVE

Police (non-European) 750 at £200	150,000	
Probation officers (non-European) 400 at £250	100,000	(Probation officers should also come under the heading 'Direct Curative')

DIRECT CURATIVE

Prisons and reformatories training institution	C	50,000	(C– Capital
			R– Running expenses)
100 students (1st year), and 100 students (2nd year), at £100	R	20,000	
Compulsory labour centres	C	60,000	
	R	15,000	
Three experimental prisons for amenables	C	200,000	
	R	40,000	
Five Lads' Hostels	C	20,000	(At present these are
	R	5,000	heavily subsidised by the Department of Social Welfare)
One additional Coloured reformatory and reformatory hostels	C	50,000	(Very much like industrial schools)
	R	20,000	
Two additional Bantu reformatories and reformatory hostels	C	100,000	
	R	40,000	
		£4,570,000	
Research		10,000	
		£4,580,000	

You will have observed that I have overspent Mr. Lewin's gift by £580,000. He tells me that this does not matter, for this is exactly what he hopes to save on the Justice Vote during the first year that the blueprint is put into operation. You will also observe that indirect preventive measures take £3,700,000 of the £4,580,000 available, i.e. 80 per cent of the total.

In my budget I have provided for five local courts. In my opinion the centralisation of courts as in Ferreirastown, Johannesburg, is a mistake. If we are going to strengthen the home and the community by spending £3½ million on them, then the court, which upholds the law of the land

and the opinion of its people, should be situated in the community confines. The greatest bulwark of the law is the opinion of the people, and we propose to spend millions to create and mould that opinion. Let us then subject the offender to the whole weight of public disapproval, and not only to the disapproval of the court itself. If the man robs and does grievous bodily harm in Orlando, let him face the court in Orlando; he will then have to face the people he has harmed, the members of his own community. The value of this deterrent is immense. For the same reason let us stop planning vast locations: the more intimate the community the more deeply felt the disapproval.

And now for the direct preventive measures. I have budgeted for 750 non-European police at £200. This £200 will include salary and other expenses. I suggest no scale, as I do not want to divert attention from the main proposal. But the day of the raw but reliable Zulu is past. It should be possible to recruit men with some education, used to urban life and understanding urban conditions. It is obvious to me that such a trained force of non-Europeans could do things that the most efficient European cannot do. It will be possible to discard or soften the pick-up-van method, for there are two reasons – amongst others – for its use. It gets a white policeman swiftly to his objective, cutting short time for warning; and it provides a measure of safety from threatening crowds. A non-European policeman would not need the same assistance or the same protection. There is no estimating the advantages to be gained from a large increase in and improvement of the non-European police establishment. Another advantage would be the lessening – to some degree – of antagonism between police and people.

A large number of these recruits would go to the C.I.D. Here again the advantages would be immense. I must here say something important about detection as a means of controlling crime. The most important control is public disapproval. The second is efficient detection; while severer punishment and stricter laws come third, and a very bad third too. Of all the direct controls of crime efficient detection has no equal. If every criminal were brought to justice, crime would not disappear, but it would decline sharply. I do not disguise the fact that increased expenditure on detection is a sign of grave defect in society; but in our society such money would be well spent.

We then proceed to an expenditure of £250 per head on 400 non-European probation officers. This measure is curative as well as preventive. Here again I do not discuss scales; the £250 includes salary and other expenses. Supervision of delinquents released from reformatories or placed under probation officers by the courts is difficult enough; but when the delinquents are Africans, and the probation officers Europeans, the difficulties are very much increased. Evening work is almost impossible, investigations are superficial, and the essential bond between boy and officer is weak indeed. The number of relapses amongst supervision cases would drop appreciably if non-Europeans were recruited for this important work.

We may now turn to the direct curative methods. It will be necessary to justify compulsory labour centres, experimental prisons for amenable prisoners, and a prisons and reformatories training institution. That veteran in the fight for penal reform, the Hon. F. E. T. Krause, has for years urged the reform of our prison system, and the relegation of the idea of punishment to the background where it belongs, and the substitution for it of the two ideas of the reform of the offender, and the protection of society. If we accept as sound the idea that committal to an institution, be it gaol or reformatory or hostel, is for the purpose of treatment and protection, then short-term imprisonment has no justification, for it affords no time for treatment and no kind of protection. For these reasons it should be abolished. We must first decide then whether an offender needs institutional treatment or not. If he does, then he must go to an institution for a minimum period, and there would not be much purpose in making this period less than twelve months. If he does not need institutional treatment, but if his offence is such that the public interest would not be served by the imposition of a fine, or by placing on probation, or such other measure, then he should be ordered to report at a compulsory labour centre. I do not suggest a large number of these, for they are admittedly experimental, and I suspect that they would be extremely difficult undertakings in their early stages. There would be malingering, absenteeism and abscondence, and it would be easy to lose heart and to revert to the old short-term imprisonment. But they should be tried, and in the right hands the right atmosphere would be created, the right methods would be found. I do not suggest how many there should be, because a small centre serving a compact community might be found far more effective than a large centre serving a greater area. All these things we must discover, and it is urgent to discover them, because thousands upon thousands of Africans go to prison for offences which do not justify imprisonment.

The more serious offenders would go to institutions. Any modern penal reformer would pick out for separate treatment those offenders who need a relatively short period of treatment, in other words the amenable offenders. This term 'amenable' does not necessarily mean 'first offender', though many first offenders are amenable.

Quite apart from psychological and psychiatrical treatment, there is one very simple method of treatment which in South Africa is not applied at all but which should be applied to all amenable offenders. This is quite simply to make a community of the offenders, to increase with passage of time the freedom they enjoy, the responsibilities they shoulder, the privileges they earn, the temptations they encounter, till they are ready to return to society under the supervision of officers attached to the staff of the institution. This is moral education, and it is what they will need most. And alongside of it will be such vocational and other education as in process of time will be found valuable.

I cannot stress enough the importance of this moral education. Inside the institution one says nothing to the offender of the shortcomings of society; one is concerned only with his shortcomings. He is made to feel – however confused may be our own minds – that he is responsible for his actions, and that temptation must be resisted by the good man. His upward progress is made visible by the according of privileges and responsibilities; for the first time maybe in his life he undergoes the remedial experience of public recognition and approval. Privileges and responsibilities are given in public, and he affirms publicly his receipt of them and his determination to deserve them. Offenders, wise though they may be in the ways of the world, are children in their desire to win approval, and who knows but that here one has stumbled upon the deepest hunger of all mankind – to count for something in the eyes of one's neighbours. It should be clear that, however moving this picture of a programme may be, the programme is based on scientific and not sentimental considerations. The prison for amenable offenders would be strict, not soft and directionless. Rebuke would be stern, disgrace not unknown. But once accorded, they would be done with, and the patient work of rebuilding and re-education would be immediately renewed.

I have no doubts of this prison as I have of the compulsory labour centre. It can be done. Half of its prisoners would be free, helping unconsciously in the work of moral rehabilitation. Many of the free would go to live in open buildings outside the prison walls. These three experimental prisons would be near the three large cities of South Africa, Johannesburg, Durban and Cape Town. The final stage of freedom would be to go to work in the town and to return to the open building at night, or to live in the town, all under the supervision of the prison probation staff.

These experimental prisons need not be grim and austere. They should be reasonably safe, but they need not be fortresses. Half of the prisoners are free, and that is a guarantee against riot and rebellion. What of the man who consistently fails to respond to such treatment? It is clear to me that no human power is ever likely to reform him, and if he is a danger to society, the sooner he is removed to a fortress the better. But even there he should be able to lead some sort of human life. I add that the Prisons Regulations must be re-written for such experimental prisons; for under the present regulations the creation of such a remedial community is utterly impossible.

For such prisons I put £200,000 and £40,000 on the estimates. And I put a further sum of £50,000 for the training of staff to run them. If the training institutions and the experimental prisons are successful, further reform of the penal system will be hard upon their heels.

For non-European children there are some six or seven pre-reformatory hostels. I place money for five more on the estimates, but I would insist that school-going children and working children should be housed in separate hostels. Such hostels are run by private endeavour, but are heavily subsidised by the Social Welfare Department. They are invaluable in the treatment of children who do not need the stricter methods of the reformatory.

I place £50,000 and £20,000 for one more Coloured reformatory with reformatory hostels situated in the adjacent town, in which reformatory boys would complete the last lap of reformatory treatment while working in the town. Any present-day South African reformatory would do much better work if 20 per cent of its more mature pupils were removed from the top, and 20 per cent of its more amenable and younger pupils were removed from the bottom. But the most important thing is to remove those at the top. This money is for that purpose.

I place £100,000 and £40,000 on the estimates for two similar reformatories for Native children. There are 550 boys at Diepkloof, and 110 should be taken from the top and 110 from the bottom. These latter 110, boys of 10 to 15 years of age, should be retained longer and would soon therefore increase to, say, 165. Such a reformatory could be controlled by the wink of the eye of a good Principal.

I have made no provision for Youth Brigades, on the lines of the Special Service Battalion. But given the guarantee that these Brigades will lead somewhere, Mr. Lewin will provide the money tomorrow. It is no use dressing people up, and giving them nowhere to go.

I have now exhausted Mr. Lewin's gift, but I add one further item of £10,000 for research. I am sure no one will grudge it. It is an extraordinary thing that our country spends so much on the control and cure of crime, and never examines the results of its methods. Well, this is a beginning.

That is my blueprint, Mr. Chairman. If we fail to carry out indirect **preventive measures, we shall** have to spend more and more on direct preventive and direct curative measures. But each extra £ of this money will have less and less purchasing power. More and more sweeping measures will have to be taken, all less and less effective; more and more money buying less and less.

But ultimately, Mr. Chairman, it is not money and expenditure that will buy us immunity from crime and criminals. Just as a prison will become quieter and more controllable as it grants significance to its prisoners, so will society become quieter and more controllable as it grants significance to its members. Significance is more than mere social and economic independence; it implies a mutual relationship, and give and take. And as man is freed to give his talents, his brains, his vigour, to his country, so less and less will he be attracted by evil. If a man is not free to fulfil his nature, then he will defile his nature. This is the dilemma of European South Africa, that it is afraid to let men defile their natures, and equally afraid to let them fulfil them. It is courage, even more than money, that we need.

[*Common Sense*, July 1946.]

This is my own, my native land

South Africa, land of my birth, and land of my children's birth. South Africa, part of the black continent into which my forebears came seeking a home and a future. They introduced some Indians for their convenience, and with the forebears of the Afrikaners conquered the black men, created a coloured people, and found some Jews in their company, so making a country which is interesting, exciting, depressing, frightening. To make things worse my forebears went to war with the forebears of the Afrikaners, on account of natives and mineral riches and general cussedness, adding thus a further racial tension to a collection which was of already satisfactory comprehensiveness.

This is my country, in which I must find myself, and a very hard thing it is to do. I found it easiest to harbour no hatred or fear or suspicion or contempt of the Jews; that was the result of home upbringing. But while my home was tolerantly inclined towards natives, a typical urban Natal trait, it was on its guard against Indians and Afrikaners, about which latter its knowledge was almost exactly nil. In fact they and all their friends still say 'Of course she's Afrikaans', a phrase pregnant with meaning; whereas I have learnt to say 'She's an Afrikaner' without any 'of course' about it.

Indeed I may boast that this was my first victory. I learned Afrikaans, and although I speak English better, I have a trick of accent which makes it difficult for all but the discerning to find me out. I even attended the great Voortrekker Celebrations in 1938 and, armed with a beard, heard truths (and untruths) about my forebears and contemporaries, which would have made the first turn in their graves and the second riot in the streets. Some I listened to while under the shower, and I commend this method to both my English and Afrikaans-speaking friends. I have in fact, without changing fundamentally my political views, overcome entirely any fears, suspicion or hatred of Afrikaners, and have come to hold those I know in deep and abiding affection.

Eleven years in Johannesburg have done much to remove my remaining fears and suspicions, that is, of Africans, Indians and coloured people. In this however I do not pretend to have progressed so far as along the Afrikaner road. The fear and bewilderment are more deep-seated, and yield more reluctantly to the promptings of reason and morality. But I do claim to be in a fairly favourable position to look intelligently on the South African scene, and to write something about it which may appropriately be accepted by the periodical called *Common Sense*.

In the first place I believe that English–Afrikaner tensions are yielding slowly to time, sense and place. I believe for example that the fiery protestations of past Afrikaners are losing their power to inflame vigour; that concentration camps, Boer Wars, persecutions of Afrikaans and Afrikaners, are losing their power to influence. They were inflammatory only while they had fuel to feed them, and today there is little. I have served under Afrikaner chiefs for most of my professional life; the Union has never had a Prime Minister that was not an Afrikaner; and the *Transvaler* has lately admitted that the language struggle hasn't much left to struggle for, a result for which it is in no small measure responsible.

All this means that the Afrikaner sense of inferiority, which in the past has been responsible for its fair share of hostility, is on the decline. It was partly born of military defeat, but that is being slowly forgotten, and what is more, it is foolish anyway to go on feeling inferior because your small nation was quite gloriously defeated by a big one. It is still kept alive however by the initial maladjustments of the Afrikaner to urban and industrial life. As these disappear, so will the sense of inferiority disappear. I have been privileged to watch the development of a large group of young, energetic Afrikaners at Diepkloof Reformatory, doing well in their profession; and I have seen hostility, suspicion and fear disappear, for the quite simple reason that there was nothing real for them to feed upon. I venture then the objective conclusion that one of the supports of extreme Nationalism is crumbling.

With these things in mind, I am sometimes surprised by the gloom and uncertainty with which some of my English-speaking contemporaries move through a world in which I am so much at home. For they also suffer from a sense of inferiority. This I ascribe to two things, one that they are numerically in the minority, two that they are not bilingual. If they were bilingual, they would soon learn the truth of General Pienaar's recent pronouncement that the differences between Afrikaans- and English-speaking people are less profound than most people suppose. Some of my contemporaries still believe that Afrikaners are an alien, brooding and dangerous race; they cloak this fear by beating their chests and their drums, and laughing because two Afrikaans translators don't produce identical versions of an English original.

These contemporaries of mine are at bottom afraid of an Afrikaner bloc. It is interesting to examine this fear. It is largely the fear of unilingual people who can't, because of their disability, see Afrikaners as individuals. In my view there is only one possible foundation for an Afrikaner bloc; all other possible foundations have been destroyed by time, sense and the growing Afrikaner confidence in their ability to adapt. The one possible foundation is a common Afrikaner resolve to resist all non-European advance.

Here my own group of young Afrikaners cannot so safely be taken as a guide. For they, working in an institution for young native delinquents, have been compelled by the sheer logic of fact to recognise the forces that are on the one hand destroying the old Bantu society, and on the other hand hindering the growth of the new. And filled with a sense of vocation that liberates a man from his fears and sets free a host of constructive ideas and impulses, they have to a great extent broken through the crust of uninformed group opinion, which I may add is a more difficult thing for an Afrikaner than for an English-speaking South African to do. I am not of course suggesting that they have in the process ceased to be true Afrikaners, nor that there is no return, especially at a time of crisis, along the road that they have come.

Is a true Afrikaner one who resists utterly all non-European advance? It would be fair to say that there are large numbers of Afrikaners, and of English-speaking South Africans, who believe this to be so. Yet it cannot be accepted, for acceptance implies that the true Afrikaner, unlike other races, is deaf to the promptings of reason and morality. The world is obviously a changing world, and world opinion has never been so sensitive to the rights of minorities and voiceless majorities. The Afrikaner who intelligently understands his own development and who knows how conquest confirmed him in his own struggle, clearly – and probably very painfully – sees the inevitability of a similar non-European struggle. He sees clearly too, for no one today follows international events more thoughtfully, that world opinion hardens against attempts at repression. If he is very intelligent, he realises that unresolved national conflicts lead to war on the grand scale. And he is usually well-informed, for he reads both the *Transvaler* and the *Star*, finding often, no doubt, that truth is no stranger than fiction.

The Afrikaner intellectual is forced too, on moral grounds, to re-examine such consoling phrases as 'hewer of wood and drawer of water', and to compare the contention that God made the races different with its shaky corollary of white domination. I think that one may expect that Afrikaner religion, which is inevitably and quite understandably shot through and through with extreme nationalism, will be progressively purified as the supports of extreme nationalism crumble; and that there will be more and more searching Christian examination of the view that it is right to secure one's advance by denying advance to others, as well as more searching intellectual examination of the view that such a programme is possible at all.

The great fear of all Europeans is, of course, not the Afrikaner bloc on the one side or the mighty English culture on the other, but the non-European bloc. If you give the non-Europeans rights and power, and assist their advance, what will they do to you when they get them? It is a more real danger, for non-European nationalism is likely to be more extreme and vengeful than Afrikaner nationalism ever was. I have been forced into what for me is a strange position; I have become a convinced adherent of the British Commonwealth of Nations, after passing through a period, not exactly of republicanism, but of sensitiveness about the 'Land of Hope and Glory'. I passed through this phase partly because I was ashamed of the Boer War, and partly because I thought – wrongly I find – that the only way really to understand the Afrikaner was to acquire some of his grievances. Now however, having become a determined believer in opportunity for non-Europeans, equally determined that this should not be at the expense of any other human beings, I find that the only guarantee of rights for all is membership of a larger body that cannot tolerate, because of its nature, injustice towards any man; I am indeed convinced that the British Commonwealth, or any other international body that may succeed it, is the only guarantee of Afrikaner continuance. I offer this singular conclusion, which is not as far as I know the child of repressed wishes, to my Afrikaner friends, for their thoughtful or derisive consideration.

The ultimate question – the practical, not the moral question – is simple to state: Is it possible to prevent non-European advance? There are many who think that it is perfectly possible, provided that we are not afraid of our destiny as a Herrenvolk. There are many again, I for one, who think it quite impossible. Among these latter are many Nationalists, with lively memories of their own struggle, but who have not yet found courage nor themselves sufficiently to speak this particular truth. It is for their emancipation that I thirst as a hart after the water-brooks; for who can better guide us in this land of fears and hates than those who have conquered their own?

Even were we to accept the view that it is impossible to prevent non-European advance, there is none of us able to predict the course or the results of such advance. That however is far less important than to start fashioning in our minds the picture of a South Africa in which the fruits of the earth and of man's long political struggle are available to all with malice towards none. To my mind there are only two other courses, one is to leave South Africa as soon as convenient, the other is to assert our divine destiny, until we are blown, President and storm-troopers and all, to Kingdom Come.

The Prison House

I ran from the prison house but they captured me
And he met me there at the door with a face of doom
And motioned me to go to his private room
And he took my rank from me, and gave me the hell
Of his tongue, and ordered me to the runaway cell
With the chains and the walls, and the long night days, and
    the gloom.

And once on leave that goes to the well-behaved
I jumped in fright from the very brothel bed
And through the midnight streets like a mad thing fled
Sobbing with fear lest the door be closed on me
And in silence he let me pass, he let me be,
No word but your clothing's disarranged, he said.

And once in a place where I was, I told a man
Whence I was come, and who was in charge, and he
Said God, but I never thought in my life to see
A man from that place, and I wish to God I was there,
Yes, I wish I was there. So I went back on air
And he smiled at me at the door, he smiled at me.

And once when he drew the blood from my rebel flesh
With foul and magnificent words I cursed and reviled
His name and his house and his works, and drunk with my
    pain and wild
I seized the whip from his hands and slashed him again
And again and again, and made him pay for my pain,
Till I fell at his feet and wept on the stone like a child.

He can take the hide from my back, the sight from my eyes,
The lust of my loins and the sounds of the earth from me,
Fruit's taste, and the scent of the flowers and the salt of the sea,
The thoughts of the mind, and the words of music and fire
That comforted me, so long as he does not require
These chains that now are become as garments to me.

[1947. Penal Reform Pamphlets No. 2, Penal Reform League of South Africa, 1948.]

Freedom as a Reformatory Instrument

I was privileged to spend some eight months in visiting prisons and correctional schools in Sweden, England, some of the states of the U.S.A., and the Province of Ontario in Canada. All of these countries have accepted wholeheartedly the view that the duty of society towards delinquent children is one of re-education, just as we have accepted it in South Africa. In this field therefore, one travels to learn refinement and improvement of methods already established.

But in the field of adult delinquency a very different position obtains, for we are none of us clear as to our objectives. We hold simultaneously several theories in regard to adult treatment. The purpose of such treatment may be to punish and deter and to teach that crime does not pay; or we may hold that the protection of society is our main objective, and this may – or may not – lead us to place the main emphasis on safe custody; or we may come out boldly and regard re-education as our main purpose.

It is clear that it is difficult to reconcile these divergent aims. Bernard Shaw regards punishment and re-education as totally incompatible; and too great an emphasis on safe custody may well take the heart out of any educational programme. This dilemma is everywhere apparent, and the modern attempt at synthesis is to regard the protection of society as the primary aim, and within the limits thus set to achieve as far as possible the secondary aims. This seems the most satisfactory solution, and from a practical point of view it is the only thing to do.

It has, however, one important result. Inevitably we tend to discard punishment, and even deterrence, as a deliberate aim. We assume more and more that what punishment there is will be incidental; we regard deprivation of liberty as the inevitable accompaniment of a method which in fact has quite another aim. We are, however, more reluctant to discard deterrence; we like to feel that outraged society, through the penal instrument, upholds the law and discourages wrong-doing. I do not think we need relinquish this proposition entirely; being sent to prison will still remain an unattractive, painful and even unthinkable prospect for most people. But I think we must relinquish the proposition in so far as it proposed that the prison itself must carry out an active attempt at deterrence. In other words, let the prison deter those who walk outside it; but for those inside it let it concentrate rather on the redemptive and reformatory possibilities.

But even this definition of function does not clear away all dilemma. For the protection of society and the re-education of the offender are not so easily reconciled. One of the means of protection is safe custody, and one of the means of re-education is physical freedom. It was in fact my interest in this very dilemma that prompted me to undertake my visits, and it was absorbing to note the various attempts at reconciliation; the most common was of course the most obvious, namely freedom in custody, but this is a compromise rather than a synthesis, and I shall deal with it at length.

To my mind the most successful attempt at synthesis is being made in Sweden, and this attempt I propose to describe, taking as example the well-known prison at Hall.

THE HALL EXPERIMENT

Hall is not a 'cream of the milk' experiment, such as is found at Wakefield Camp in England. Wakefield Camp selects its men from other prisons and gives them physical freedom; Hall prepares its own candiates. Both have their virtues, but Wakefield is a finishing school, Hall is a training school. A man goes to Hall with no freedom; he enters the custodial block. If he does well, he goes to the semi-custodial block, and thereafter to the free block. The great difference between the Wakefield experiment and the Hall experiment is that Hall is an established prison providing reformatory treatment for certain types over the whole period of their detention, whereas Wakefield is an experimental prison offering considerable freedom to good-conduct prisoners who are reaching the end of their sentence and have no longer any great incentive to escape. There are profound educational and psychological differences between the two methods, and quite apart from that, the percentage of Swedish prisoners enjoying this treatment is much higher than in any other country, justifying the view that in Sweden a reformatory method is being confidently applied, while in other countries a safe risk is being tentatively taken. There is all the difference between the confident *use* of freedom as a reformatory instrument and the cautious *grant* of freedom; this latter may well be a concession to those persistent gadflies, the penal reformers.

In passing I make it clear that I have chosen Wakefield for the purpose of emphasising the contrast between a safe risk on the one hand and a real experiment on the other. It is not my intention to deny the value of Wakefield Camp; on the contrary it is the certain precursor of bolder experiment.

REFORMATORY AND CUSTODIAL DETENTION

It is clear that the Hall experiment, and any similar experiment, will fail if the wrong people are experimented with. There are numerous offenders who would not respond to these methods, and of these there are three notable classes:

(1) serious and dangerous offenders whose escape would endanger both society and the new experiment;

(2) less serious offenders who must be imprisoned, but who would not respond to reformatory methods;

(3) trifling offenders who do not need imprisonment. In South Africa, however, hundreds of thousands of these (mainly non-Europeans) are sent to prison.

For these classes one would advocate:

(1) Severe custodial prisons.

(2) Ordinary custodial prisons.

(3) Quite other methods, such as compulsory attendance, compulsory labour, and reduction in amounts imposed as fines for non-Europeans.

To these above add the reformatory prisons, special institutions for special cases, etc., and we have the whole range of penal institutions. The question now is, who goes to which?

In other words, the success of any diversified penal programme depends on sending the right people to the right places. Above all, the success of the reformatory institutions depends entirely on keeping types (1) and (2) out of them.

THE TASK OF DIAGNOSIS, SENTENCE AND ALLOCATION

This problem has received more attention in the States than in other countries. In California there is an interesting solution. The Court determines guilt, and pronounces sentence which by law lies between fixed minima and maxima. Thereafter the sentenced person is handed over to the Adult Authority, which allocates him to an institution, the actual period of detention to depend on his own response to treatment. The observer will note that minimum and maximum are often so widely separated as to grant powers of life and almost of death to the Adult Authority. The Youth Authority has even wider powers (except that its control ends at age 25), for it may on the one hand order probation, or on the other commit the youthful offender to a thorough-going penal institution.

In Ontario there is another interesting situation. The Court determines sentence, and if this sentence is over two years, the prisoner goes to a Federal penitentiary and will be a custodial case. If sentence is under two years, the offender (be he old or young) is handed over to the Department of Reform Institutions, one of the most enlightened penal authorities in the British Commonwealth. But this simple solution has one grave weakness; there is no guarantee that the offender sentenced to less than two years is reformable, and no guarantee that the other is not. When this difficulty is overcome, the placing of all reformatory cases under one authority will be seen to be a great achievement. I would not hesitate to predict that the Ontario Department of Reform Institutions would then make far greater use of freedom as a reformatory instrument, and would take a yet higher place among the world's most enlightened authorities.

It is my own prediction that no great penal progress will be achieved until the Courts distinguish between reformatory and custodial sentences, and that penal authorities will be afraid to use freedom until this is done. They will compromise by attempting all kinds of minor reforms within a framework of custody, and they will justify themselves by saying that the risks are unwarranted. And of course they are right; the risks will always be too great until this primary distinction is made. Once the distinction is made, we shall be astonished by the risks which can safely be taken by a reformatory institution.

In South Africa there has been considerable discussion of this important problem. One suggestion is that the Prison Authority must diversify its institutions, and allot prisoners appropriately. My own opinion is that the distinction is too important to be left to a Prisons Authority; that the distinction would carry more weight if it were made by the Court; that the prisoner will inevitably, if the distinction goes against him, cherish a grievance against the Authority which will hinder any progress he might have made.

Another suggestion is that the task of sentence and allocation should be undertaken by a third agency, a diagnostic and expert body. But because this suggestion is repugnant to British and Anglo-Saxon ideas of justice, and even to their Courts (which being human, one must note, may fear the loss of authority), I myself have always made the suggestion that the presiding officer of the Court, or some other judicial officer, should preside over the diagnostic body. I have however further revised my opinion, and consider that the diagnostic body should recommend to the Court that the Court should pass sentence and make it clear whether the sentence is reformatory or custodial, and that the decision of the Court should be subject to review, especially where the Court rejects in whole or in part the recommendation of the diagnostic body. Thus we would achieve a distribution of responsibility which would be very important.

I make the further point that the making of an early distinction between reformatory and custodial sentences will materially affect the length of sentence. A reformatory sentence should in general be about two years in length (with additional time for supervision, as in the Children's Act), a severe custodial sentence is likely to be much longer, and an ordinary custodial sentence about the same or less. It is very important that the prisoner should know more or less what he is in for, and I think that the Californian method is open to the gravest criticism on this score. It may sound well in theory to tell a prisoner that the prison term depends on his response, but it can have the most profound and disturbing psychological results. To this I make one exception; under no circumstances should a serious and dangerous offender be released automatically at the end of sentence, and it will be the duty of the diagnostic body to prevent such releases, its recommendation of course needing the approval of the Courts.

I believe that this fundamental distinction between reformatory and custodial detention is appreciated by our present Director of Prisons;[1] all his latest reforms point to such an appreciation. He chooses as a ready-made criterion the distinction between first and other offenders. As a rough criterion there is none better, but a diagnostic body would exclude some first offenders, and include some second and perhaps even third offenders, as suitable for reformatory treatment. I myself prefer a distinction between reformables and non-reformables, and prefer to see the distinction made by the Courts, believing that it would carry more weight, and even cause some offenders to say, 'Well, perhaps I am reformable after all.'

I note, however, that the Federal Prison System of the U.S.A., which has the most impressively diversified range of institutions in the world, makes its own allocations. On the other hand, it is as cautious as most authorities in its use of freedom as a reformatory instrument.

CRIME AND PUBLIC OPINION HINDER EXPERIMENTATION

It must not be supposed, as I am afraid many penal reformers do

[1] It is to be noted that this was written in 1947.

suppose, that the real obstacle to the use of freedom is the stupidity and timidity and sadistic natures of penal authorities. One meets many bright people who know exactly what prisons should do, and one is tempted to wonder how many would last just one month if their experiments went awry. I do not suppose that Sweden or Switzerland or Holland has a monopoly of intelligent and progressive thinkers and administrators.

But Sweden has a public opinion which at the best is actively sympathetic and at the worst is indifferent to changes in penal methods. This again I do not suppose to be entirely due to the enlightened nature of Swedish public opinion. Swedish opinion is at the best actively sympathetic and at the worst indifferent because Swedish crime is not the worrying problem that it is in other countries. This is because the country has a relatively high standard of living, a homogeneous population well distributed, and because it has been able to pursue, relatively unhindered by war, an active programme of social reform over many decades. It is, thanks to these factors and to the qualities of its people, one of the most highly civilised countries in the world, with a deep regard for law and order.

As soon as crime becomes a worrying problem, there is a marked decrease of sympathy for penal reforms. I should not hesitate to declare that important penal reforms will take as long to achieve in South Africa as in any country. Crime in England, America and South Africa is given great publicity; penal and correctional institutions in England and America are always under the spotlight, and failures and irregularities are widely advertised. At the present moment English newspapers are four- and six-page affairs, but hardly a day passed during my stay in that country without its account of some prison or Borstal misfortune. The effect on some institutions was marked; that subtle atmospheric tension was heightened, and there was an absence of that confidence and naturalness that mark the efficient institution.

The effect of crime itself on public opinion is, paradoxically and conclusively, to be seen in Sweden itself. For while crime is not serious, traffic offences, notably drunken and dangerous driving, are a source of anxiety. The same community that tolerates a humane and dispassionate approach to ordinary crime asks for sterner measures in regard to dangerous traffic offenders. Here is obviously a profound inconsistency, but it is a natural inconsistency and is to be expected when anxiety and other emotional factors disturb the operation of dispassionate judgement. One is forced to conclude that, the more concerned we are about crime, the less likely are we to prescribe scientific treatment for the offender. One is compelled to adopt the strange view that the country which least needs enlightened penal methods is most likely to achieve them. This is unfortunate, but all penal reformers must reckon with it; penal progress is in its essence a compromise between rational theories, themselves often emotionally charged, and emotional reactions, which can of course always be rationalised.

This inevitability of compromise can be made however to yield one advantage. The public is more likely to approve of scientific (which in general means more humane) treatment for those offenders regarded as reformable. It will not tolerate such treatment for mixed collections of reformable and custodial cases. If we therefore press for the making of this important distinction, we shall at last be able to make progress in reformatory institutions and for the time being leave custodial institutions to pursue their accustomed way.

THE BLIND ALLEY OF MINOR REFORMS

I am afraid that this paragraph has a harsh title. But I wish to press further this demand for a distinction between reformable and custodial prisoners. Most of the prison reforms that I saw outside Sweden are reforms within the framework of custody, and leave out of account the importance of freedom and responsibility as the supreme reformatory instruments. It may be argued that the minor reforms must precede the major, but my argument is that it is only the major reforms which will give real meaning to the minor. In British prisons I saw a great number of minor reforms, all of which tend to humanise these institutions. But to me it is clear that without the exercise of freedom and responsibility any programme of minor reforms is robbed of the greater part of its educational meaning. If our great aim is to restore self-respect and self-confidence, to inculcate ideals of conduct and responsibility, we cannot do so, except partially, by allowing longer hair, giving more cigarettes, encouraging chaplains, organising classes, distributing more books, all in custody. The great prison of Sing-Sing has done a great deal of this, under the shadow of the great walls and the machine-guns. But while Sing-Sing is expected to cater for life-sentences and ordinary sentences in one institution, much of this reform is meaningless.

PRIVILEGES IN CUSTODY

There are great and substantial advances being made in this field. Prisons all over the world are being humanised. Smoking is permitted at certain times; in some prisons it appears to be permitted at all times, and cigarette butts litter the floors in a famous American prison. Clothing has been improved, and the hair may be grown, in some English prisons to world-championship lengths. Prison food is good, and I ate many a prison meal with relish. Conversation between prisoners and visitors is in some prisons perfectly free, and the barrier between prisoner and visitor had disappeared, with few untoward results, I was told. Letters and books are rationed, but the ration has grown more generous.

Here again I must give the palm to Sweden for the use of imagination in the granting of privileges in custody, but I must mention again that the Swedish institutions are so free of tension that greater risks are more easily taken.

Attempts are also made in many countries to give more freedom within the walls and under the machine-guns. While I am prejudiced against this, I nevertheless recognise it as an advance. At Langholmen, though it is a custodial prison, football is played outside the walls; at Chelmsford open army huts are used within the walls; at Englewood, Colorado, there is an elaborate system of promotion within the enclosure.

REVISION OF REGULATIONS

All over the world regulations have been revised and relaxed. I found that it was always the poor institution that objected to this. A weak superintendent and weak staff always hide behind regulations. In the magnificently disciplined prison of Atlanta, for example, the regulations permit many things that we do not allow in South Africa. It must be admitted of course that the strictness or otherwise of the regulations must to some large extent depend on the arrangement of the buildings, and it would be foolish to relax regulations in a prison not adapted for good supervision.

PLANNING OF BUILDINGS

In fact this whole question of the arrangement and planning of buildings is of the greatest importance. The last century has left us with a legacy of custodial buildings ill adapted to modern ideas. Heroic efforts are being made, especially in England, to adapt such buildings, but progress in this direction cannot go far. The outmoded prison building, with its radial construction, its landings and wire nets, is almost unadaptable, and should be kept for strict custodial cases, until such time as proper custodial prisons can be built away from the towns.

This does not mean that the new buildings of America are perfect. Here one has an entrance hall leading to a long central passage, and from this the other passages branch off to every department of the great institution. All passages are of course enclosed, and the whole prison is, so to speak, under one roof. Now this is a great advance as far as custodial buildings are concerned, but many of these institutions claim to be reformatory. With the exception of Hall in Sweden I did not see one reformatory institution for adults which was built and planned with imagination; that is, I did not see one institution where the arrangement rather than the nature of the buildings provided a large measure of the security and facilitated the supervision. This however is no architect's failure; it is a failure on the part of the penal authority. Many of these prisons boast that they are 'un-walled'; but in fact they are as secure as any walled prison, and actually provide less physical freedom than many 'walled' institutions.

EDUCATIONAL AND RECREATIONAL FACILITIES

At one time the great question would have been 'why should such a man receive education?' But today more and more do we regard deprivation of liberty as the sufficient consequence of the wrongful act, and we are pre-pared to do almost anything for a prisoner which may result in his be-coming an asset and not a liability. All over the world advances are to be seen, though I must admit that they would impress a penal reformer rather than an educator; on the whole the special needs of such an unusual edu-cational programme are imperfectly understood. Women teachers are used in American prisons, and they told me that they had never experienced any rudeness or difficulty from their students.

Recreational facilities are also being increasingly provided. In Swedish prisons physical training is provided, and in some American prisons it goes on all day long; the question as to whether prisoners deserve it is just not heard at all. Swedish prisoners even have Turkish baths! They go into these wonderful rooms once a week, and come out as clean as men can be. What would I not give for such a bath at Diepkloof Reformatory!

PRISON OCCUPATION AND REMUNERATION

In Sweden and some American states the remuneration for prison work is comparatively high. A prisoner in Hall can on the average earn 1s. 6d. per day, and the more generous allowances are usually of this order. Some prisons maintain canteens for the benefit of prisoners.

Penal reformers however still press, and will continue to press, for full wages for prisoners. From this full wage will be deducted firstly a charge for the feeding and lodging of the prisoner, secondly an allowance for dependants, and thirdly an amount which will enable compensation to be paid to those physically or otherwise injured by the prisoner. Here there is no sentimentality involved; the reasons for this demand are hard, business-like and scientific.

But such a reform will not be accomplished in our lifetime. It involves too radical a departure from tradition, especially the tradition of punishment. It involves also a fundamental conflict with certain established interests, which wrongly hold that the provision of full occupation and remuneration means that law-abiding citizens will be deprived of them. Yet there is one very real difficulty that must not be overlooked; is this full occupation and remuneration to be continued in times when the outside world suffers from unemployment? The public must receive some kind of guarantee against such an eventuality, and penal reformers would be advised to include such a guarantee in their programmes.

And again, what kind of occupation should it be? It is clear that the traditional occupation of mailbags and the like makes both full occupation and full remuneration impossible. I wish that my readers could see the factory shops of the great Federal prison of Atlanta, which runs like a great machine. I am convinced that the thoroughgoing factory plan is the only possible plan for prison occupation in an industrial country, and certainly the only possible plan under which the payment of full wages can become anything more than a pipe-dream.

FACILITIES FOR SPECIALISED TREATMENT

It is clear that a prison authority encounters many behaviour problems which do not yield to an institutional programme devised to correct old habits and establish new ones. Essentially the task of a prison is to establish a remedial community, which by mere participation in its life will restore self-respect, re-establish ideals, encourage industry, reward diligence, maintain home contacts, and fix the eyes and wills of its prisoners on the real and eventual goals of the wider community. A great deal can be done by this remedial community to meet the needs of its members, and the great proportion of the work of reformation must be done by just such simple and indirect methods.

But there will remain many difficult cases, some of whom will be able to benefit from the institutional programme as soon as some preliminary adjustment is made. This is the work of specialists, and no reformatory prison can do without them. To them should be entrusted the task of allocation of occupation, to them should be referred resentful and rebellious prisoners, and they should advise the disciplinary authority in all matters of serious punishment. They should advise the disciplinary authority in all such matters as transfer to stricter custody, the use of confinement, and the all-important question of release.

There is one real difficulty here. The presence of such specialists can lead to friction between themselves and the disciplinary authority, especially when the latter entertains an inferiority-feeling towards the specialists, and is jealous and fearful of its position. In some prisons the psychiatrist and the superintendent are not on speaking terms. This is partly due to the fact that the psychiatrist does not always appreciate the problems of the disciplinary authority, and partly due to the fact that the superintendent is fearful of losing his position to the psychiatrist. Sometimes the expert despises the official, and sometimes the official regards the psychiatrist as a sentimental mollycoddler who does not understand prisoners.

This is inevitable so long as there is too great a disparity between the qualifications of superintendent and psychiatrist. But once this difficulty is removed, the problem is more easily solved, for it then becomes a problem of personal adjustment. No qualified superintendent needs to fear advice, nor would he feel humiliated in seeking the advice of a specialist on a specialised problem.

However we are not likely for many years to have psychiatrists in prisons. There are not enough to go round. But there is one step we could take now. At present difficult problems like those listed above are solved (or rather dealt with) by the existing machinery. Profound behaviour problems are therefore dealt with as disciplinary problems, and equally profound damage is done to human personalities. Even now we could set aside an efficient and intelligent officer in each prison whose task it would be to pay special attention to grave behaviour and other problems, which cannot possibly be dealt with satisfactorily as a part of routine. I predict that this simple step would go far to reducing the number of antagonisms, feuds, and hatreds that so disfigure prison life.

TRAINING OF STAFF

There is no indication in any country that the authorities feel strongly about the need for training staff. In the U.S.A. there is a highly competitive system of examinations to be found in many states; in England there is a training school at Wakefield which provides a two-weeks' course for prison officers; and in all countries, South Africa not excepted, there is a tendency to demand a higher standard of education from candidates for the service. At one time I was strongly in favour of a two-year course of training for recruits, and pointed to the new South African Railways and Harbours Training School as an example to be followed. I still think it would be a minor reform of the greatest importance, but I am now doubtful of its financial practicability. It would cost a lot of money, and we are desperately short of buildings and institutions suitable for our new purposes. I have also learned from experience what can be done with untrained men of natural ability and strength of character. I have indeed come to the mundane conclusion that improvements in the salary scale will at this stage secure better material than the provision of training.

But one thing must be pointed out. There is always great danger in a system which recruits untrained and less qualified men at the bottom, and accepts more highly qualified men at the intermediate stages. It seems to me that if you accept untrained and less qualified men at the bottom, it is both right and wrong to let them reach the top. For this reason alone I would now press for a one-year training course for all recruits, on full pay, this to be followed by a one-year probationary period. If we did that, we would in this respect be the most advanced country in the world.

I am sure it is a grave error not to train prison staff, and I have no hesitation in stating that, apart from the senior officials, I found an alarming number of thwarted, time-marking, and quite unenthusiastic men in the world's prison services. One has only to read their professional journals to discover this, but in addition I had the advantage of a hundred private and unofficial conversations.

AFTER-CARE SERVICES

With the exception of Sweden, there is no really developed after-care service to be found anywhere. In fact prisons everywhere have everything to learn from those authorities that deal with children. At some children's institutions, no less than twelve and a half per cent of the staff is engaged on after-care work. In Swedish prisons there are the 'social curators' to study the past and plan the future of prisoners. On release, however, the prisoner is sent to the State Labour Office, and it is the duty of this office to find him employment. I was sorry I was unable to discover the value of this, for I am intensely suspicious of any such arrangement.

Nor did I see anything that convinced me that penal authorities really did much to safeguard the prisoner during the inevitably unstable and dangerous period immediately after release, nor did I see any institution that itself provided any kind of transitional stage between institution and community.

It was interesting to me to note that the leading children's institutions of the U.S.A. believed that it was very important to do their own after-care and to note that this had developed further into a lively interest in the child's past and his family, extending even to a thoroughgoing attempt to improve the family situation before the child's release.

I am convinced that this is the right way to go, and that only when the Prisons Department appoints its own after-care staff will any real headway be made. I see no reason also why our reformatory prisons should not have their own city working-men's hostels, where a man might serve the last portion of his prison-term, and so be prepared still further for release to the community.

I still maintain, however, at the risk of being tedious, that the real value of all these minor reforms will be lost if they are introduced in a framework of custody, except in the first stages of a prison sentence. It is interesting to note that it is a policy of 'safety first' to cling to custodial methods for reformable prisoners. In this way too much of the final risk is borne by the community. It is interesting too to note that the community concurs in this. It bears with equanimity damage inflicted on it by a prisoner who has 'served his time', but resents similar damage from an absconder from a penal institution. It takes courage therefore to use freedom as a reformatory instrument, and my argument is reinforced, namely that the Prisons Department should not bear alone the responsibility for classification and allocation.

I predict however that once we establish truly reformatory institutions, many of these reforms will come as the day follows the dawn. A reformatory institution will go on changing itself, and there is no knowing where it will end. I predict that ever-increasing physical freedom will be a characteristic of such an institution, and that we will be astonished by the risks that will be naturally, and, to a large extent, safely taken. I predict that ex-prisoners in trouble or out of work will come back to the institution for help and advice, and that such institutions will prove a far greater safeguard to the community fearful of crime than any amount of safe custody. I predict that, even when the institution fails, its failures will be less likely to turn to that brutal and violent form of crime that so disturbs South Africa.

Parallel to this reformatory programme there must be a custodial programme. Transfer from one to the other should be possible, with safeguards. The custodial institution should not be harsh and punitive; it is dangerous to require that a violent and cruel criminal should be violently and cruelly treated. It is far more sensible to require that he should be safely detained until he can safely be released. Whether this needs seven or seventeen years is something that we must learn from experience; but provision must be made if necessary for further detention after the 'time is served'.

These are the bare bones of the enlightened prison system:

(1) Abolish as far as possible short-term imprisonment.

(2) Distinguish between reformatory and custodial imprisonment.

(3) Distinguish between severe custodial and ordinary custodial imprisonment.

(4) Use freedom as the prime reformatory instrument.

(5) Establish a special reformatory institution for the last two years to be

served by severe custodial cases.

If the protection of society is our supreme aim, this is the way to achieve it, not by more use, but by more intelligent use of imprisonment. And we need not travel round the world to find how to use freedom as a reformatory instrument; for the truth is, that, except for countries whose problems are far less urgent than our own, we know as much, and as little, as anybody else.

[An address delivered at a national conference convened by the Penal Reform League of South Africa for the discussion of the recommendations of the Lansdown Commission on Penal and Prison Reform. The Commission's Report was made public in March 1948. Penal Reform Pamphlets No. 3, Penal Reform League of South Africa, 1949.]

Juvenile Delinquency and Its Treatment

I have had the privilege of working for thirteen years for a Department of State that has tried ably and honestly to give full effect to the provisions of the magnificent Children's Act of 1937. My work has been concerned with Native children, and it has been my experience that in the Courts and in the institutions South Africa has tried to discharge honestly its duty to such children. It is quite wrong to believe that a Native child delinquent will get an inferior kind of justice from the Courts, and that he will be sent to a reformatory for the most trifling of offences. The past histories of reformatory pupils show for the greater part that some drastic action was needed; if there is any marked differentiation to be seen, it is in the difference between rural and urban courts, and I suspect that this is equally true of white children. A rural court commits much more readily to a reformatory than an urban court. Offences which appear trifling in Johannesburg are regarded more seriously in a small village, and in general the Johannesburg delinquent has one or two more previous convictions than his country cousin. In fact, the general tendency in larger centres is often to let the delinquency reach a dangerous stage before the child is committed. On the other hand many a rural or village child is committed to a reformatory when a kind of finger-tip control would have been sufficient to avert his delinquent progress. Of course there is a reason for this, and it is the poverty of our resources for dealing with the rural and village child. One notes therefore with gratitude the extension of the machinery of the Social Welfare Department to the more remote centres. The Department nevertheless faces a dilemma here, for it is highly probable that the country as a whole would have benefited more from a further expansion of such services in the larger centres where juvenile delinquency is really an urgent problem than from any rural extension. I hope however to return later to what I hope will be a constructive and reasonable criticism of the whole matter of the function of a Social Welfare Department in relation to delinquent children.

The gradual extension of educational methods in our industrial schools is past history. But a further great step was taken in 1934, when reformatories were transferred to the Union Education Department from the Department of Prisons. And this step was consolidated in the great Children's Act of 1937, which legislated for the whole problem of delinquency from the cradle to the first years of manhood. This legislation has had a profound influence on our reformatories, and has changed them out of all recognition. I even had the extraordinary experience, almost unknown to Public Servants, of administering the Diepkloof Reformatory for some years under no regulations at all, and this meant a freedom to experiment such as comes to few of us in our lifetimes. And when the regulations came, they were based on the practices of the institutions, and have never restricted and confined them.

The foundation of these regulations, and indeed of the Children's Act itself, was the recognition of the profound truth that a law-breaking child is a child, that he has closer affinities to the child than to the law-breaker, and that as a child he has to be helped and protected, not judged and punished. This recognition was long delayed, partly due to the theories of heredity, which regarded the child as uneducable, and to our ultra-moralistic attitude to the whole question of free-will and choice. But the growing volume of evidence that laid such heavy responsibility on environmental influences could no longer be denied. And with this growing scientific understanding came also a realisation of the grave responsibility and duty of society towards its delinquent children, and that they were being expected to resist forces that a child least of all can resist.

I should like to set out briefly the guiding principles that should guide every civilised society in its dealings with delinquent children:

(1) At all costs the delinquency should be detected early. For delinquency roots itself, and if it is associated with profound inadequacies and inferiorities and insecurities, and if it roots itself in a child who is being denied the deep needs of his own nature, it may well prove ineradicable.

(2) If at all possible, the child must be taught to adjust in the very environment where he is failing.

(3) If removal of the child is necessary, it should be to an environment as like that of the home as can be achieved, e.g. to foster-parents or to a hostel-home.

(4) Only if this fails, or if it is from the outset impracticable, should he be removed to the industrial school or reformatory.

(5) If he is to be removed at all, attention should be turned, during his absence, to the home in which, and perhaps because of which, his delinquency developed.

If these guiding principles are to be followed, society will need the following range of devices:

(1) The Child Guidance Clinic, to which parent or teacher or probation officer may repair for guidance and help.

(2) The Nursery School, where parents can learn as much as children, and where wayward and dangerous tendencies may be speedily discovered and checked.

(3) The establishment of a service of Visiting Teachers attached to ordinary schools, so that our schools can assume a duty which is theirs and theirs alone, a duty that has been unrecognised for far too many years.

(4) If the delinquency continues to develop, and if it appears that more serious action must be taken, there should be available in our larger cities a series of observation centres, capable of giving to our Courts information and recommendations in regard to the best treatment for such children. Such duties have in the past been entrusted to Probation Officer and Court, but there is no doubt that neither of these is in a position to discharge them adequately. I do not think we need be afraid of an arrangement by which the observation centre, the place of safety, and the place of detention, are all together. And while we are about it why not have the Children's Court and the Juvenile Court there as well? And why not a Boys' Centre and Girls' Centre as well, so that all welfare activities for children can be together? I can think of no better way to remove the stigma which must attach to a Children's Court and a Juvenile Court situated in a great Magistrates' Court Building devoted to the tasks of judging and punishing.

(5) The whole scheme of foster-parents should be developed and encouraged, so that, if a child is to be removed, he at least has the chance of staying in a home. I do not conceal the great difficulties here; for foster parents are born, and if they are to be made, there exists in this country no means of making, i.e. of training them. Nor must one conceal the fact that the adoption of a child of 7 or 10 or 12 is a very different proposition from the adoption of a baby. Nor the fact that there are few people ready to consider the adoption of a child of 7 or 10 or 12, especially if he has been in trouble. Nor the fact that some of these people would be actuated by motives far from pure. Nothing will come of this recommendation until one day the Social Welfare Department makes it a special task for one of its most intelligent and imaginative officers. We can express the pious hope, but the difficulties are immense.

(6) After the foster-home comes the hostel-home. If the original home, for all its defects, has real affection for the child, the hostel-home should be near the original home. There is no knowing what the original home may learn from the hostel-home. But if there is no affection, or if it is a dangerous affection, sometimes cruel, sometimes indulgent, corrupting

and degrading, it may be necessary to remove the child to a distance, and perhaps for ever.

(7) There may be reasons why removal to a home is impracticable. There is then the industrial school. The Commission recommends the establishment of such schools for Indian, Coloured, and Native children. Our system of Industrial Schools for European children is much more highly developed, but it is pleasing to be able to report that a Coloured Industrial School has been established at Ottery, and that a Native Industrial School is to be established at Lenz. One of the immediate effects of these schools will be to remove the younger and more amenable children from reformatories, a reform that is long overdue.

(8) That will still however leave two large incompatible classes at present treated in the one reformatory institution, namely, the child who is still amenable to treatment, and the mature and hardened delinquent. It would be unwise to divide one from the other on an age basis alone, and indeed I regard this as one of the greatest weaknesses in the practice of countries throughout the world. In many countries, in Great Britain for example, and in many of the States of the U.S.A., an arbitrary line is drawn at 16. But many of the younger group are hardened and intractable, and many in the older group are educable and amenable. I would not hesitate to propose that the Porter Reformatory for Coloured boys and the Diepkloof Reformatory for Native boys, should each be divided into two institutions, one for the amenable pupils of the age-group 15–21, and the other for the hardened pupils of the age-group 17–21. If there are 500 pupils so to be classified, they should not be divided into two groups of 250 each, but into groups of 400 and 100 respectively. These two latter groups would be more homogeneous than the two former; for the Theory of Mean Distribution holds here as well as in other spheres.

(9) The last and very important link in this range of devices is the release-hostel, to which released children from reformatories and industrial schools can be sent during the unstable months immediately following release. This is the most dangerous period in the life of the reformatory boy (or girl, I am sure); it is the period in which not only must he make many readjustments to community conditions, but it is the period during which he himself feels perhaps that he has become a man and wishes to have money, clothes and popularity. Indeed the dangers of this initial period are so many that it is surprising sometimes that a boy overcomes them at all; and the release-hostel is an invaluable method of helping him over this dangerous and unstable period. I might make two observations here. One is that the hostel-home boy and the release-hostel boy are two quite different characters, and that it is very unwise to attempt to make any

hostel fulfil the double purpose; the other is that some children will not go to the release-hostel at all, but will proceed direct to their own homes.

This range of devices is reasonably complete. It will be noted of course that, as one progresses down the scale, the treatment slowly loses its intimate and personal nature, and takes on the sterner qualities associated with discipline and order. This has given rise to the assertion that to place a child in an institution is to doom him for ever, because he is deprived of the personal attention that he requires. But there is another and more reassuring side to this question, for education of this special kind, and I believe of any kind at all, has a two-fold aspect. Education is not solely a matter of the impact of personality on personality; it is just as importantly a matter of the impact of environment on personality, and it is the task of an institution to create a remedial community, by the mere participation in whose life the child is strengthened in habits of industry, obedience, reliability, punctuality and trustworthiness. Indeed it is very wrong to suppose that education is solely a matter of instruction, teaching, preaching, admonition and correction. There may be times when this is necessary, but the greatest tasks of education must be carried out by a non-instructing, non-teaching, non-preaching, non-admonishing community, in which a child is led on from stage to stage to participate in a mode of living in which the great silent forces of example, and of laws and customs unconsciously adopted and obeyed, are the greatest operating factors. The child may well have reached a stage when he is unable to profit any further from personal and intimate attention, from instruction and admonition, unless these things are actively and plainly related to the life of the community in which he shares.

We need therefore not be concerned about the dangers of institutionalisation, if that institution is a purposeful and meaningful community, in which the child passes from stage to stage, each advance bringing with it greater privileges, greater responsibilities, and greater physical freedom. He is living and learning, and as he advances the institutional supports are removed from him one by one, so that when he is ready to leave he has acquired some self-trust, some self-reliance, some self-respect.

You must not understand me to say that personal and intimate attention is unnecessary, that psychiatric and psychological services have no value, that an institution must not be comprised of a number of smaller groups which compensate for the defects of mass education. But this I must point out, that in my long experience the child who needs the most individual attention is often the least likely ever to be cured. Some children go out of their way to attract individual attention. We had a boy at Diepkloof who, whenever he was made free, broke into staff-houses. The whole behaviour was so purposeless that one suspected at once that the real purpose was not the apparent purpose, that he suffered from deep disturbances that the ordinary educator could not understand. It is in such cases that expert advice is necessary, but it is also in such cases that the delinquent behaviour is most difficult to correct. The final truth must be stated in this way, that the greater part of the educational burden must be carried by the remedial community itself, and that individual attention must be given only at those points where the child is obviously not participating easily, almost unconsciously, in the communal life.

I believe there is one more important thing that must be said about the modern reformatory method. It is still widely supposed that the prime function of the reformatory is to imprint on the tender mind the great lesson that crime does not pay. It is supposed that this can be done by strictness, hardness, austerity and deprivation. But it is quite wrong to suppose that a child is delinquent solely because he has lacked this kind of treatment. A child is more often delinquent because he has been deprived of other and far more fundamental needs, of security, affection, and outlets for his creative and emotional impulses. The change in him is remarkable when these deep needs are satisfied. His insolence, secretiveness, untimely independence, disobedience, disappear when he lives in the kind of community in which he finds, consciously or unconsciously, a meaning and purpose for his own life. It is quite wrong to suppose that the privileges and opportunities of an institution are evidences of pampering and sentimental benevolence. They are designed to restore self-reliance, self-respect and self-trust. They are tests of growth, providing a wealth of information in regard to the way in which the child is responding to remedial measures.

An ex-magistrate has just published a book in which he expresses a low opinion of reformatory institutions, and in which he suggests that the Government would do far better to spend more money on a few sticks and canes. Such a statement cannot be allowed to pass unchallenged in a Conference of this kind. Sharp and swift punishment may succeed in some cases, but they are cases of superficial delinquency. When a child is suffering from deep inadequacies and inferiorities, from the deep wounds that the bad home can inflict upon him, he is an easy prey for the destructive forces of the bad environment, and who would dare to suppose that there is any magic in a stick or cane that can undo in a few moments of pain the lifelong effects of such dark and powerful factors? Not only our intellects, but our consciences also, are revolted by such a superficial and cruel hypothesis.

I might add here that this ex-magistrate has never to my knowledge made any investigation whatever of the effectiveness of reformatory institutions, nor has he made any study whatever of available statistics; certainly not that conscientious and thorough investigation that alone would justify one in expressing an opinion.

I hope you will pardon me for having embarked on such a lengthy defence of the reformatory institution. But no one need suppose that the good reformatory will be able to undo the effects of years of neglect. It will have failures enough. We can usefully return to our first guiding principle, that at all costs delinquency should be detected early. And here we can welcome the Report of the Inter-Departmental Committee on Deviate Children, which has just produced suggestions, in importance second only to the provisions of the Children's Act, for the early detection of potential delinquents.

For where are these potential delinquents to be found, if not in the schools?

I believe that you would wish me to describe very briefly the immediate past attitude of the schools towards such potential delinquents. Headmasters did not want them. Teachers did not want them. It was possible to frame an almost unanswerable argument against the involvement of the schools in this new and extraneous problem. Teachers, no doubt aware of the extraordinary complications I have already described to you, failed to see how they could possibly attack a problem that ramified so widely and deeply into the world outside the school. I once taught at a school in Natal where a boy was found pilfering in the town, and nothing less than expulsion was considered the right and only step. But expulsion where to? what to? Was the school, that had taken over such a grave and important charge from the town, to wash its hands of it, and to send the child on, to reformatory or prison? It is a poor society that has such a poverty of devices.

EARLY DETECTION OF DELINQUENCY

We have already laid it down that one of the cardinal principles in the treatment of problem children is that they should be discovered early and that every attempt should be made to enable them to adjust themselves in the very environment in which they are failing. One realises of course that this cannot always be done; for it is often true that the environment in which they are failing is the direct cause of their failure. If a child is the offspring of idle and selfish and drunken and irresponsible parents, nothing short of reformation of his parents will offer any hope for his recovery. But this is an extreme case. It is often the ignorance and unwisdom of parents that is the cause of his trouble; and they are very often fully conscious of

51

their responsibility, but attempt to discharge it in foolish and dangerous ways. It has happened more than once that we have taken a boy, who in the reformatory has shown every sign of recovery, to his home, and that we have told his parents, 'Here is your child back again; we have found him a good and obedient and willing pupil, and it is our hope that you will find him to be a good and obedient and willing son;' whereupon one of the parents, heavy perhaps with the memories of past hurts and wrongs, has said to us, 'I am glad to hear what you say, but it astonishes me, for of his goodness and obedience and willingness we have never seen any sign.' One can well imagine the effect of such a welcome upon a child who has perhaps formed some inarticulate resolve to trouble his parents no longer. I have again quoted an extreme case to you; sometimes no words are spoken but the constraint of the welcome says as much. It is for this reason, and for others, that we have developed a system of regular leave for boys from the Witwatersrand and Pretoria, so that a beginning at least shall be made with the establishment of a bond between pupil and parent. And we supervise these leaves carefully, visiting the parents regularly, and trying to form some idea of the relationship that is growing up.

But how much better it would be if these antagonisms and resentments could be laid bare long before any child gets to the reformatory. For where the feelings have grown up between child and parent, the whole problem of delinquency is so much more complicated and difficult of solution. Now I have every hope that the proposals of the Committee on Deviate Children will lead to just such an advance. For if the schools and the Provincial Education authorities recognise their undoubted responsibility, and if the proposal is carried out to appoint Visiting Teachers to investigate just such dangerous situations before they develop too far, there is every hope that fewer children will find themselves in trouble.

THE VISITING TEACHER

This Visiting Teacher should be, not only a teacher, not only a social worker, but of course a lover of children. As soon as the telltale signs are observed, of truancy, of pilfering, of sullenness, of impatience with authority, of precocious sexual behaviour, of abnormal fearfulness, of cruelty, the Visiting Teacher will visit the home and the parents, interview the child, and try to piece together the whole dangerous situation that, although under our own eyes, eludes us until the child breaks out into some piece of behaviour so flagrant that it can no longer be ignored. This situation is very like the hidden ogre that is to be found in the puzzle pictures of children's books. Once we have seen it, we wonder how ever we could have missed it. That will be the task of the Visiting Teacher, to find the ogre, who has so far been missed in the hundred other distractions and duties of a teacher's life.

The Visiting Teacher will of course make use of the other agencies that can help her in her task, not the least notable being the Child Guidance Clinic. For here are other experts, skilled in the detection and elucidation of just such problems as we are discussing. The task of the Visiting Teacher will be to marshal and use all the social agencies that are to hand, and to try to straighten out the environmental and individual tangles before it is too late, before child and parent, school and teacher, policeman and magistrate, reformatory and prison, are caught up in one disastrous and overwhelming complexity that is completely and utterly helpless to save the life of a bewildered and equally helpless human being that was once a child. Surely no effort is too exacting, no sacrifice too great, for such a purpose.

SOCIAL WELFARE MACHINERY

The Visiting Teacher may find that the home situation is so complex and difficult that additional effort is required that no Visiting Teacher can undertake. Here the vast machinery of the Social Welfare Department is to our hand. The rehabilitation of a home, in cases where this is possible, is a task which may require vast resources. And here I venture a few constructive suggestions in regard to the right use of our Social Welfare machinery for such a purpose. I am leaving the Public Service and could wish to say nothing that would wound the feelings of colleagues with whom I have worked so long and so fruitfully. But the fact remains that when any organisation is rapidly expanded, the general problem of coordination is apt to overwhelm an equally important problem, namely the preservation of specific functions and responsibilities. In other words, when there takes place a general and welcome expansion of social welfare activities, that specific activity which is concerned primarily with the direct care of human beings is apt to be absorbed and lost. I believe this has happened. I believe that the Probation Officer, the man who is concerned primarily with the direct care of children in trouble, has been swallowed up by the Social Welfare Officer. What will happen then? One important thing will happen, namely that those social welfare activities which can be inspected, audited, and checked, will be given preference over those which cannot be. And the man who spends hours wrestling with the problem of one wayward child will be inevitably weighed down by the fact that his monthly returns are overdue, that the records of the very child he is trying to save are incomplete, and that the paper-work in connection with a dozen other duties is days behind.

This is perhaps a grave statement to make, and I would not make it if I did not believe it to be true; I certainly would not make it unless I could produce evidence to prove it. But much of this evidence I do not produce here, believing that it would have precisely the wounding and hurting effect that I wish to avoid. But one proof I must produce. It is, for example, the duty of officers supervising children released from reformatories to submit six-monthly reports on such children. This, as far as Native children released from the Diepkloof Reformatory are concerned, has never been done until recently, when the Union Education Department made representations to the Social Welfare Department. These reports are now coming in, and in the great majority of cases the supervising officer reports that he no longer knows where the child is, and recommends his discharge from the Provisions of the Children's Act. Thus one of the wisest and most far-seeing provisions of the Act, providing for the supervision of children released from institutions, is in truth a dead letter.

I can only suppose that Social Welfare Officers find it impossible to carry out the duties laid on them by the Act, and this is a serious state of affairs. The constructive suggestion I wish to make is this, that a certain percentage of Social Welfare Officers in any centre should be confined solely and wholly to the important duty of the direct care and supervision of children, and that, if any work is to be neglected, let such burden fall equally on the Social Welfare and the Probation divisions, not on one alone. I think we would be shocked if we knew what percentage of the time and effort of the Social Welfare field staff is spent on the direct care and supervision of children.

In all such matters the vigilance of the public is the only guarantee that this whole new proposal of Visiting Teachers, investigating the problems of children before they go too far, calling in the assistance of Social Welfare Officers, and in general giving to the ordinary school a new and magnificent duty, will be carried out.

I trust that this survey of the whole field of Juvenile Delinquency and its treatment has been interesting for you. For it is the context in which the recommendations of the Penal Reform Commission take their relevant and important place. If it is true that society begins to realise its own deep responsibility for those who break its laws, how much more is this true for children? I hope that the hopes of all of us who work for a more enlightened and more efficient penal practice are going to be realised. But we have great cause to be thankful that many of these hopes have already been realised in relation to delinquent children, in our magnificent Children's Act, that states, in the language beloved of lawyers, the very simple truth that a child is a child, and as such is to be helped and protected, not judged and punished. For children are not delinquent always because they are naughty, children are not insolent always because they are naughty, and children do not break the law always because they are naughty, except in a very superficial sense. They are often delinquent because they have been denied the lives of children because the home has failed to perform its nourishing and protective functions. Children are often insolent because they are independent and defiant, because life has forced them to reach out beyond their natures. When we grow up, there is suffering and tragedy waiting for us all; within the limits that even a child's life sets, there should be happiness and security and affection and guidance. Given these things there is every chance and hope that he will grow up to find some meaning and significance for his life, and be spared the tragic and bitter lot of those who break the country's laws.

PART TWO

1948-1953

In these years Alan Paton lived mainly on the south coast of Natal. He wrote the novel *Too Late the Phalarope* (1953) and some of the Diepkloof stories which were to appear in *Debbie Go Home* (1961, published in the U.S.A. as *Tales from a Troubled Land*), and he began to work on his biography of Jan Hofmeyr. He received a number of literary awards, and visited Britain and America, but at the same time, as many of the poems of this period show, he was constantly haunted by the injustices of South African society.

[1948. Not previously published.]

Bulstrode's Daughter

Bulstrode's little daughter was playing with my daughter and son. I didn't like Bulstrode, he was a coarse and insensitive man, whose conversation was limited to the deterioration of India since the British had left. Therefore I felt some concern when the tall Indian who had joined the ship at Beira brought his small daughter and set her down in the centre of the small group.

'Play with them,' he said, 'they won't eat you.'

I should say that the little Indian girl was about four years old. My own daughter is about eight, with a strongly developed protective affection for smaller children. She took the little Indian girl's hand at once.

'Come and jump,' she said.

She had tied one end of the skipping-rope to a railing, and was holding the other, and Bulstrode's daughter and my small son had been jumping over it. The little Indian girl did not want to jump, but her father persuaded her to try it. She was successful, and went back readily to jump again. Soon all three were jumping.

There was no colour-bar on the ship, but there was a mere handful of Indians amongst the first-class passengers. They kept very much to themselves, and I understood that most of them ate specially prepared foods in a special place of their own. The other classes of passengers were almost entirely made up of Indians. But the tall Indian and his wife ate with us in the first-class dining-saloon. I noticed that the South African passengers talked to them freely, as though it were a relief to be free of restrictions. But I felt uncomfortable about Bulstrode's daughter.

The tall Indian watched the jumping with a benign expression. He looked a man of the world and must have known its ways. I admired the way he took our goodwill for granted.

The game was going on merrily when Bulstrode came up. He surveyed the scene for a moment, and then went up and took his daughter away. She said, 'Why, Daddy, why?'

'I'll tell you why,' he said.

As he went past me he said, looking at me and then at the tall Indian, 'Damned impudence.'

I stood up and went to my daughter and took the rope from her.

'You jump too,' I said.

While they were jumping I said to the tall Indian, 'I apologise.'

He smiled at me.

'These things happen,' he said.

Then the gong went for the children's meal. My daughter took the small Indian girl with her, and the tall Indian and I followed them to the saloon. The children sat at one of the long tables, but there were not enough of them to fill all the places. There was plenty of room for Bulstrode's daughter, but Bulstrode called the steward and told him to set a place at one of the other tables. The steward tried to explain something, but his English was inadequate, and it was impossible to know what he was intending to convey. His inability, although it was accompanied by smiles and humility, angered Bulstrode, and he demanded to see the chief steward. The tall Indian intervened.

'Let me rather move my daughter,' he said in English.

While I had no wish to antagonise Bulstrode, I felt that such a thing would be intolerable.

'I hope you won't,' I said. 'I have no objection to your daughter sitting with my children.'

Then I felt that was rather defensive, so I added, 'I wish my children to sit with your daughter.'

Bulstrode shouted at the steward, 'Call the chief steward, I said.'

The steward looked for assistance to the tall Indian, who spoke to him in some language I could not understand, and the steward went for his chief, and soon returned with him. The chief steward listened impassively to Bulstrode, and then to the tall Indian, who again offered to move his child, and then to me, who expressed the wish for my children to sit with the small Indian girl. By this time some of the other white passengers were listening interestedly to the conversation. The chief steward, still impassively, ordered the steward to set a place at one of the other tables for Bulstrode's daughter. The little girl protested at being put to sit alone, but her father said to her viciously, 'Do what you're told.'

Bulstrode lost no time in telling the first-class passengers of his firm stand. He was in fact telling them at the bar a few minutes later.

'I'm sorry you couldn't support me, Penfold,' he said to me coldly.

'I couldn't,' I said. 'I would never dream of humiliating a child in that fashion.'

'It's not a question of the child,' he said. 'It's a matter of principle. In fact it's you who are hurting the child. You're giving her a false idea of things.'

'The colour-bar is not a principle,' I said. 'It's made by stupid men.'

I thought he would explode. Instead he turned his back on me and ignored me.

That evening I was sorry to see that some of the other white children were sitting with Bulstrode's daughter. The tall Indian was very unhappy about it.

'You should have let me move my daughter,' he said.

'You would have been wrong,' I said. 'That would have prevented a person like myself from taking a stand.'

'I am grateful to you,' he said.

By this time, amongst the parents of younger children at least, there were two distinct parties, those who supported Bulstrode, and those who did not. After dinner on that evening we had a cinema show, and the Bulstrode supporters, who had attended at least one previous mixed show, stayed away. That was about as far as matters went, for our Indian passengers were very unobtrusive. When the show was over, the tall Indian spoke to me.

'I did a foolish thing,' he said, 'bringing my small daughter to play. But you see she is the only Indian child in the first class.'

'I hope you'll bring her tomorrow,' I said.

'If you insist,' he said.

'My daughter will be very disappointed if you don't.'

He smiled.

'Then I'll bring her,' he said.

'Good.'

'We have taught her that the colour-bar is evil,' he said. 'If I had been a South African Indian I probably wouldn't have brought her. But I am trying to teach her that the barriers in India itself are evil, that all human beings are one. In her small way she may one day add to the peace of the world.'

As we turned the corner the captain was addressing Bulstrode.

'If you want to complain,' he said, 'you must do so to our Head Office in London. Their instructions are explicit, no colour-bar on the Company's ships.'

'I'll raise hell,' said Bulstrode.

'I should think you would be good at it,' said the Captain. 'Good-night, sir.'

He turned away and greeted me cheerfully, and we talked for a few moments about nothing in particular. When he left me, I looked for the tall Indian. He was standing by himself at the rail, and seemed to be speaking to himself. Then he saw me and smiled.

'Were you praying?' I asked.

'Not praying,' he said. 'I was reciting.'

'May I ask what it was?'

'I was saying, *O love, return to the dying world, as the light of morning, shining in all regions, latitudes and households of high heaven within the heart.*'

'Is that from one of your Indian poets?' I asked.

'You could call her that,' he said, 'though I do not know if she ever was in India. It was Edith Sitwell who wrote that.'

He looked out at the sea.

'She went on,' he said, '*and wash the stain from the darkened hands of the universal Cain.* You and I must remember that. It's not what an Englishman does to an Indian, or a German to a Jew. It's what a man does to a man.'

[Anerley, 8.8.1948. Not previously published.]

To Walt Whitman

Barefooted boy on Paumanok's shore,
I, not a boy any longer,
I, having waited longer than you,
Being a man now, dare not wait any longer,
For in me too there are a thousand songs,
And some more sorrowful than yours.

And why did he not sing before? Why, duties,
Duties and resolutions, programmes and crusades,
Solemn undertakings, religious obligations,
And plans to revolutionise the world,
All crowded in upon him, till night came,
And pen stared at paper, waiting for a voice
That never spoke. So head fell on arms
And pen on paper, and the singer slept
With no song sung, waking again with day
To duties and resolutions, programmes and crusades,
And solemn undertakings. Yes, and woke afraid
That the great living host of tumbling words
Was a delusion, a brood of children
Locked within a womb that ne'er would open.
He pressed his ears to the dividing wall
Hearing the crying to be born, and knew
With joy them yet alive, and knew with fear
Them yet unborn. And all the while a voice
Mocked him for barrenness, a mocker struck
The full-bellied womb with careless hands
Striking the frail, the tender things,
Saying, bring them forth, the singing children,
The gay and lovely ones, the sorrowful,

Mocking and saying, bring them forth,
Singer without a song.

And once when he awoke so, deep afraid
Hearing the voice, the voice, the mocking voice,
Saying, bring them forth, the singing children,
The gay and lovely ones, the sorrowful,
Bring them forth, singer without a song,
He stopped his ears, shrinking from this tormenting,
But this voice possessed him, entered his body
By what way he knew not, filling the heart,
The mind, the soul, calling from within him,
Louder than any voice he ever knew,
Until he heard, he who had waited endlessly,
Until he heard, astonished, scarcely believing,
It was commanding, not mocking any longer,
Commanding, bring them forth, the singing children,
The gay and lovely ones, the sorrowful.
And when he would have spoken, it spoke before him,
Saying all he thought of saying, duties,
Resolutions, plans, programmes and crusades,
All these a time are ended, go and sing.
And he, astonished, scarcely believing, cried
What shall I sing? And this voice said, sing
What else but Africa, songs of Africa,
The thousand sorrowful songs?

So now, great brother, I am ready to sing now.
These songs shall be presented to you
And what does it matter if they are unworthy,
If they are not so gay and sorrowful as I thought,
For I have a feeling to give them to you,
I, not really a stranger, have a desire to speak to you
And why not speak to you with these?

Only the child is no more

The sea roars as ever it did
The great green walls travel landwards
Rearing up with magnificence
Their wind-blown manes.

His wonderment I recapture here
I remember his eyes shining
I remember his ears hearing
Unbelievable music.

I hear it now, but the high notes
Of excitement are gone
I hear now deeper
More sorrowful notes.

All is the same as ever it was
The river, the reed lagoon
The white birds, the rocks on the shore
Only the child is no more.

[Johannesburg, 4.11.1948. Not previously published.]

Dancing Boy

Small boy I remember you
I remember you used to dance here
By the roadside
And the white people stopped in their cars
And when you had finished dancing
Gave money to you.

Sir, I am the one indeed
I remember you stopped in your car
And when I had finished dancing
Gave money to me.

Small boy you are the one indeed
But why are you not dancing?
Do you not dance here any more?

Sir, I do not dance here any more
For one day when I was dancing
A white man stopped here in his car
And he came at me trembling
Like nothing I had seen before
And he thrust money at me
Great piles of paper money
Into my very hands and cried
For God's sake and for Christ's sake
Do not dance here any more.

I took this money to my father
And he said to me
It's a deep thing and a dark thing
And I do not understand it
But you must not dance there any more.

Sir, that is why
Although I am the one indeed
I do not dance here any more.

[December 1948. *The Forum*, 26.2.1949.]

On the Death of J. H. Hofmeyr

Toll iron bell toll extolling bell
The toll is taken from the brave and the broken
Consoling bell toll
But toll the brave soul
Where no brave words are spoken

Strike iron bell strike ironic bell
Strike the bright name
From the dark scrolls
Of the blind nation
Strike sorrow strike shame
Into the blind souls

Clap iron bell clap iron clapper
Clap your iron hands together
Clap the loud applause
That life denied him
Clap the dead man
And if you can
The dead man's cause
Clap in beside him

Strike iron bell
Strike iron hammer
Strike deaf man's ears
Lest man's earth hears
Heaven's clanging and clamour

Clap iron bell clap iron clapper
And drown the clapping of the million million
Who clap the great batsman returning
To his Captain's pavilion

[Anerley, 1949.]

To a Small Boy who Died at Diepkloof Reformatory

Small offender, small innocent child
With no conception or comprehension
Of the vast machinery set in motion
By your trivial transgression,
Of the great forces of authority,
Of judges, magistrates, and lawyers,
Psychologists, psychiatrists, and doctors,
Principals, police, and sociologists,
Kept moving and alive by your delinquency,
This day, and under the shining sun
Do I commit your body to the earth
Oh child, oh lost and lonely one.

Clerks are moved to action by your dying;
Your documents, all neatly put together,
Are transferred from the living to the dead,
Here is the document of birth
Saying that you were born and where and when,
But giving no hint of joy or sorrow,
Or if the sun shone, or if the rain was falling,
Or what bird flew singing over the roof
Where your mother travailed. And here your name
Meaning in white man's tongue, he is arrived,
But to what end or purpose is not said.

Here is the last certificate of Death;
Forestalling authority he sets you free,
You that did once arrive have now departed
And are enfolded in the sole embrace
Of kindness that earth ever gave to you.
So negligent in life, in death belatedly

She pours her generous abundance on you
And rains her bounty on the quivering wood
And swaddles you about, where neither hail nor tempest,
Neither wind nor snow nor any heat of sun
Shall now offend you, and the thin cold spears
Of the highveld rain that once so pierced you
In falling on your grave shall press you closer
To the deep repentant heart.

Here is the warrant of committal,
For this offence, oh small and lonely one,
For this offence in whose commission
Millions of men are in complicity
You are committed. So do I commit you,
Your frail body to the waiting ground,
Your dust to the dust of the veld,—
Fly home-bound soul to the great Judge-President
Who unencumbered by the pressing need
To give society protection, may pass on you
The sentence of the indeterminate compassion.

[Anerley, 1949. Not previously published.]

In the Umtwalumi Valley

In the deep valley of the Umtwalumi
In its tribal valley with its kaffirboom
Red, red, and red again along the banks
We in our swiftly moving car
Pass small boys on the road walking
And they call out in their own language
For pleasure or hope of gain, I cannot say,
Their salutations, father, father.

Yes, I will not forget your salutations
I sit here pondering the deep meanings
The solemn and sacred meanings
Of your salutations
I sit here pondering the obligations
The solemn and sacred obligations
Of your words shouted in passing.

[Anerley, 1949.]

Samuel

The black boy rose from his bed
And came to me willingly
And master, master, he said,
Why did you call for me?

But I told him I called no word
And he said to me sheepishly
I must have dreamt that I heard
The master calling me.

And again he rose from his bed
And came to me willingly
And master, master, he said
Why did you call for me?

But I told him I called no word
And he said to me with shame
I dreamt again that I heard
The master calling my name.

And yet again from his bed
He came to me willingly
And master, master, he said
Why did you call for me?

Now God is great I know
But He can't quite understand
Or why should He summon so
Black boys in a white man's land?

I did not call, I said,
And I have no mind to call
For God's sake go to your bed
And answer no more at all.

The Discardment

We gave her a discardment
A trifle, a thing no longer to be worn,
Its purpose served, its life done.
She put it on with exclamations
Her eyes shone, she called and cried,
The great bulk of her pirouetted
She danced and mimed, sang snatches of a song.
She called out blessings in her native tongue
Called to her fellow servants
To strangers and to passers-by
To all the continent of Africa
To see this wonder, to participate
In this intolerable joy.

And so for nothing
Is purchased loyalty and trust
And the unquestioning obedience
Of the earth's most rare simplicity
So for nothing
The destruction of a world.

[Anerley, 1949. Not previously published.]

The Stock Exchange

And he said – it was two in the morning then –
Let us hurry home, sleep, rise, bath, and dress
And meet on the floor of the Stock Exchange
And there you and I shall stand up and cry out
Against injustices.

And I said, I can hardly wait for daylight,
I can hardly wait to stand up and cry out
Against injustices.

So we went to the floor of the Stock Exchange
And I failed to see him though I looked everywhere
And he failed to see me though he looked everywhere
And we failed therefore to stand up and cry out
Against injustices.

But we are meeting again some time soon
To work out some better, even more vivid plan
Whereby we shall stand up and cry out
Against injustices.

[1949? *Contrast*, December 1961.]

I have approached

I have approached a moment of sterility
I shall not write any more awhile
For there is nothing more meretricious
Than to play with words.
Yet they are all there within me
The great living host of them
The gentle, the compassionate
The bitter and the scornful
The solemn and the sorrowful
The words of the childhood that will not come again.
But they do not come out for nothing
They do not form themselves into meanings
Unless some price has been paid for them
Unless some deep thing is felt that runs
Like a living flame through their shapes and forms
So that they catch fire and fuse themselves
Into glowing incandescences
Or if the felt thing is deep indeed,
Into conflagrations, so that the pen
Smokes in the hand, and the hand
Burns to the bone, and the paper chars
Under the heat of composition.
Therefore words, stay where you are awhile
Till I am able to call you out,
Till I am able to call you with authentic voice
So that the great living host of you
Tumble out and form immediately
Into parties, commandos, and battalions
Briefly saluting and wheeling away instantly
To waken the sleeping consciences
To call back to duty the absenting obligations
To assault again, night and day, month and year
The fortresses and bastions of our fears.

[A talk given in the U.S.A., 7.11.1949. Not previously published.]

Why I write

I haven't written very much. I wrote one book whose reverberations and consequences still continue to astonish me, and since I wrote it I have written some thirty or forty pieces which for want of a better name I shall call poems. Where some of these are illustrative of some point I want to make, I shall venture to use them to illustrate such a point.

This book and these poems are about South Africa. I write about South Africa because it is the only place I know to write about. But I write about it because I must write about it. What I have written about South Africa appears to have the property of being able to move people who know nothing about it. I know of course that there are things about life in South Africa which are common to life anywhere, that fears and hopes and griefs and joys are common to all men. But what astonishes me is that people, disregarding, yet not altogether disregarding, the South African shades and tones and colours, find that these fears and hopes and griefs and joys are their own. This encourages me, and makes me feel a strong desire to write again.

But just as strong as the desire to write again is the fear to write again. This is not only because I fear to write another book which will compare badly with its predecessor; it is because the mere giving of South African shades and tones and colours to universal hopes and griefs and joys is a fearful thing for a South African to attempt. I must tell you briefly why this is so.[1]

There are eleven to twelve million people in the Union of South Africa. Of these only two and one-half million are white, three-fifths of these being Afrikaans-speaking, two-fifths English-speaking. There are one million of what we call 'coloured' people, the descendants of the racial mixture which took place before white custom and law hardened against it, and forbade it, under the influence of the white man's intense determination to survive on a black continent. There are about one-quarter million

[1] The following passage is an excerpt from the *New York Herald Tribune*, 26.10.1949, 'The Grave Problems of South Africa' by Alan Paton.

Indians, whose forefathers were brought out by the English settlers to work on the sugar farms of Natal. And there are eight million black people, the people of the African tribes.

The Afrikaans-speaking people are the descendants of the Dutch who first came to the Cape of Good Hope, which Francis Drake, the navigator, described as the fairest cape in all the circumference of the earth. These people did not come to Africa to settle, but the fertile valleys and great mountains of the Cape bound them with a spell. The primitive Bushmen and Hottentots could not stand up against this new thing that came out of Europe, and they melted away. But this new thing that came out of Europe changed also; under the influence of the isolation of these vast spaces, and the hardships and loneliness of this patriarchal life, the people from Europe and the language from Holland changed too. Something of Africa entered into it and changed it. This the people themselves recognised and they called themselves the Afrikaners, and their new and simple and flexible and beautiful language they called Afrikaans; their love of this new country was profound and passionate.

But still another change awaited them. As the Afrikaners moved yet farther north they encountered the warlike tribes of the black African people. A long and bloody warfare ensued between them. Their opponents were numerous and savage and determined, and the history of this encounter is one of terror and violence. The black people became truly a part of the white man's mind. Under the influence of this danger, the Afrikaner attitude toward black men hardened. The safety and survival of this small band of white people was seen to be dependent on the rigid separation of white and black. It became the law that the relationship between white and black was to be that between master and servant; and it became the iron law that between white men and black women, between black men and white women, there was to be no other relationship but this. Land was set aside for the conquered tribes, but, as we see so clearly today, never enough.

And yet still another powerful influence entered into the making of the Afrikaner soul. In 1806 the English came to the Cape during the Napoleonic Wars. They came initially, not as settlers, but as governors, officials, missionaries, teachers, traders, and fortune-seekers. Their attitude to the black man was quite different from that of the Afrikaner. The black man was not their enemy; he was their business. This fundamental incompatibility between two policies was to influence our history for many years. In fact this incompatibility reached a climactic point in 1836, when many of the Afrikaner trekkers, abandoning all that they had so far gained, set out on the greatest trek of all, into the heart of the sub-continent, in order to escape this new and alien culture. There they set up the republics of the Transvaal and the Orange Free State. The position now was that the coastal regions of South Africa were English, and that the great interior plateau was Afrikaner.

A new dramatic factor then entered the picture. In the interior of this South Africa, in the very heart of the country to which the Afrikaner trekkers had gone to escape British rule, the richest gold of the world was discovered. The great modern, vigorous city of Johannesburg was born in a collection of tents and huts. Gold-seekers, many of them British, poured into the Transvaal. The Afrikaners watched with fear and anger and despair this new intrusion of the old enemy. The newcomers wanted the franchise; the Afrikaners dared not give it to them. And so we reached the second great climax, of the Anglo–Boer War, in 1899. The century-long incompatibility of a pastoral, agricultural, conservative community, and a commercial, industrial community became abundantly apparent.

In 1902 the Afrikaners capitulated, and the British conscience, which was not to permit the British Crown ever again to engage in such a war, brought about the magnanimous settlement of 1906, by which self-government was restored to the defeated republics. A great wave of good-will spread throughout the country, and four years later the Cape of Good Hope, the Orange Free State, the Transvaal and Natal came together to form the Union of South Africa, under the leadership of three defeated Afrikaner generals, General Botha, General Smuts and General Hertzog.

But reconciliation was not so easily achieved. War, even when it is followed by magnanimity, leaves wounds not so easily healed. Twenty thousand Afrikaner women and children died in the camps set up for their reception, mostly of typhoid fever. This was not easily forgotten. But more important, the Afrikaner saw the danger that he would be swallowed up and lost in the great British culture. He also was afraid that the traditional English policy of *laissez-faire* toward the black people would lead to his engulfment. So he set about again to re-establish his separateness and distinctness. He established cultural societies for the protection of his customs, history and language. And he succeeded magnificently, largely because of his fiery independent spirit, and largely because the ballot box had been put into his hands by his British enemy. So emerged what is called Afrikaner Nationalism, the persistent and implacable urge that eventually, in 1948, defeated General Smuts, to the astonishment of every part of the civilised world.

In the meantime the position of the black people was changing beyond recognition. The cities of Johannesburg, Cape Town and Durban were rapidly growing, and inevitably began to attract from their impoverished

Reserves a never-ending stream of black people seeking work and city lights. Problems of housing, crime and deterioration began to increase in intensity. This is indeed the central theme of my novel *Cry, the Beloved Country*. The white people of South Africa became more and more afraid of engulfment. This was one of the great reasons why we put the Nationalists in power; we became afraid of the *laissez-faire* policy of the Smuts government, and returned a party that advocated control and separation as the only solutions of our rapidly growing problems.

And so we have returned, for the time at least, to the old policies of survival and separation. It is the white settler on a black continent who is speaking through the mouthpiece of the Malan government.

But you must not imagine that this white settler is motivated solely by fear. He, too, is a human creature; he, too, has not lived upon the earth without being influenced by great human ideas, notably by the ideas of Christianity. Therefore, he, too, is a divided creature, torn between his fears for his safety and his desire for survival on the one hand, and on the other those ideas of justice and love which are at the very heart of his religion. What we are indeed witnessing today is a struggle in the hearts of men, white men, between the claims of justice and survival, between the claims of conscience and fear.[2]

When one surveys this history, and the country in which this history was made, one is filled with a compassion for all the races that have been caught up and involved in this situation that is apparently without solutions. One feels compassion for those who struggle to hold what they have, and those that struggle to get more than they have; one feels compassion for those who are caught in the vice of these opposing struggles, many of whom do not understand the nature of the thing in which they are caught; one feels compassion for those who desire above all else to live lives of peace and ordinariness, and who want to leave some kind of future for their children; and all this compassion is caught up and made one in an immense compassion for something that is greater than them all, namely the vast and beautiful country that suffers it all.

Yet it is not easy to capture the deep and solemn undertones of all this suffering and to put them into words. I do not mean it is not easy from the point of view of writing; that depends on one's gifts. I mean it is not easy if one is a white South African. For one is writing about men's fears, and men do not want to have their fears written about. There is one thing that has I believe so far made my writing acceptable, and that is that I have not mocked at or sneered at or laughed about man's fears. I believe that one

[2]The excerpt from the *New York Herald Tribune* ends here.

may write at such a level that men look at themselves sorrowfully instead of looking at the writer vengefully. But one is often fearful that one will not be able to reach that level. In any case there are men who don't want their fears written about at any level, who hate just as much to have them written about with compassion as they would hate any other way.

There is another reason to fear writing. For with whatever compassion one writes about men's fears, one must always write about them with truth. That is equally fundamental. For it is obviously impossible to produce anything but counterfeit compassion for counterfeit truth. And the truth is not an easy thing to write. There come to the mind a hundred stories, as dramatic, as tragic, as terrible, as any stories that any country can produce. And simultaneously with the story comes the fear to write it, because many of these stories relate truths that men fear, and there is no fear greater than the fear we have of those who are afraid. In South Africa there are many white men who wish to follow their conscience rather than their fears. But no sooner do they emancipate themselves from their own fears, than they experience a new fear; they find now that they fear those who are not emancipated, and who regard with anger and detestation those who are. This second fear, which is my own, is well known in South Africa. It is not of course unknown in other countries, but it is more intense in South Africa, because in some way one is made to feel that a loyalty to truth and conscience is in fact a gigantic racial treachery.

I shall read you at this point a piece, which we shall call a poem, which describes this second fear, although it does so in what might almost be called a light-hearted manner:

['The Stock Exchange', see page 73.]

It is an interesting fact that some of my friends find this piece, which was written with a teasing rather than an earnest intention, bitter and painful. This will show, I think, how seriously we take our problems, when we do take them. It is a very significant fact that last year, in a new and important anthology of South African verse, a mere fraction of the total number of poems contained any of those deep and solemn undertones of which I have spoken. It is a significant fact that our novelists in general avoid the most significant themes.

Here the Afrikaans-speaking novelist at one time enjoyed an advantage, because he was able in his novels, with the complete and warm approval of the group to which he belonged, to draw on the rich and colourful history of his people, and also to write about the wild life of Africa in a way that has I believe seldom been surpassed in any literature. But even this advantage is passing away; the long political struggle of the Afrikaner seems to have reached its high point, and the wild life of Africa is less well understood by a country that is growing more and more urban and industrial. Therefore sooner or later the Afrikaner novelist will have to use the men and women of the present. He will find himself simultaneously attracted and repelled by the themes and stories that come into his mind; and he will find himself in a serious dilemma, for to handle a great theme honestly may bring down upon him the disapproval of those who understand its implications, while to handle it dishonestly will certainly bring down on him the disapproval of those who understand life and literature. The English-speaking novelist also finds himself in this dilemma, but not to the same extent, because he belongs to a group which because of its history has succeeded in making literary judgements less dependent on racial and political judgements. Nevertheless he is a white South African, and there is today in him a noticeable tendency to blur again the clear line of demarcation between literary and political judgements. What happens indeed is this, that our writers, who have a storehouse of new material as rich as any in the world, must, because of considerations not literary at all, select and discard and disguise in such a way that the raw material loses much of its original beauty and strength.

One cannot, if one is to write at all, allow oneself to be bound by these fears. One must, while possessing them, disown them. One must, while paying attention to them, not pay attention to them. I wish to write, but to me it is intolerable that raw material should lose its original beauty and strength under my hands. I have a respect for raw material which is at least as great as my respect for the considerations of expediency. But these two respects, the one balanced against the other, do not produce writing, they merely produce a state of equilibrium, a state of not writing. Therefore I am perhaps more than other people dependent on a final compulsion to push me off the fence. This compulsion may come in several ways; if it is through compassion, then such a piece is produced as I shall read to you now:

['In the Umtwalumi Valley', see page 70.]

So is produced something that is more or less acceptable. I must note however that its content is not particularly provocative, and that the mere pondering of moral issues is not an unacceptable social occupation. I must also point out that this is only a poet writing. And for several reasons that we have no time to consider now, society scrutinises novels and novelists far more searchingly than it does poets and poetry.

This compulsion may at another time come in the shape of anger, in which case is produced a piece of this kind.

DURBAN

The voice of God over Durban crying
Over the white men and the Indians
Over the merchants and the politicians
Of the proud city.

The voice of Christ over Durban crying
No, not the meek and the mild Jesus,
But he who drove from the temple
The money-changers.

Come down O Lord of Man and Heaven
To a round table of white men and Indians
That when you have finished instructing us
We may crucify you.

Now while this piece is not likely to be popular, it is placed in a city that is predominantly English-speaking, and it is therefore, for reasons I have already discussed with you, less likely to arouse very deep displeasure.

This compulsion may come again as a compound feeling of guilt and compassion, to produce this piece:

['Indian Woman', see page 100.]

Here the poet, by using himself as the guilty person, accuses only by implication; and I must add, too, that when a poet pronounces a judgement in this odd and roundabout fashion, it is not always completely understood, and those who completely understand it are on the whole less likely to be antagonised by it.

Now I suspect that this whole question of the writer and his susceptibility to social approval and disapproval, that the whole question of the extent of his triumph over or his defeat by these forces, that the whole question of the devices to which he resorts to avoid social disapproval, that the whole question of the choice and handling of raw material, are questions already known, even if in different forms and intensities, by other writers in other countries. And I must make it clear that this whole process of adaptation is only partly conscious and deliberate, and is in a large measure unconscious and natural.

There is no country in the world today that is not fearful. The whole world is fearful. South Africa is no exception. But its fears are complicated and intensified by its own complex racial structure. In this country writing is confined almost entirely to white people, English- and Afrikaans-speaking. In their writing they have to a great extent adopted certain conventions, one of which is to pretend that they do not hear the deep undertones of which I have already spoken. There may be two reasons for this; one may be that the writer himself does not hear or does not wish to hear the undertones or does not wish to write about them even if he does hear them, the other may be that he is afraid of bringing into his writing undertones that so many do not wish to hear. But when a writer does bring these undertones into his work, he too adopts certain devices, conscious and unconscious, which will enable his work to gain social approval, or at least to escape any great social disapproval.

But why does he write at all? Why doesn't he take up some easy thing like politics or publishing? Or why if he writes, does he not follow the conventions? I once wrote an answer to this question, in one of those pieces that I call poems. I claim no merit for it, it merely answers the question.

COULD YOU NOT WRITE OTHERWISE?

Could you not write otherwise, this woman said to me,
Could you not write of things really poetical?
Of many-coloured birds dipping their beaks
Into many-coloured flowers?
Of mine machinery standing up, you know,
Gaunt, full of meaning, against the sky?

Must you write always of black men and Indians,
Of half-castes and Jews, Englishmen and Afrikaners,
Of problems insoluble and secret fears
That are best forgotten?
You read the paper, you post your letters,
You buy at the store like any normal being.
Why then must you write such things?

Madam, really, since you ask the question,
Really, Madam, I do not like to mention it
But there is a voice that I cannot silence.
It seems I have lived for this, to obey it
To pour out the life-long accumulation
Of a thousand sorrowful songs.
I did not ask for this destination
I did not ask to write these same particular songs

Simple I was, I wished to write but words,
And melodies that had no meanings but their music
And songs that had no meaning but their song.
But the deep notes and the undertones
Kept sounding themselves, kept insistently
Intruding themselves, like a prisoned tide
That under the shining and the sunlit sea
In caverns and corridors goes underground thundering.

Madam, I have no wish to be cut off from you
I have no wish to hurt you with the meanings
Of the land where you were born
It was with unbelieving ears I heard
My artless songs become the groans and cries of men.
And you, why you may pity me also,
For what do I do when such a voice is speaking,
What can I speak but what it wishes spoken?

I regret to import such a note into this discussion, but I undertook to answer this question, and it seems that I cannot honestly avoid it. I have so far written very little; but what I have written has been produced under compulsions, emotional compulsions. Some people have described this writing as sentimentality; if so, there has been a gross failure on my part to obey with dignity the emotional compulsions.

Therefore ultimately I have written because I must; and in the future I doubt if I shall do any writing for any other reason. This does not mean that I shall not try to discipline myself as well. I shall not sit down in a chair and wait for words to come out of my mouth. But in the last resort, if I do not think much of the words that are coming, I shall probably return to some other occupation. How could I dare continue to write books, and have people that I respect read them and say, using even my own question against me, 'Why does this fellow write at all?'

[U.S.A., 1949. Not previously published.]

No Place for Adoration

I saw the famous gust of wind in Eloff Street
It came without notice, shaking the blinds and awnings
Ten thousand people backed to the wall to let it pass
And all Johannesburg was awed and silent,
Save for an old prostitute woman, her body long past pleasure
Who ran into the halted traffic, holding up hands to heaven
And crying my Lord and my God, so that the whole city laughed
This being no place for adoration.

[Lane's Flat, California, 18.12.1949. *South African Outlook*, 1.7.1953.]

A Psalm of the Forest

I have seen my Lord in the forest, He walks from tree to tree
    laying His hands upon them.
The yellowwoods stand upright and proud that He comes amongst
    them, the chestnut throws down blooms at His feet.
The thorns withdraw their branches before Him, they will not
    again be used shamefully against Him.
The wild fig makes a shade for Him, and no more denies Him.
The monkeys chatter and skip about in the branches, they peer
    at Him from behind their fingers,
They shower Him with berries and fruits, they shake the owls
    and the nightjars from their hiding places,
They stir the whole forest, they screw up their faces,
They say to each other unceasingly, it is the Lord.
The mothers cuff their children, and elder brothers the younger,
But they jump from tree to tree before Him, they bring down
    the leaves like rain,
Nothing can bring them to order, they are excited to see the Lord.
And the winds move in the upper branches, they dash them like
    cymbals together,
They gather from all the four corners, and the waterfalls shout
    and thunder,
The whole forest is filled with roaring, with an acknowledgement,
    and a glory.

[Lane's Flat, California, 1949. S.P.C.K., London, 1959.]

Meditation for a Young Boy Confirmed

I

I rise from my dream, and take suddenly this pen and this paper
For I have seen with my eyes a certain beloved person, who lives
    in a distant country,
I have seen hands laid upon him, I have heard the Lord asked to
    defend him,
I have seen him kneel with trust and reverence, and the innocence
    of him smote me in the inward parts.
I remembered him with most deep affection, I regarded him with
    fear and with trembling,
For life is waiting for him, to wrest the innocence from his young
    boy's eyes,
So I write urgently for this beloved person, and indeed for all
    beloved persons,
I write indeed for any person, whoever may find something in
    these words.

II

I see him there young and very innocent, he still confides many
    things to many persons,
I know what is waiting for him, I see enemies and dragons and
    apparitions,
I know them all, I am familiar with them, I walk amongst them
    carelessly,
I walk amongst them having a truce with them, but I cannot make
    a truce with them for any other person,
I cannot make a truce with them for any young and reverent person,
    nor any gentle child;
Therefore though I myself walk through them carelessly, today
    they fill me with most anxious trembling.

86

III

My son writes to me, Today I made my first communion,
I was rather nervous, but everything went off satisfactorily.
I see him communicating, I observe that he believes himself to be
    in the presence of the One and Everlasting and Most Loving God,
I observe him at the altar rails, I observe his heart is beating,
I observe that he is anxious to behave correctly, I know that he will
    blush if he makes some error,
I observe that he stretches out his hands, that he partakes of the
    bread and wine,
I observe that he returns to his place, that he casts down his eyes
    and does not look about him.

IV

I watch him with old and knowledgeable and very old eyes, I am
    aware that he has been indoctrinated,
I am aware that his choice is contingent, that I have allowed him
    to commit himself deeply,
I am aware that he is neither a Buddhist nor a Muslim, that his
    circumstances have hardly permitted him to consider these religions.
I am aware that the whole world is not confirmed, that the whole
    world does not communicate,
I am aware that some climate has changed in the world, therefore
    I write these words to him.

V

I say to my son, These are the visible and outward forms,
These are the inarticulate gestures, the humble and supplicating
    hands of the blind reached out,
This is the reaching out of children's hands for the wild bird, these
    are the hands stretched out for water in the dry and barren land.
This is the searching in a forest for a treasure, buried long since
    under a tree with branches,
This is the searching in the snowstorm for the long-waited letter,
    the lost white paper that has blown away,
This is the savage seeking a tune from the harp, the man raking
    the ashes for the charm in the burned-down house.
This is man thrusting his head through the stars, searching the void
    for the Incomprehensible and Holy;
Keep for it always your reverence and earnestness, these are men
    searching here,

They stretch out their hands for no star, for no knowledge however
    weighty,

They reach out humbly, supplicating, not more than a cubit's length

That haply they may touch the hem of the robe of the Infinite and
    Everlasting God.

VI

This kneeling, this singing, this reading from ancient books,

This acknowledgement that the burden is intolerable, this promise
    of amendment,

This humble access, this putting out of the hands,

This taking of the bread and wine, this return to your place not
    glancing about you,

This solemn acceptance and the thousand sins that will follow it,
    this thousand sins and the repenting of them,

This dedication and this apostasy, this apostasy and this restoration,

This thousand restorations and this thousand apostasies,

Take and accept them all, be not affronted nor dismayed by them.

They are a net of holes to capture essence, a shell to house the
    thunder of an ocean,

A discipline of petty acts to catch Creation, a rune of words to hold
    One Living Word,

A Ladder built by men of sticks and stones, whereby they hope to
    reach to heaven.

VII

You will observe that virgins do not bear children, and that dead
    men are not resurrected;

You will read in the newspapers of wars and disasters, but they will
    report miracles with impatience.

You will be distressed, you will not wish to repudiate your
    commitment,

You will not wish to disappoint your parents, you will suffer deep
    troubling of the soul,

You will cry out like David before you, My God, my God, why hast
    thou forsaken me?

Do not hastily concede this territory, do not retreat immediately,

Pass over the slender bridges, pick your road quickly through the
    marshes,

Observe the frail planks left by your predecessors, the stones gained
    only by leaping;

Press on to the higher ground, to the great hills and the mountains
From whose heights men survey the eternal country, and the city
    that has no need of moon or sun.
But do not lie to yourself, admit this is the journey of the heart.

VIII

Listen to my opinion, accept or reject it.
The intellect is like a searchlight, it probes the darkness to and fro
    unceasingly,
Its rays at their limit describe a great sphere, and this is the universe
    of the intellect,
But this is not the universe of God, and God is not captured in it.
We do not search the darkness for him, and pronounce that he is
    not there,
Nor do we hold him caught in the beam, and declare him to be
    exposed and humbled.
Our intellect is of finite glory, but God is of Infinite Glory;
It cannot make or unmake the Creator, it is he who created it.
It can rebel, but it is a proud and desolate rebellion;
We may yet fly to the stars, we may yet fire our guns and wake to
    echoing the waste mountains of long-dead places,
But all that we do shall be of the order of what is done already,
    our searchlights fall back from the edge of the outermost void,
They fall back, they are exhausted, who shall make them rise higher?
Shall we say of the intellect, we shall devise means to exalt it?
Shall we say of our created nature, we shall otherwise create it?
No, we must say to the poets and to the humble, what moves in the
    outermost void?

IX

Do not pronounce judgement on the Infinite, nor suppose God to
    be like a bad Prime Minister,
Do not suppose him powerless, or if powerful malignant,
Do not address your mind to criticism of the Creator, do not pretend
    to know his categories,
Do not take his Universe in your hand, and point out its defects
    with condescension.
Do not think he is a greater potentate, a manner of President of
    the United Galaxies,
Do not think that because you know so few human beings, that he
    is in a comparable though more favourable position.

Do not think it absurd that he should know every sparrow, or the
number of the hairs of your head,
Do not compare him with yourself, nor suppose your human love
to be an example to shame him.
He is not greater than Plato or Lincoln, nor superior to Shakespeare
and Beethoven,
He is their God, their powers and their gifts proceeded from him,
In infinite darkness they pored with their fingers over the first word
of the Book of his Knowledge.

X

This is not reason, men do call it faith.
If ten men came to me, now some I should confound, and by some
be confounded,
And those I do confound shall leave me for an easier victory,
And those that me confounded shall find elsewhere defeat.
And who, to God found in an argument, will put out supplicating
hands?
I do not lie to you, I tell you plainly,
I do not presume to bring my knowledge into his presence, I go
there humbly.
All this I recommend to you, it is the heart of worship.

XI

Such was the brief, such was the lonely life,
Such was the bondage of the earth, such was the misery,
Such was the reaching out, such was the separation,
That my Lord tore the curtain from the skies, and in compassion
He took upon himself all angry things, the scourge, the thorn, the
nail, the utter separation;
And spoke such words as made me tremble, and laid his yoke upon me
And bound me with these chains, that I have worn with no especial
grace.
Why then I did accept this miracle, and being what I am some lesser
miracles,
And then I did accept this Faith, and being what I am some certain
Articles,
And then I did accept this Law, and being what I am some
regulations,
Why then I worshipped him, and being what I am knelt in some pew
And heard some organ play and some bells peal, and heard some

people sing,
And heard about some money that was wanted, and heard some sin
was preached against,
And heard some message given by some man, sometimes with great
distinction, sometimes with none.
I made this humble access, I too stretched out my hands,
Sometimes I saw him not, and sometimes clearly, though with my
inward eyes.
I stayed there on my knees, I saw his feet approaching,
I saw the mark of the nails, I did not dare to look fully at them,
I longed to behold him, I did not dare to behold him,
I said in my heart to him, I who in sins and doubts and in my
grievous separation reach out my hands,
Reach out your hands and touch me, O most Holy One.

XII

I see my son is wearing long trousers, I tremble at this;
I see he goes forward confidently, he does not know so fully his own
gentleness.
Go forward, eager and reverent child, see here I begin to take my
hands away from you,
I shall see you walk careless on the edges of the precipice, but if you
wish you shall hear no word come out of me;
My whole soul will be sick with apprehension, but I shall not disobey
you.
Life sees you coming, she sees you come with assurance towards her,
She lies in wait for you, she cannot but hurt you;
Go forward, go forward, I hold the bandages and ointments ready,
And if you would go elsewhere and lie alone with your wounds, why
I shall not intrude upon you,
If you would seek the help of some other person, I shall not come
forcing myself upon you.

XIII

If you should fall into sin, innocent one, that is the way of this
pilgrimage;
Struggle against it, not for one fraction of a moment concede its
dominion.
It will occasion you grief and sorrow, it will torment you,
But hate not God, nor turn from him in shame or self-reproach;
He has seen many such, his compassion is as great as his Creation.

Be tempted and fall and return, return and be tempted and fall
A thousand times and a thousand, even to a thousand thousand.
For out of this tribulation there comes a peace, deep in the soul and
    surer than any dream,
And in the old and knowledgeable eyes there dwells, perhaps, some
    child's simplicity
That even asks for gifts and prays for sons.

XIV

Listen to one more word from me, now that I begin to take my hands
    from you.
Now God be thanked for this so brief possession, so full of joy,
This zest for life, this keen anticipation of some quite trivial thing,
This ingenuity for making occupations, these programmes strictly
    adhered to,
This typewriter sadly out of gear, on which were thundered out
    messages, poems, plays, and proclamations,
These rages, these lunatic stampings, these threats of leaving home,
For these withdrawals of affection, when you sat pouting like a pigeon,
For these restorations, at all costs to be accepted gravely, even with
    penitence,
For this reverence, this eagerness, this confidence in many persons,
For all these gifts we give our thanks.

XV

I see him communicating, I observe that he believes himself to be in
    the presence of the One and Everlasting and Most Loving God,
I observe that he goes to the altar rails, I observe his heart is beating,
I observe that he is anxious to behave correctly, I know he will blush
    if he makes some error,
I observe his humble access, his putting out of his hands,
I observe that he returns to his place, not glancing about him, I
    watch him with old and knowledgeable and very old eyes,
I say to myself, So would I wish to communicate.

XVI

I put my pen down, round me the world is dark and all men lie
    asleep.
But I have written urgently for this beloved person, and indeed for
    all beloved persons

I have written urgently for this my son, and for all sons and daughters,
And indeed for any person, whoever may find something in these words.

[1950. *The Lance*, St. George's Presbyterian Church, Johannesburg, Christmas 1950.]

The Gift

I had not long been at school. I was six years old and clever, and it was not long before I distinguished myself indoors. But outdoors in the playground I was quiet and gentle, and stood against the brick walls in the sun, watching them play. I would have played had they asked me to, but no one did, so I kept myself to myself.

I remember one occasion on which I attracted attention. I wore a pair of shoes that did not lace up, but had a strap that went over the instep and was fastened by a button. These shoes some knowing fellows pronounced to be girls' shoes, but I denied it, not hotly or angrily, but no doubt quietly and gently. I had no idea that such a small matter could attract such great attention, but soon there was a crowd of boys around me, and the knowing ones again pronounced the shoes to be girls' shoes. They were supported, too, by all the other knowing and manly and strong-looking boys, and indeed by all those who spoke at all, for no one spoke a word on my behalf. So I spoke for myself, quietly and gently, that these were boys' shoes. Then a big and manly and strong-looking boy angrily put his arm lengthwise in front of his chest, and if he had flung it out he would have caught me in the face. I could not shrink against the wall because I had my back to it already, and whether some pity was excited in him or whether he was afraid of authority I do not know, but he brought his arm down again and contented himself by asserting again that these were girls' shoes and by looking at me to see if I would deny it. But I did not deny it again.

Maybe I was too meek to satisfy whatever desire they might have had, for they drifted away and left me, and left some others, too, not so manly or strong-looking as those who had gone, but not so quiet and gentle as myself. One of them said, when the others were safely gone, those are not girls' shoes, and I smiled at him timidly and gratefully. Perhaps he saw that I might have attached myself to him, and perhaps he had no wish and even some fear to go any further, for he, too, left me, and there I was standing alone, thinking only to myself, these shoes look like girls' shoes. I lifted one foot and put it on the other, so hiding one shoe, but the other could not be hidden, and I thought of some plan to hide them both.

I walked along to the big school verandah and sat down there on one of the benches, for there I could put both my feet under the bench, and thus hide the shoes. But I had not been sitting there long when a teacher came to me and said, sitting, sitting, go and play in the sun. She said, aren't you well, but I had no great experience of telling lies, so I told her I was well, and she said, then go into the sun, it's against the rules to sit here now.

That is what I was like. But this is not really my story. My story is stranger than that. It has stayed with me all my life, and keeps on coming back to me, two or three times every year, at times perhaps when I think too much about myself. It has not always done that; for many years it lay sleeping in the depths of my memory, and then suddenly I remembered it. When I first remembered it, it astonished me, and filled me with pain and shame and pity. I write it down now because it seems foolish to feel pain and shame about it. The pity I feel still, but the astonishment is gone, not quite gone, but turned into a kind of wonder at what went on in the mind of a quiet child put out into the world.

It was another day at school. I stood in my usual place against the wall, and the playground was full of the cries and calls of boys playing and pushing. They, and I in much smaller measure, had got used to the shoes that looked like girls' shoes, and they left me in peace.

Near where I stood, a gate opened out into the street, and I could see all the people that passed by the school. It was the middle of the day, and we had all eaten the food, usually sandwiches, that our mothers gave us to bring. But it was poor food for a day like this, for without warning a wind had sprung up, and the weather had suddenly turned cold and bitter. Yet it was with dismay that I saw coming up the street towards the gate of the school, the black boy who worked as a servant in our house. He carried a basket, and over the top of the basket was a clean white cloth. I knew at once that it was food, no doubt hot food, that my mother had sent because of the sudden bitterness of the day. And I knew, too, that this would attract more attention to me and embarrass me, so I went further along the wall so as not to be seen by the boy. I had not been standing there long when one of the schoolboys came to me and said, 'Your boy's here, with a basket.'

'What boy?' I asked.

'Your boy,' he said. 'The boy that works at your house.'

I shook my head, denying finally and completely that such a boy could be there.

'I'll bring him to you,' he said.

So he brought the boy, and of course it was our boy, and we both knew it as well as any two human beings could, but while he smiled at me uncertainly because of the strangeness of the place, I shook my head.

'That's not our boy,' I said.

Some of the schoolboys spoke to him, and I heard him telling them privately, not openly, because my attitude confused him, that he was certainly my mother's boy, and that I was certainly the young master of the house, and that my mother had sent me something warm to eat and drink. But I denied it resolutely.

Then one of the schoolboys brought him nearer with his basket and took off the white cloth, and there was a jug with a cup in the mouth of it, and another white cloth in which something was wrapped up. The schoolboy took the cup out of the mouth of the jug, and it was steaming.

'Cocoa!' he said, smelling it. 'Hot cocoa!'

He opened the second white cloth, and there were the scones that my mother had baked. And I knew that while they were hot she had opened them, not with a knife but with her fingers, and had dropped butter into them, to melt and sink yellow and sweet, into their very hearts. Even then, as I now remember, I thought of my mother thinking of me at school, and I was touched and therefore ashamed, but I resolutely denied that this was our boy, and so denied that it was my mother's work. And by this time all the attention that I feared had been directed at me, and at the black servant and the cocoa and the scones, so that half the school was there, watching the strange spectacle of a boy who would not claim so timely and desirable a gift.

Then one of the manly and strong-looking boys said to me, 'Come on, it's your mother's boy.'

But I denied it.

Then he said, 'What are you going to do with it?'

'It's not mine,' I said.

'Can I have it?' he asked.

'It's not mine,' I said stubbornly.

'Can I have it?' he asked again.

So persistent was he in asking my permission that he forced me to acknowledge some kind of ownership, and at last I said unwillingly, 'It's not mine, but you can have it.'

So he shared it with his friends, the cocoa and the scones. Our black boy held the basket patiently, and what he thought of it I do not know. When they had finished he put the jug and the cup back into the basket and covered them with the white cloth. Then he saluted me and went out of the gate down the street. But, of course, I did not acknowledge his salute, for what had I to do with this unknown boy?

Then the schoolbell rang, and I went back indoors with relief, where whatever attention I attracted would be warm and pleasurable.

As I remember, my mother asked me when I returned if this strange story was true, and I did not lie to her, as I had done to the boys at school. I do not remember that she spoke any further; I do not remember that she patted my head or smiled in any special way at me; I do not remember that she ever told the story to my father or my brother, but I am almost sure she did not, because my brother would have plagued me with it. I have no doubt that she kept it in her heart.

And so would any mother keep it in her heart. For this is one for whom she fears, going forward and retreating, now confident, now afraid, making his way from her womb into the world.

[1948–52. Not previously published.]

The Laughing Girls

I hear the noise of the loud laughing girls
Laughing around the house, distracting me
And should I go to them and say
Go away and leave me some silence
For I am writing the sorrowful meanings
Of your race, why they would laugh at me
And say in their own tongue to one another
This man is mad. They would laugh more loudly
Derisively, not apprehending
The sorrowful meaning of themselves.

But should I go to them and say
Go away and leave me some silence
Or I shall telephone to the police,
Why they would leave me then
Still laughing perhaps, but less loudly,
Half bravely and half afraid,
Their laughter dying away down the street,
Saying in their own tongue to one another,
Yes let us move away. They would laugh half bravely,
Half afraid, yet dimly apprehending
The sorrowful meaning of themselves.

[1948–52. Not previously published.]

Black Woman Teacher

Black woman teacher in distant Bavendaland
Nameless woman teacher teaching your life out
Far from the lights and the sounds
   of the tumultuous cities
I said to you, your work is noted
Your humble work is noted and remembered
It is known there in Johannesburg.

I did not lie to you, your work is noted
Your humble work is noted and remembered
By some of us, here and there,
   in the tumultuous cities
Yet had it not been so I could have lied to you
To see the glad light in the eyes
The shy and earnest pride
That your humble work was noted and remembered
By the might and power and glory of the land.

[1948–52. Not previously published.]

Indian Woman

You, Indian woman in the rain,
Do you not see me coming?
Do you not see it is a white person coming
In his automobile?
What, you will not yield?
Neither will I then
And the brown–coloured mud
Rises in a fountain bespattering
Your stubborn garments.

My God, but your hair is white as snow
I did not know you were so old, Indian woman
For had I known you were so old
I would have conceded something
I would have bespattered you
Not quite so venomously.

[The third Peter Ainslie Memorial Lecture on Christian Unity, delivered in the City Hall, Grahamstown, 29.8.1951. Rhodes University, 1951.]

Christian Unity: A South African View

When the Archbishop of Cape Town delivered the first Peter Ainslie Memorial Lecture, he entitled it 'Christian Unity : An Anglican View'. He was followed by the Revd. Sidney Berry with the lecture 'Christian Unity: A Realistic View'. I beg to follow the example of my predecessors, and to entitle this third lecture, which I am honoured to be asked to deliver, 'Christian Unity : A South African View'. I should truly have said, 'Christian Unity : A White South African View', but I thought that such a title could be found distasteful. But here I say frankly that that is what it is, and that a black South African would present something significantly different. Perhaps he will one day, and then he can call his lecture 'Another South African View', so that we can perhaps out of mutual charity show a better front to the world than we can show to ourselves.

Christian Unity – a South African view. It must be clear that such a discussion must inevitably be a discussion of racial affairs. We call South Africa a multi-racial society, and it is clear that any real South African cannot but cherish the ideal of achieving some kind of unity out of such diversity. We differ widely in our ideas of how this is to be done; but I cannot believe that any one of us would dare to suggest that it need not be done.

I myself have undergone one unforgettable experience of racial unity. It was when Edith Rheinallt Jones[1] died, and a great congregation of white people, black people, coloured people, Indian people, not all Christians, assembled in St. George's, Johannesburg, to give thanks for her life and works. It was one of the overwhelming experiences of my life. I felt that I had no control of the deep feelings of pain and joy that moved so powerfully in me. It was not mere sorrow or thankfulness but something transcending both, the sense, almost of awe, that some great quality of the dead woman had caused to be caught and held before us, accessible for a brief space to human eyes, a vision of the oneness of mankind, and of our South African society. It was as though we had all ventured out from a thousand

[1] See pages 239–241.

tributaries and backwaters, and had entrusted ourselves for a moment to some broad river, which bore us on irresistibly, with a power that both exalted and terrified, towards some ocean dimly apprehended.

But joyful though it is to see such a vision, it is also painful, because it is a vision and must be withdrawn. This vision of the glory of God and the oneness of mankind was evoked by an exceptional occasion. It is comparable with the vision seen by St. Peter in Joppa; and in that seen by St. John in the island that was called Patmos, of a city that had no need of moon and sun, into which was brought the honour and glory of all the nations of the earth. One sometimes finds that one is transported, not asking, not seeking, by some accident or event, whether within or without oneself, to some place where some vision is seen; but one cannot stay or live there, one has to return, one has to leave the Church Universal and to return to the Church that one knows, in some street under some trees, with its priest, predikant, or minister, its dioceses, rings, districts, its synods, conferences, or assemblies, and there one has to fashion something for oneself. Let us then so return.

We return therefore to a country where policies of racial separation are already warp and woof of our national life. The Native Reserves, the city locations, the British protectorates, our school system, accommodation for travellers, provision for the sick in hospitals (whether in separate hospitals or separate wards), bathing-beaches and a hundred other examples can be given of this, all dating back many years. It seems quite inevitable that the coming of European settlers or invaders or missionaries or officials or traders to any African country should immediately, by reasons of education, culture, religion, and social habits, cause the evolution of a pattern of life which emphasises the differences between the newcomer and the indigene. This pattern can be seen in every African country, even when it is a territory administered by European officials in the interests of an indigenous population. But the pattern in South Africa was more striking than in all the rest, because the relationship between white and black was from its beginnings that of enemy and enemy, and because the necessity for *survival*, for the survival of a white people on a black continent, was the ultimate basis of all secular policy. In such days there was no relationship possible except two, that is enemy and enemy, or master and servant ; and any other relationship of person and person was to be kept remote and austere, never becoming that of friend and friend, and above all never becoming, except at the cost of being made outcast, that of man and woman. The qualified tolerance which had been extended to the Chief Surgeon when he married the Hottentot woman, Eva, changed in a century and a half, under the influence of this struggle for survival, into a massive disapproval, and in another century and a half this disapproval was translated into law. In all this, religion played a great part, as it has always done in the national struggles of the Afrikaner people. This religion was Christian, but the dangers of frontier life, the wanderings and privations, the very nature of the land itself, caused to come especially vivid and alive the stories of the Israelites, their destiny as a chosen people, and the necessity to hold themselves elect and apart.

This feeling of necessity to separate oneself and to hold oneself apart was strengthened by the arrival of the British and other missionaries whose aim was the salvation of souls and not the ensuring of survival. These missionaries in their turn posed questions to the British authorities; they preached the brotherhood of man and raised difficult moral questions, so that the authorities were caught and vacillated between the opposing considerations of the rights of the settlers and the rights of the conquered. This vacillation, and in particular the unwillingness of the authorities to reject the implications of equality in any ideal of brotherhood, an unwillingness reinforced by powerful sections of public opinion in Britain, was the main cause of the Great Trek, which Hofmeyr in his history[2] called 'The Dividing Asunder'. And it was in truth a Dividing Asunder, a division which was sharpened by external events for another sixty or seventy years, and persists powerfully in memory and action till this very day.

So there arose that strange and baffling paradox, which is part true, part untrue, that in respect of the non-white population of South Africa, the Afrikaner and English views are irreconcilable. No one can doubt that it was initially an incompatibility of views that caused the Dividing Asunder, but it is widely acknowledged that today these views are not so incompatible as supposed. The truth is that quite irrelevant to these issues are joined other issues, notably those concerned with our continuing in the Commonwealth, which to English-speaking South Africans is a guarantee of *their* survival. It is as though the events of the last sixty years of the 19th century brought about a shifting to the poles, and no matter what tropical delight is thrown down between us, we each cling to our own ice and snow.

This situation, this historical situation, has profoundly affected our churches, so that we find that on the question of apartheid, the English-speaking churches and the three Dutch Reformed churches appear in general to be ranged on opposite sides. They agree on one thing, that one has no right to seek the approval of the Scriptures for what are the secular policies of the State. But in all their other pronouncements it is a conclusion that is inescapable that the Dutch Reformed churches regard the pre-

[2] J. H. Hofmeyr, *South Africa*, Ernest Benn, London, 1931.

servation of racial difference and integrity as a solemn duty, and consider that only by the separation of non-white peoples will they be able to escape the disabilities imposed on them by life in a mixed society; while the English-speaking churches stress man's dignity as a child of God, and find in men's common humanity a fact of greater significance than men's differences. Yet the first would claim that they have not lost sight of man's dignity as a child of God, and that indeed they advocate separation as a means of his attaining it, while the second would disclaim any intention of turning South Africa into a mixed and degenerate country. Underneath all this lies amongst other things the fear of miscegenation, which the first abhors and would prevent, while the second would judge it to be left to the self-respect of the various developing communities. One cannot escape the conclusion that the two sides are looking at the matter from different places. Nor can one justly neglect to state that the present Government, though a secular body, must derive many of its ideas and purposes from the Dutch Reformed churches. The Dutch Reformed churches stand to the present Government in a relationship which has never before existed between any South African church and any South African government. Nor should one omit to mention the fear of the English-speaking churches that the Dutch Reformed Church may become an instrument of State and that there are groups in the D.R.C. who are desirous of establishing a closer and more permanent relationship between the State and the Church. Nor should one omit to state that there are groups within the D.R.C. who believe that a Church, while having respect for the temporal authority, should under no circumstances yield one tittle of its independence as a sovereign body whose head is the Lord.

The Nederduits Gereformeerde or Hervormde Kerk (the strongest of the D.R. churches) did indeed make an important pronouncement when it said that the only just apartheid was total apartheid. Leslie Hewson, in addressing the Rosettenville Conference of the Christian Council in 1949, said that there was an element of idealism in the contemporary statement of apartheid which could not be ignored, and which made it unjust to consider it as a purely selfish policy of separation. Professor Hoernlé,[3] not, I believe, a professing Christian, but revered by Christians because of his clear and courageous thought, declared himself towards the end of his life in favour of 'separate areas of liberty' as the only alternative to domination; yet he added that he thought total separation impracticable. To this I would add only one observation, which is not moral in nature. It is frequently stated, and on high authority, that it will take a great many years

[3] Alfred Hoernlé, Professor of Philosophy at the University of the Witwatersrand and one of the founders of the South African Institute of Race Relations.

to realise the ideals of apartheid. Some think it will take a century. But I do not think we will get a century. I do not wish here to talk at length of changes in Asia, of changes and impending changes in Africa, nor of changes of heart and attitude in America and Europe; but such changes are taking place and the world is going to look different whether there is war or not, and whoever wins it. We are living in a moving world, and it is necessary for Christians to re-examine statements of moral principle and programmes of moral action so that that which is of Christ and eternal may be separated from that which is of time and place.

It is frequently said and thought that the incompatibility of the English-speaking and Afrikaans-speaking churches is so profound that any kind of co-operation is beyond realisation. Each side fears that co-operation will be at the cost of some sacred ideal or principle. At one time the Dutch Reformed churches were represented on the Christian Council; I hope they will be again and there are thousands on each side who hope for it, not with the intention of converting or appeasing, but of trying to find some common ground. It may well be that it will be idle to seek agreement on policies and plans; but if out of it comes some discovery of a common love for South Africa and all its peoples, that would be something. It would be something to discover that love and to proceed from it. It would be something to dispel the not uncommon beliefs that the English love only Africans, and the Afrikaners only themselves. I cannot believe that there is no common ground, even though it may be uncomfortable at first to crowd so many people on to so small a space. It seems to me to be not worth any sacrifice of principle, but worth any sacrifice of pride, a matter of the greatest importance that we should speak about some things with a united Christian voice.

Failure to achieve even such limited co-operation can, I believe, lead to only one thing; it will mean not only bitter and unfruitful strife, but we shall be so occupied with this internal strife that we shall be unable to adapt ourselves, as we must, to the great forces stirring in our continent and the world. Let no man suppose that he can achieve any kind of unity in our multiracial society without recognition of and adaptation to the changes of the larger world. Let no man suppose that an imposed unity can do anything but break apart.

By this I do not suggest that a fully representative Christian Council guarantees the attainment of Christian unity. But it at least creates some of the conditions antecedent to it. It should be a Council in which any man can say what for him is right and true; and whatever languages are spoken there, at least if a man speaks one of the official languages, it should be without benefit of translation.

Can this be done? Well, let me say that if it cannot be done, it is less likely to be due to devotion to God and principle, and more likely to be due to the pride of race and the corruption of history.

But differences between these groups of churches concern not only the question of race within the larger society, but the question of race within the churches themselves. It is impossible on this occasion to give any historical account of this and the observations that follow must not be regarded as an attempt to do so.

In 1829 the Kaapse Ring of the N.G. Kerk, replying to the Kerkraad of Somerset West, stated that people of colour should be admitted together with others to the Lord's Table. In the same year the Kerkraad of Swartland received a similar reply, but both Kerkraads found the decision unacceptable. In 1845 the Kerkraad of Swellendam threatened secession. In 1857, on the motion of the Revd. Andrew Murray, the Synod, while regarding it as both desirable and scriptural that converted heathens should be received into the existing congregation, agreed that they should meet in a separate building, if their reception should, on account of the weakness of some, hinder the advancement of Christ's cause. This was the beginning of the church policy of separation, which today is practised in all but a few churches. In 1880 a separate missionary Church was established. The present position is therefore that a separation of communicants and worshippers is almost completely established in the N.G. Kerk.

In the Church of the Province of South Africa (the Anglican Church) a person of colour seeking to receive communion or to worship with a predominantly white congregation might create embarrassment and might not; it is most unlikely that he would be refused. In some churches such persons come regularly, and usually sit at the back of the church. In a cathedral their presence would excite no comment, even if they came to the altar rails amongst white communicants. In a small church they would probably come last. In one small church which I know such communicants sit at the back, occupying both sides of the aisle; but the arrangement is that first those on one side, then those on the other, go up to the altar rails. This is interrupted, however, when all the white communicants from the one side have communicated; for then all the white communicants from the other go forward. The harshness of this arrangement is softened by the action of the white churchwarden who comes up last of all. Thus the Christians of colour, who by the first act are reminded of their separateness, are by the second symbolically restored.

I give this example with no intention, however, of belittling my own church; it has a proud record of raising its voice in defence of the meek and poor, and I could give a further and quite different account of some of its other arrangements. The truth is that all South African churches mirror, some more, some less fully, the existing social arrangements, and this truth should keep us humble. It is interesting to quote in this connection from the first Referaat of the Bloemfontein Congress:

'With a few exceptions all the Christian Churches of South Africa use separate church formations for non-whites. In the case of the exceptions justice is not done to the non-white; he must usually sit at the back and gets little or no say in matters of church management.'

That is partly the truth but it must be supplemented if the whole truth is to be set down.

Now I think it quite possible that there will arise cases of mixed congregations of English-speaking churches where separation will yet be brought about, partly because the presence of Christians of colour poses uncomfortable problems, partly because of a sincere belief that their spiritual interests will thus better be served, partly because of residential considerations. I also think it possible that there will arise other cases of mixed congregations where the presence of non-white Christians will challenge that particular society to achieve a more truly Christian fellowship. Among English-speaking church leaders, not only because they are leaders and more forward-looking, but also because they deal with aspects of church organisation that make such developments more desirable and practicable, there is a clear tendency to seek for points of contact and to create such contacts in an effort to heal the wounds of separation, for separation deals wounds as well as justice.

I think it fair to say that while both Afrikaans-speaking and English-speaking churches in their pronouncements on separation, re-affirm their belief in the unity of all mankind in Christ, the English-speaking churches seem to require, as it were because of some need of the soul, some *visible* sign of that unity. I take it that the decision of the Grahamstown District of the Methodist Church to hold, for the first time in 1950, joint ministerial sessions was an expression of such a need. So also is the Wilgespruit Fellowship Centre in the Transvaal, where hard work is being done to provide a meeting-place where Christians of all races might meet together to worship, study, and work.

It seems that the English-speaking churches will tend to adopt more such measures, not merely for the purpose of *consultation*, not only for the purpose of *co-operation* and *collaboration*, but for the purpose of affirming and experiencing a true unity in Christ.

These things manifest themselves more easily in English-speaking churches for two reasons, one because their historical approach was always different, but also because the English-speaking people of South Africa have never had to reckon with a powerful internal group opinion; for I take Afrikaner group opinion to be one of the most powerful in the world.

Yet there are evidences that at least more consultation will take place between white and non-white members of the Dutch Reformed churches; this is at the moment high level and explorative, but I am sure that the intention is not only to learn to know one another's minds, but also to affirm and experience a truer unity. How far it will go, I cannot say.

Why is it that so many Christians desire some *visible* symbol of the unity of Christendom? Why is it that the sight of a great and silent mixed congregation, humble before its Creator, can move one so intolerably? Why is it that in many congregations there is a growing desire to know more of their sister congregations in the locations, more than the mere knowledge that such congregations are there? Such desires may derive from guilt as well as love, and they may be inhibited by fear. But why are they there? What is that in us which is moved and shaken by Chesterton's great hymn?

> O God of earth and altar,
> Bow down and hear our cry,
> Our earthly rulers falter,
> Our people drift and die.
> The walls of gold entomb us,
> The swords of scorn divide,
> Take not Thy thunder from us
> But take away our pride.
>
> From all that terror teaches,
> From lies of tongue and pen,
> From all the easy speeches
> That comfort cruel men,
> From sale and profanation
> Of honour and the sword,
> From sleep and from damnation,
> Deliver us, good Lord!
>
> Tie in a living tether
> The prince and priest and thrall,
> Bind all our lives together,
> Smite us and save us all.
> In ire and exaltation
> Aflame with faith, and free,
> Lift up a living nation
> A single sword to Thee.

What moves us indeed, but the vision that it gives to us of the unity of mankind? What we dread about separation is not residential or territorial separation, or the existence of separate congregations in Parktown and Orlando, or the provisions of separate hospitals and churches and schools, but the profound separation of man from man. We have a conviction that if separation of man from man goes beyond practical and utilitarian considerations, and becomes itself elevated into some kind of morality, then we shall shortly find ourselves separated from our God. In so far as separation policy can be an act of love, we are not so greatly concerned; but if separation policy becomes the act of fear or of self-interest, we fear that we shall shut ourselves off from God. It is this knowledge, I believe, which prevents many of us from regarding separation policy as an act desired by God, no matter how lofty may be some of the motives inspiring it.

There is another possibility that must be considered, and that is that the failure of a Church to show forth the unity of mankind may result in its decay. The growth of strong African sections of both Afrikaans-speaking and English-speaking churches is to be attributed to the devoted work of missionaries, rather than to the examples of other Christians. But it is difficult to keep the convert's eyes on Christ so that he will not have a chance to look at Christians. The missionary churches of the world, who have a great knowledge of Africa and a great desire to see it Christian, watch with hope and fear the behaviour of white Christian churches on the continent; and believe that the white Christian inhabitants of Africa have it in their power to bring missionary work to an end, not by withholding their gifts, but by withholding their love. Nor must we forget that the faith of Communism is often more warm and vital than that which we ourselves show.

It must also be considered possible that the Christian standpoint, that morality has no end but to serve the ends of love, may bring a Church into conflict with the State. It must be considered possible that a Church, in its attempts to achieve the outward and visible expressions of love, might come into conflict with a State morality that disapproves of such attempts. In that case there is nothing to do but humbly to seek the will of God, and to do it. Our Lord advised or commanded us to render unto Caesar the things which are Caesar's, and unto God the things which are God's. But we have no certitude that the choice would ever be posed so finally and so fatefully; it could be posed partially and tentatively. In that case it would be the duty of any Church, no matter whether it found itself alone or in company, to seek the will of God for itself, and to do it.

You remember that in Dostoevsky's story, Christ revisited the earth during the Inquisition, and the Grand Inquisitor flung Him into prison, where he visited Him, and reviled Him, saying:

'"Know too that I have been in the wilderness, I too have lived on roots and locusts, I too prized the freedom with which Thou hast blessed men, and I too was striving to stand among Thy elect. But I awakened and would not serve madness. I turned back and joined the ranks of those who have corrected Thy work. Tomorrow Thou shalt see that obedient flock who at a sign from me will hasten to heap up the hot cinders about the pile on which I shall burn Thee for coming to hinder us. For if anyone deserved our fires, it is Thou."

'When the Inquisitor ceased speaking he waited for some time for his Prisoner to answer him. His silence weighed down upon him. He saw that the Prisoner had listened intently all the time, looking gently in his face, and evidently not wishing to reply. The old man longed for Him to say something, however bitter and terrible. But He suddenly approached the old man in silence and softly kissed him on his bloodless aged lips. That was all His answer. The old man shuddered. His lips moved. He went to the door, opened it, and said to Him, "Go, and come no more . . . come not at all, never, never!" And he let Him out into the dark alleys of the town.'

How we fear, and how we should fear, to offend against that love. The fearful thing about the Christian morality of love is not its gentleness, but its uncompromisingness. How magnificent it would be to achieve Christian unity in South Africa, and how important! How magnificent it would be, if with our social arrangements we could achieve the Divine arrangement! How magnificent it would be to free ourselves from the corruption of history, or to render the right things unto Caesar, and the right things unto God, and both approve us. But until this Heaven be realised on this earth, and even while we try to realise this Heaven on this earth, we have our persisting duty to be obedient to the law of love. Therefore, while we strive to obey the laws, this is our law; and while we wish to serve the State, Christ is our Lord. There is no other way for a Church.

Sanna

The village lies in Sabbath heat
The dog lies in the sun
But stern and strict the elders go
They pass me one by one.

The alien traffic swirls and blows
The dust about the street
But stern and strict the elders go
In any dust or heat.

And careless words are spoken
By idlers of the place
But stern and strict the elders go
To hear the words of grace.

And stern and strict the sabbath clothes
And stern the eyes above
And stern and strict the elders go
To hear the words of love.

And Sanna follows all demure
And plays her little part
The child of love moves in her womb
And terror in her heart.

[1948–52. Not previously published.]

Anxiety Song of an Englishman

Down here where we talked of the Empire
From morning till night, and heard not a word
Of Afrikaans spoken, now come the great engines
And the Afrikaners stand on the footplates
And look confidently down through the hissing steam
As though they themselves had manufactured them
Yes they look down confidently at me
From a great height it seems, and turn a lever
And move off majestically and contemptuously
To the next station, to dwarf some other person.

[1948–52. Not previously published.]

The Joke

Let me relate a small affair.
A room. Johannesburg. Ten of us there.
One said, don't think that I presume
But if a bomb fell on this room
Why that would end the liberal cause.
Oh my the laughs! the loud guffaws!

Why, even now, I choke
Over that joke.

We mean nothing evil towards you

Black man, we are going to shut you off
We are going to set you apart, now and forever.
We mean nothing evil towards you
You shall have your own place, your own institutions.
Your tribal customs shall flourish unhindered
You shall lie all day long in the sun if you wish it
All the things that civilisation has stolen
Shall be restored. You shall take wives
Unhindered by our alien prohibitions
Fat-bellied children shall play innocently
Under the wide-branching trees of the lush country
Where you yourselves were born.
Boys shall go playing in the reed lagoons
Of far Ingwavuma, the old names
Shall recover old magic, milk and honey
Shall flow in the long-forsaken places
We mean nothing evil towards you.

A fresh new wind shall blow through your territory
Under your hands freed from our commandment
You shall build what shall astonish you.
The ravished land shall take on virginity
The rocks and the shales of the desolate country
Shall acquire the fertility of the fruitful earth.
Chance-gotten children shall return to the womb
To re-emerge with sanctions and live pattern lives
Of due obedience to authority and age.
Morality shall be recovered, the grave
And fearless bearing, the strange innocence
Of the tribal eyes, and all the sorrows
Of these hundred years shall pass away

This is our reparation, our repayment
Of the incomputable debt.
We mean nothing evil towards you.

Can you for whom we have made this reparation
Not give us something also, not petition
The gods of all the tribes we recreate
To call you back in one migration
North to the beating heart of Africa?
Can you not make a magic that will silence conscience,
Put peace behind the frowning vigilant eyes,
That will regardless of Space and Time
Wipe you from the face of the earth?
But without pain . . .
For we mean nothing evil towards you.

Our resolve is immutable, our hands tremble
Only with the greatness of our resolution.
We are going to set you apart, now and forever,
We mean nothing evil towards you.

[10.11.1952. Not previously published.]

Piet van der Merwe goes to Heaven

When Piet van der Merwe went to Heaven he was disconcerted to find that the head of the Reception Office was a black man but he was even more disconcerted to find that it was his old servant Joseph. He had always regarded Joseph as a good-for-nothing scoundrel, and what was more, he had thoroughly disapproved of Joseph's active support of the Roman Church, which as everyone knows is a harlot sitting on seven mountains.

Joseph gave no sign of recognition, but made his old master sit down so that his name and other information could be entered in the Great Book.

'What is your name, man?' asked Joseph.

Piet was up in a flash.

'Listen,' he said, 'I will not be called *man* by you or any other black creature.'

'You will be called *man* and no other name,' said Joseph.

He opened a little book at a certain page, and showed it to Piet; and sure enough it was written there, *man* and *woman* shall be the only titles in Heaven, save when it shall please the Lord to bestow the title of *beloved*, which is reserved for His Saints.

'I see it,' said Piet grimly.

'Then what is your name, man?'

Piet swallowed, and then he said in a choking voice, 'My name is Piet van der Merwe, you black bastard.'

'It is not forbidden', said Joseph, 'to call a man a bastard, but it is forbidden to call him a black one.'

And at last Piet van der Merwe had given all the required information.

'Where would you like to sleep, man?'

'I should like to sleep', said Piet, 'anywhere except with coloured bastards.'

'I beg to point out', said Joseph firmly, 'that the word *bastard* may not be used with any adjective of colour or race.'

And Piet swallowed.

'However,' continued Joseph, 'special arrangements are made for

116

people with your views. There are special quarters for those who do not wish to live with people of another colour.'

'Now you are talking,' said Piet. 'In my Father's house are many mansions.'

'It must however be noted', said Joseph, 'that the Lord does not visit any colour-bar mansion. Nor does He bestow the title *beloved* on any occupant of any such mansion.'

'Well, you can't have everything,' said Piet.

'I shall send for a messenger to take you to your mansion, man. I hope . . .'

'You mind your own business, you black bastard.'

'You have offended three times,' said Joseph, 'and if you offend again, you will be sent to an international mansion.'

'I shan't offend again,' said Piet. 'You . . .'

And here the messenger appeared, a small black boy in uniform and gloves. Piet looked at him suspiciously.

'Is he from my mansion?' he asked.

'In your mansion,' said Joseph, 'all messengers, lift-boys, and servants, are black; but the superintendent is a European.'

'That's good,' said Piet.

He turned to the messenger.

'Take me to my mansion, boy,' he said.

The messenger bowed low to Joseph.

'Stay well, beloved,' he said.

Then he turned to Piet van der Merwe.

'Come on, man,' he said.

[1953. *Africa South*, April–June 1957.]

My Great Discovery

After much exploratory
Work in my laboratory
I made an epoch-making
Breath-taking
Discovery.

Can you not picture me?
Can you not see me there,
Wild eyes, disordered hair,
With fanatical persistence
And white-robed assistants
In masks,
And flasks
Smoking, choking
Everywhere?

I cannot give to such as you
The reasoning which led me to
This epoch-making
Breath-taking
Discovery.
For if you look
At all the poems in this book
You will observe that I have undertaken
And have so far remained unshaken
In my quite revolutionary plan
To write so that the common man
May understand.
Therefore I cánnot give to you
The reasoning which led me to
My great discovery.

Well, this discovery
Was simple as could be
Five straight injections
Position, lumbar
In colour, umber
Taste, very like cucumber
Effect, inducing slumber
And if I may remind you
Five in number –
These five injections could erase
In just as many days
The pigmentation
From any nation.

I sat astounded
Completely dumbfounded
By the epoch-making
Breath-taking
Discovery.
Being a scientist, delighted
Being South African, affrighted
In Great Britain, knighted.
I seized the telephone
And in a voice unlike my own
(Not through dissembling
But through trembling)
Government, I said
The girl said, what division?
I said, no divisions any more.
She said, I mean what section?
I said, no sections any more.
She said, I'll report you,
(Or deport you,
I can't quite say
I'm not au fait
With recent legislation)
I said, you go ahead
Or I shall plunge the nation
Into a conflagration.
I know that shocked her
She said, you need the Doctor

I said, yes get the Doctor
And all the Cabinet,
For I can change the pigmentation
Of any nation.
To cut the story short
She gave a kind of snort
And got the real big Boss
Who said, of coss, of coss,
Come up at once.

It is no kind of pret
To face a Cabinet
They were astounded
And dumbfounded.
One said, Good Lord
And hummed and hawed
And one was suave
Just like the papers say.
And one was gay
And said this is the day
For if the pigmentation
Of any nation
Can suffer alteration
Why the whole fact of race
Takes on another face.
But another Minister
Looking quite sinister
Just like the papers say
Said this suggestion
Requires digestion
Let's meet another day.

And so again I met
The Cabinet
And this same Minister
Still looking sinister
Said, does this alteration
Of the pigmentation
Of any nation,
Just work from black to white
Or do you think it might

Change also white to black?
And I replied
All full of pride
The recipe can be supplied
For any shade
In beige or jade
In snow or jet
Or violet.
Then sir, he said, I here submit
A list of those to be
Changed with this recipe.
He pushed the list across
To the big Boss.
My eyes are fine
A shiver went right down my spine
The leading name was mine.

I reached into my pocket
And pressed the radar switch
That sent the radar rocket
Which
Blew up the laboratory
And all work exploratory
Plus my assistants
Whom at this distance
I spared the degradation
The gross humiliation
Of working for a caitiff
Who had gone naitiff.

PART THREE

1953-1968

This period coincides with the life of the Liberal Party of South Africa, which was formed in May 1953 and was forced out of existence by the Political Interference Act of 1968. Alan Paton was one of the founders of the party; he became national chairman in 1956, and in 1958 national president, a position he held until the party was dissolved. These were fifteen years of intense political and social activity and involvement. It was in this period that the political articles later collected and published as *The Long View* (1968) were written. But at the same time Alan Paton produced three books of other kinds: *Debbie Go Home* (1961), a collection of short stories; *Hofmeyr* (1964), a biography; and *Instrument of Thy Peace* (1968), a book of meditations. He travelled fairly frequently in the 1950s, lecturing several times in the United States and in Britain; but in 1960 his passport was withdrawn by the South African Government.

[1953–4. Not previously published.]

My Sense of Humour

My friends are angry with me
Because I have lost
My sense of humour.

They remind me of occasions
When I have had the room rolling
With my wit.

They weep with despair
Over my sorrowful book
And sombre verses.

Well I too have pondered
This sad matter
With regret.

The truth is I have struggled
To get my humour
Into its harness.

But it bucks like a beast
And rears and kicks and will not get
Between the shafts.

I have a suspicion
It does not like the strange carriage
I am driving.

I feel like saying to it
I do not like it either.
Obey, like myself.

[Long Island, 1954. Not previously published.]

The General

The General could hardly get over the smallness of the town. In memory it had seemed much bigger. But the mountain was the same as ever, bringing back to him, now that he saw it, things that he had forgotten. And how clearly he remembered the magic of its name, Hunger Mountain. And how clearly he remembered that he had to keep the magic for himself, because no one else had understood it; except maybe, his father and his mother, but certainly no one else that he knew. It was just a mountain, wasn't it, called Hunger Mountain because someone had known hunger there, someone had died maybe, in some bygone day, and what else was there to say? Ah, there was a lot more to say, but perhaps you couldn't say it, only feel it; and perhaps if you could say it, that would be just as hard to understand.

When he came to the gate of 'Arlington', he was assailed, no, rather assaulted, by memory. Through the trees he could see the farmhouse and the guest huts, and it was just as he remembered it, to the great oak that stood outside it, and the fowls running about the yard. It was here that they had come for so many of their holidays. It was in these trees that Catherine and he had built houses, small houses a foot high, forked sticks stuck upright into the earth, then the roofsticks laid in the forks, and on the roofsticks the roof of leaves, the walls built of miniature bricks made from the claypit by 'Arlington' stream. It was a labour of love, beginning after breakfast, reluctantly suspended for lunch, kept up till the sun was going down. Then shockingly, unbelievably, Catherine had died, and left him desolate. He could remember, even now, the dark room, the sweet odours, and most terribly, the still form, the white face of his companion, of one who a week ago was so alive. He could hear her voice, 'David, I think we ought to do this, don't you?' She was older than he, she was the leader, but not bossily. They were both inventive, imaginative; they talked to each other very like two people talking to themselves, in fact they did talk a great deal to themselves even when together.

Her death left him alone, and after it his father and mother paid him a

125

great deal of attention. The other children at the holiday farm were already engaged, and more than that, were of superior and indifferent years. Nevertheless, he knew, even at that age, that he was not just imaginative and sensitive, but that he was fearful. Home was easy enough, and church too, anywhere that he went with his father and mother. School was hard, and the streets. Boys were quick to see when you were fearful, and played on it. But you could get home, and read your books, and play in the yard. It was all safe there. If you could live all your life there, it would be wonderful.

'You have to go out, David,' his mother had said. 'We all have to go out. We can't stay inside for ever.'

Then she would catch him up and kiss him, and hold him away from her, and look into his eyes, which was a trick of hers.

'Do you know what I mean?' she would say.

He would nod his head, not able to assent with words, because he knew what she meant, but what she said was pitiless, and he could not assent with words.

Now along the road from the farmhouse to the gate where he was standing, was coming a white-haired woman. She smiled at him, noting with interest the signs that this must be a soldier of some distinction.

'You have been standing here so long', she said, 'that I thought I would come and see if I could help you.'

They introduced themselves. She was Elizabeth Garrison, the widowed owner of 'Arlington'; he General David Masterson, from the big camp at Deep River. She opened the gate, and he took his car to the big oak by the house and walked back to meet her. She gave him tea in the dining-room that he remembered, noisy with many people; and he could smell the smells that captured him long ago, of a farm kitchen and a farm pantry.

Then he left her to walk before lunch, first along green and gently rising slopes, after which begin the man-made plantations girdling the base of Hunger Mountain, and after them the mountain itself, now rising majestically, here in sheer walls, there in steep kloofs, filled with chichi bush. The chichi bush was itself something that he had quite forgotten, but the moment he saw it, and took one of its leaves in his hand, he remembered leaning over from the horse Scout to pluck some kind of switch with which to urge the old fellow to a faster pace. He had never plucked the switch, for Scout had suddenly started off at demonic speed, throwing his years aside, becoming an engine of tumultuous power, going faster and faster as though nothing could be fast enough. He himself was first filled with terror and then with exaltation, part of him holding on for dear life, part of him suddenly torn loose and freed. As he passed the others, they laughed and shouted and cheered, but he had no time or chance to reply to them, being fully occupied with the business of staying where he was. Then the path grew steeper, and Scout came to a grinding halt.

'Well, David,' said one of the older men, 'I never saw you look so fierce before.'

'I had to be fierce,' he had replied. 'Otherwise I couldn't have stayed on.'

He was now approaching the girdle of trees. He did not suppose that they were the same trees as those of thirty-four years ago. Trees grew fast and did not stand long in this timber-hungry country. But their present appearance was just as he remembered them. It was dark in there. Something had urged him in, he remembered, just as something had caused him to keep on looking back to the sunlit mountainside. The trees stretched away before him, long lanes of quietness paved with gold-brown needles.

He had gone in farther, feeling brave because he knew he was afraid. If John Marshall had been there, he would have gone in like a grown-up, shouting to hear his voice in the silence, and he himself would have followed John with no fear at all. It was a strange and great friendship. John was the older boy, strong, self-confident, athletic; it was a wonderful thing to have been befriended by him, and marked the turning-point of his life.

He remembered the time that Chick Duncan, for no reason at all, had begun to torment him on the way home from school. From cruel words Chick had passed on to cruel acts, until he had pinned him down on the ground, with knees moving up and down cruelly on his upper arms; he had struck him in the face and banged his head on the ground. He had not been afraid at first, having been many a time the object of Chick's attention, but as the blows became more and more vicious, and as he could feel that Chick's reasonless anger was growing into something beyond his control, he began to fear for his life. He was saved by approaching voices, and Chick suddenly rose from off him.

'If you tell, I'll kill you,' Chick had said.

He had tried to go quietly into the house, so that he would get a chance to wash the blood from his teeth and brush his hair. But so different was this from his daily habit of going at once to his mother with all the news of school that she had come looking for him, and had seen his pitiful state.

'What happened?' she asked.

He could not tell her at first. It seemed to him that not even she had the right to know the distress of his soul.

'This can't be allowed,' she said. 'It can't be allowed. Who did it?'

Then she said, 'Well, if you won't tell me who did it, tell me if it was someone bigger than you.'

He nodded to that.

'Was it Chick Duncan?' she asked.

His silence was enough.

'I'll clean you up,' she said.

She cleaned him up, and with her trick, held him away from her and looked at him, so that he saw the pity and anger in her eyes.

But while his father wrestled with the problem of whether to report the whole matter to the headmaster, John Marshall had discovered it all for himself, and he had given Chick Duncan the hiding of his life. So began their friendship, as one of guardian and ward; no one ever dared to touch him again.

In 1914 he had been twenty years old, training to become a schoolmaster. He and John had gone off to the wars. He had long known that his rapid rise in the army was due to his friendship with John, not because John had been in any position to advance him, but because from their friendship had come his new self-confidence and strength. Though he disliked war, he was not terrified by it. Given responsibility he put fear from his mind. He had come out of it all with honour, a beloved officer. His name was always coupled with John's but he knew that it was John who was the great soldier. He and John decided together to remain in the army, and he had thought that no one knew but himself that he had done it because of John. In the darkness of the pine forest he smiled to himself, at the innocence of such a thought. His father and mother must have known. His headmaster must have known. Even Chick Duncan, if he had thought about it, must have known. All those who had watched the growth of their friendship, and the slow gaining of strength and confidence by the shy and gentle boy, must have known. And of course John had known too.

As he came out of the forest into the sunlight, and took the path that led back to 'Arlington', he remembered his bitter experience at the hands of Colonel Temple, a hard and merciless taskmaster. Everything had been going well till Temple came. Colonel Roberts had always said, 'Masterson, I don't know what I should do without you.' But not Temple. Temple would lash out at him, and as he was leaving the room would call him back, and lash out more terribly still, saying the same things again, but in more cruel ways. He was sitting on his bed when John came in and caught the despair in his eyes before he could hide it away.

John shut the door. 'Take it easy, David,' he said, 'you'll have a breakdown if you go on like this.'

He would not have humbled himself, but John had already seen for himself. You couldn't lie about that. He supposed that his love for John was greater even than his pride, otherwise he could not have humbled himself.

'I don't know that I can take it any more,' he said.

'What does it do to you, David?'

'It's a pain, John, not a real pain, I know, but my whole inside seems full of it, a kind of aching, I don't know. Everyone must see it,' he concluded miserably.

'No one sees it,' said John, 'except Margaret and myself. And Margaret doesn't quite know what it is. I think I do.'

'I know you do.'

'In point of fact,' said John, 'you don't need to bear it any longer. Temple's going.'

The relief was immediate. But some strange humility, honesty, call it what you will, made him say, 'John, let's be frank. Temple may go away, but *I* don't go away. I stay the same.'

'I know. I've thought about that. But I couldn't advise you, David. That's private ground.'

'You're right. Who'll be in command?'

'I shall.'

He could not have hidden the joy in his eyes had he tried. But he did not try, partly because of the honesty of his love.

'You deserve it,' he said, then added, 'sir.'

John grinned. 'Not yet,' he said, 'tomorrow.'

So the dangerous period had lasted only a month, and no one saw but the two who were closest to him. It never happened again in twenty years. As John rose, so did he. His father and mother watched his progress with pride. His mother could no longer use her old trick, and hold him away from her at arm's length, and gaze at him, but he often caught her looking at him, marvelling.

In 1939 he became General Masterson. They were great names those, General Marshall, General Masterson. Everyone was glad that they were there, General Marshall in supreme command, General Masterson in command of the First, training at Deep River, till it was ready to go up North. Both of them were quiet, confident, unassuming men, with no thought higher than that of duty.

When he reached the door at 'Arlington', Mrs. Garrison was just coming out.

'Go into the dining-room,' she said. 'Lunch will soon be ready.'

To his astonishment, Margaret was there. She came to him and embraced him. He recognised at once that her embrace was maternal rather than wifely. He knew at once that she knew.

'How did you know I was here?' he asked.

'John told me.'

'How did he know?'

'I don't know. I thought you must have told him.'

Love was a strange thing, capable of many deeds, and having surprising knowledge. He had always thought John Marshall was a great man, but perhaps he was greater than that. Why, even his wife, here with her arms about him, thought perhaps that his heart was broken.

'What made you come here?' he asked. 'Hiding your car and all.'

He could feel her relaxing. She was beginning to get it.

'Did you see it in the papers?' he asked.

'It's not in the papers yet,' she said. 'John told me. Did it hurt you, David?'

'Yes, it hurt me. That's why I came here.'

'Should I not have come?'

'No, it was good that you came. You timed it well.'

She stood apart from him.

'What did John say?' she asked.

'He said he needed me here.'

That wasn't all that John had said. John had said that Judson had got the Northern Command, an Australian, a hard man, a tiger of a soldier. But he didn't tell her that.

He saw that she was weeping.

'Don't weep,' he said. 'I'm to get the Home Command.'

Then suddenly he himself was moved, but because he did not want her to see it, he left her, and went to the window, looking up at the mountain, Hunger Mountain, whose name had captured him when he was still a child. He was filled with pity for all those who, for ambition or something else, pride perhaps, duty, necessity, had to push out into a world of which they were afraid, with no one at hand to help. He knew suddenly why he himself was beloved; not for virtue or for courage, but because he could recognise his own kind.

[1955–6? Not previously published.]

The Magistrate's Daughter

She was very cold and very beautiful, and wholly apart from us. That was not only because her father was the magistrate of our village, but also because neither she nor her brother went to the village school. They were at school in the city, and wore blazers of expensive grey flannel, with badges of obscure device, very different from the crossed gun and spade of our own, and the plain English legend 'Fight and Work'.

When she came home for the holidays, she walked up and down the village street like a princess. She had grey eyes and a pale, clear face, with hollows in her cheeks which gave to her a look of ethereality. Archie Garland fell in love with her at sight. He was the captain of the school, in cricket and football and tennis, and was a tall and handsome boy. His father was the village blacksmith.

Archie was the school hero. All the boys looked up to him, and all the girls adored him, partly because he had never singled one of them out. He told no one of his passion, but walked up and down the village street. She was heartbreakingly proud, and the hollows in her cheeks were unbelievably distinguished and beautiful. He lived for these encounters. He would see her from far off, and would not take his eyes off her until he was about twenty yards from her, and then he would look rigidly ahead, and would not have known if she had looked at him or not.

He saw her the first Sunday too, at the church with her important father and impressive mother, and her younger brother in a smart dark Sunday suit. About them was this aura of unattainability, and they spoke only to the rector and the Ansons and the Crewe-Thompsons, rich farmers of the district, and to their sons and daughters, who went to those schools with the grey-flannel blazers and the badges of obscure device. And Archie Garland thought her more and more ethereal and beautiful.

'They're a nice-looking family,' said Mrs. Garland.

'They're a stuck-up lot,' said Archie's sister Mary, 'and as for that Hermione, she needs a dash of paint.'

'And what might you mean by that?' asked Mr. Garland.

'I mean, Dad, she needs colouring up.' Mary put on a snobbish voice. 'She looks so Fraightfully Fraightfully delicate, don't you know?'

Hermione! That was her name! And what a name for her! It was the first time he had ever heard it, so it wasn't a name for many. And she did not look delicate, she just had that indescribable pallor which set her off from all others, even from her own father and mother and brother. He thought of her a great deal, much more than would have been expected from one of his sanity and practicality of mind, which more than one of his teachers had commended in the end-of-term reports. They would have been astonished had they known that this dependable captain of the school, this matter-of-fact son of his father, this unquestioned ruler of five hundred souls, dreamed of saving the magistrate's daughter from fire and water and fates worse than death.

One holiday afternoon Archie arranged some cricket at the school, and the magistrate's son came and stood at the fence and watched them. Archie walked over to him and said, 'Do you want a game?'

'Yes, please. But I'm not very good.'

He wasn't very good, but he played those stylish shots that they learn at the grey-flannel schools. It was a pleasure to watch him, then suddenly he was bowled.

'Your strokes are good,' Archie told him. 'But you want to put more punch into them. You're Parker, aren't you? What's your other name?'

'David. My dad's the magistrate.'

'I'm Archie Garland. If you want to practise tomorrow, I'll bowl for you at the nets. Nine o'clock.'

The next morning Archie showed David Parker how to put more punch into his shots, and after the practice they went to Turnbull's and drank cokes. But there was no sign in the street of the magistrate's daughter.

'Do you play tennis?' asked David.

'Yes.'

'I won't be good enough for you, but we can play at our place this afternoon.'

So Archie went to the magistrate's place that afternoon. Although he was captain of the school and ruled five hundred souls, he opened the magistrate's gate with a distinct beating of the heart. The house was called 'The Residency' and by this name the magistrates' houses in all villages were distinguished from all others. The house was not otherwise distinguished, but for Archie it was not only bathed in an aura of power and authority, it was also the home of the magistrate's daughter. Before he could reach the house, he was called by David from the tennis court. The balls were brand-new, something that happened at school only when there was a big game. A servant brought out tea and scones, but there was no sign of the magistrate's daughter. He therefore lavished his devotion on her brother, and taught him how to put more punch into his strokes.

After that he was every day with David Parker, either playing cricket at the school or tennis at the Residency. The servant came always with the tea and scones, but there was never a sign of the magistrate's daughter. Never did she come to watch the tennis, and the only time he ever saw her was in the village street and that was only from that distance of never less than twenty yards.

Then came one afternoon when David Parker did not ask him to tennis. Archie thought he would go down to the station to see the Harrisons, and take the path which ran past the Residency, and then he thought he would not, because he was the captain of the school and not a first-form boy. But in the end he did. They were playing tennis there, the Ansons, and the Crewe-Thompsons, and suddenly he was ashamed of himself for having come, and would have turned back if it had not been too late. Luckily he was hidden from the court by a hedge, and of course as he passed he looked rigidly ahead.

He spent the afternoon with Geoff Harrison. More than once he thought of his foolishness, and his ears would burn, and once he surprised himself by suddenly drawing in his breath, so that Geoff Harrison said to him, 'Archie, what's the matter?', and he said with great presence of mind, 'Something I'd forgotten.'

He went back home by the railway track, and gave himself over to jealousy. He was good enough to play with David Parker, who could never have won a game if it hadn't been given to him, but he wasn't good enough to play with the Ansons and the Crewe-Thompsons and the magistrate's daughter, even though, so far as he knew, he was as good a player as any of them. When he gave himself over to jealousy the results were painful, because he thought only of those grey-flannel blazers and those heraldic badges, and the aristocratic pallor of her face. But the thing that made him most ashamed was that he found himself remembering that his father was a blacksmith, which was something he had never thought of in that way before. He would like to have returned to his normal life, but unfortunately he was in love.

In any event on the next day his jealousy was suddenly wiped away. David Parker asked him to come and play tennis with his sister and a friend who was coming to stay. His excitement he concealed from everybody. He brushed up his blazer with extra care. There was nothing to be done about the gun and the spade, but he could not help wishing that they could become a dragon spewing fire, or a mailed arm and fist showing courage and death and aristocracy.

'Are you playing singles again with that stuck-up kid?' asked Mary.

'No, I'm playing doubles.'

His sister sat up as if stung by electricity.

'With Hermione?' she asked.

'Yes.'

'You never told us you'd met her.'

Archie turned on her the gaze of a thoroughly righteous soul.

'I haven't,' he said.

'So now you're going to. How Fraightfully Fraightfully naice! And how jolly for you, dear boy.'

'Somebody's eyes are green,' said Mrs. Garland.

Mary ignored her mother and looked at her brother with disdain.

'No wonder you spent all that time cleaning up your blazer.' She stood up and made an elegant exit, flicking imaginary specks of dust from her dress. 'Au revoir, all,' she said, in what she meant to be the manner of a great lady.

He had never looked at Hermione directly, and her face was not quite the same as he had imagined it. But it was ethereally beautiful, and her pallor was as indescribable as ever. She called him Archie without fuss, and introduced him to her friend Elaine. Hermione was the stronger player, so Archie and Elaine played against the magistrate's son and daughter. He was able to play harder than usual, but could not help winning all the sets. At four o'clock the servant brought the tea, and this time Mrs. Parker came down to pour it out. It was a strange afternoon, he could hardly describe it. He got on easily with David, and his partner Elaine admired his play in genuine and generous fashion. But Mrs. Parker was like an empress, and Hermione like an empress's daughter. He said good-bye to them, and thanked them for the tennis, but they did not thank him for coming to play with them, or hope that he would come again.

The jealousy was on him again, because Hermione and Elaine had spoken of the dance that was to be given by the Crewe-Thomsons. They spoke of strangers, Hugh and Darrell and Anthony, and of how well Hugh danced. The thought of the magistrate's daughter in the arms of this Hugh filled him with a pain in some place, a kind of ache which had somehow made its way through from the mind to the body.

'Well, is she beautiful?' his sister asked. When he did not answer, she asked, 'Can she play?'

'She plays all right,' he said.

'Is she stuck-up?' And when he made no reply, she said, 'It's time to stop mooning about, brother. You're a big boy and you're growing up.'

He played once more with Hermione and Elaine, and Elaine was glad to see him. She asked him if it was true that he was captain of cricket and football and tennis, all three, and seemed to think it was something to be proud of, even though it was at a country school. He warmed towards her because she made him feel more at his ease. He called Hermione by her name for the first time, and when Mrs. Parker came down to pour out the tea he thought her less forbidding than she had been before.

At church on Sunday there was no change. David Parker said hullo to him, but Mr. and Mrs. Parker and Hermione and Elaine were busy speaking to the Ansons and the Crewe-Thompsons; in any case Mr. Garland was not much given to gossip after church.

'I can't see that she's beautiful,' said Mary. 'Looks as though her cheeks might fall in at any moment.'

'She's a nice-looking girl,' said Mrs. Garland.

'Do you think she's beautiful?' Mary asked Archie.

'I don't go round thinking whether girls are beautiful or not beautiful.'

'Oh, don't you now? You can't bluff me, Archie Garland.'

'There's one thing you should learn, miss,' said Mr. Garland, 'and that's not to talk so much about people.'

'They're a stuck-up lot, Dad, and you know it.'

'This village has been like that ever since I can remember,' said Mr. Garland. 'It's almost as though every magistrate leaves a list of the best people behind for the next magistrate. Your mother and I have never been on the list, and we've never wanted to be. But we don't waste our breath talking about those who are.'

Archie did not know whether to be pleased or otherwise when David Parker asked to see the blacksmith's shop. He could not help wondering if Hermione and Elaine and the Ansons and the Crewe-Thompsons had discussed the fact that his father was the village blacksmith, and he could not help wondering just in what manner they had discussed it. But his good sound sense came to his rescue, and he took David to the shop and handed him over to his father, and whether Honest John was pleased or amused or took it as a matter of course to have the magistrate's son in his shop, no one would have known.

'Thank you very much, sir,' said David Parker after he had seen everything, 'it was very good of you to spare me your time. It was very interesting.'

'It's a dying trade,' Honest John told the boy. 'I would have started a motor business, but Archie wanted to be a doctor. It's natural to want to go up in the world.'

At teatime at the house Mary was at her worst, holding her teacup with her fingers sprayed out affectedly, and speaking with great refinement. Archie would have been angry except that David seemed quite unaware of any mockery.

'Not a bad kid,' said Mary after he had gone. 'Are you going to ask him to our end-of-holiday dance?'

Archie hesitated, but his mother said, 'I think we must ask him, son. You can't go about with him the whole holiday, and then not ask him to our dance. And we shall have to ask Hermione and her friend as well. I'll write to Mrs. Parker tonight.'

'I hope we can come,' said David Parker to his friend. And Archie hoped they could come too, and dance in the big Garland lounge, and see one of the nicest houses in the village. The thought of dancing with Hermione, of touching her, was in itself of the nature of ecstasy. And he wanted her to see him amongst his friends, and see how they looked up to him, and he hoped that this might make her less remote and unattainable.

Dear Mrs. Garland

It is very kind of you to invite my daughter Hermione and her brother and her friend to your end-of-holiday dance. I have discussed it with my husband, and we much regret that we cannot accept your invitation. He is very strict in his outlook and believes that as the magistrate who has to dispense justice in the district, he must not run the risk of cultivating personal relationships which might one day influence him in the performance of his duties.

I hope your dance will be very successful.

Yours sincerely
Elizabeth Parker

'So that's that,' said Mrs. Garland to her daughter. 'And listen, there's to be no hurting Archie about this. He'll be hurt enough as it is. This is one time when you mustn't go round fooling.'

'Yes, Mother,' she burst out. 'How I hate them! How hateful they are! Aren't the Ansons and the Crewe-Thompsons in the district too?'

'It's no use hating them. We're going to have the best dance ever, and this girl will go back to school, and Archie can forget all about her.'

And that was the end of the holiday friendship and the cricket and the tennis. Archie did not see his friend again. And he himself felt too hurt and shamed to go into the village street. But on the last day but one of the holiday, on the day of the dance itself, there were a dozen jobs to do, and it was while doing one of them that he saw her coming up the village street. He turned abruptly into Fox's Lane, so that he need not see her pale and cruel face.

[This paper was presented at a conference of writers, publishers, editors and university teachers of English, held at the University of the Witwatersrand, Johannesburg, in July 1956. Witwatersrand University Press, 1957.]

The South African Novel in English

The South African novel written in English is to my mind quite a remarkable achievement, and not the least remarkable thing about it is that it has in the last few years begun to add to itself at an accelerated pace. This fact has been widely commented upon overseas, by which I mean in Europe and the United States of America. I can vouch from personal knowledge for the growing reputation of our fictional literature in the United States. There, we are said to be going through a renaissance; however, my own opinion is that we are not experiencing a renaissance, but a first birth. Let me say at once that I am implying no denigration whatsoever of our two forerunners, Olive Schreiner and Sarah Gertrude Millin. But since their time the body of South African fiction in English has begun to grow apace. Olive Schreiner's *Story of an African Farm* stood by itself for nearly half a century, for I do not consider that she added anything of importance to that first famous story. After that came Mrs. Millin, who proceeded single-handed to build up our literature, except for Laurens van der Post's contribution of *In a Province*, William Plomer's *Turbott Wolfe*, and May and Williams's *I am Black*. Any history of the South African novel in English will give an abiding place to our two most famous women writers.

But it is only in the last decade that our fiction has begun to develop a body; and in this year alone, 1956, there have been added to our literature three more works of substance, namely, Harry Bloom's *Episode*, Miriam Basner and Mopeli-Paulus's *Turn to the Dark*, and Gunnar Helander's story, called in America *Black Rhapsody*. This is, I think, a remarkable achievement, and I do not think the end of it is in sight. Only time can decide the lasting qualities of any of the books I have so far named, or of any of the books I have yet to name. I am not suggesting that any single one of them would find a place in the world's ten or twenty or thirty, or any other number of great novels. But they are all of them productions of quality. All of them are fit to be considered in any discussion of the South African novel in English.

The point I am making here is that the process of building up a body of fiction in English shows no signs of abating. If we go on at this rate, we are likely to build up a fictional literature second only to the great literatures of Europe and the United States of America; in other words, our literature is likely to occupy a distinguished place among the literatures of the minor nations of the world.

It is often said – and I believe that something of the kind has recently been said again by Professor Guy Butler with particular reference to South African poets – that the English-speaking South African has not yet become a true native of his country. This is not true in respect of the English-speaking writer of fiction. Nothing could be more a product of the South African scene than the South African novel in English. To take a single example, Mr. Harry Bloom's *Episode* is South African through and through. No one but a South African could have written it. This might be a fascinating subject to explore. Why does the South African novel differ from our poetry in this important respect?

I would admit without argument that the English-speaking South African is more of a European than the Afrikaner, that his churches, schools and politics offer proof of this. But it is not true of his novels. There is an obvious and perhaps platitudinous explanation of this. In the novel the novelist is observing, interpreting and communicating his interpretation of life. And he lives life here, and what is more, he is absolutely fascinated by it. At Christmas time he may – though I doubt it – buy one of those anathematised Christmas cards showing the holly bush red with berries and the snow deep on the ground – but when he writes, he writes of the thorn tree, and the sun pouring down out of the southern sky. The truth is that we English-speaking South Africans are not English but South African. When we talk of 'home' we mean the country in which the great majority of us were born, which commands our affection, and excites our desire to write of what we know and understand.

Before I proceed I should like to examine for a moment the theory so often put forward, that the novel itself is in its decline, that, for example, the limited number of plots and situations has been exhausted, and that each new novel tends to be a copy of one that has already been written. This theory attaches far too much importance to the basic elements of any story, and far too little to the environment in which the events take place, and far too little to the actual skill in writing which the creator of the story possesses. I attach no importance whatever to this theory. We in South Africa have an environment so incredibly rich and complex and strange that, even if a writer lacked the superlative gifts, he could still with reasonable ones write a story which would excite the interest of the outside world. But not only the outside world; he can excite the interest of our own. He can interpret South Africa in such a way that countless numbers of readers will respond to his vision, they will be excited by a revelation, not of something they do not know, but of something they do know, revealed to them in such a way that what they dimly sensed is suddenly illuminated, sometimes brightly, sometimes by an arrow of light that pierces the very heart, causing an emotional storm of grief, recognition, pain, exaltation, guilt and joy.

It is life, not any structural pattern, that is the making of any story. And life in South Africa is so fantastic, so deep and wide and rich, that it shows no signs of being exhausted. The son of a former Governor-General goes to prison because he believes the laws are unjust. A coloured boy kills himself because he cannot face expulsion from a white school. A small black boy finds himself marooned on a quarry-face, and is brought to safety by a brave white man, who is greeted on descending by a great crowd, mostly Indians and Africans, who cry out to him, 'Thank you, sir. God bless you, sir. White man, God bless you.'[1] In a dangerous race-riot an African woman takes an Afrikaner woman to the safety of her house, and there they pray together for South Africa. South Africa teems with such stories, born out of the danger and complexity of our country. There has never been anything quite like it before. If we write of these things with honesty and skill and, if we are so blessed, with genius, our country and the whole world will listen to us. The story is as old as man, or certainly as old as language; and as long as language lasts, so will the story.

To suggest that the story, the novel, is on the decline, is to my mind comparable to suggesting that the painting of still-lifes or portraits, or landscapes, is drawing near its end, or that the art of biography is finished. This is surely nonsense. It seems certain to me that if the writing of South African stories were to come to an end, one must seek for quite other causes, which at the moment show no sign of coming into being. I believe that this theory comes from countries, European countries, which are pessimistic about the future of their continent, and in whose societies life seems to be losing its exciting qualities. I suggest that pessimism and hopelessness, while legitimate themes, cannot compare with that perpetual renewal which is characteristic of the United States, but is of no country more characteristic than of our own. Everything lies before us. A period of change, upheaval, tension, and creation lies ahead. That is life, that is the very stuff of which stories are made. Even the attempts of our Government to impose tranquillity upon us are part of this pulsing life, for they

[1] See the story on page 179.

provoke, and must inevitably provoke, fears, hopes and resistances. Speaking as a writer, and not as a politician, I say that the future seems full of promise.

It could of course be suggested by those who know my political interests and ideals, that I am confusing politics with life. Or it might be said that I am confusing race questions with life. Yet I would be the first to recognise the qualities of Elizabeth Webster's *Expiring Frog*, which is a true story of South Africa. I would be the first to recognise those of Sarah Gertrude Millin's novels which do not concern themselves primarily with questions of race. I would be the first to recognise Frank Brownlee's *Cattle Thief*, and Allister Miller's *Mamisa*, which deal with a race group rather than a race question. These are all authentic and distinguished works. I understand what Dan Jacobson means when he says he looks forward to the day when one need not write about race.

Yet there is nothing fundamental in writing about race, and nothing fundamental in not writing about race. I grow quite impatient with the reviewer who welcomes a novel because the author has freed himself from the current obsession with race. I suspect quite frankly that the reviewer does not like to confront racial questions, that he is employing not a literary yardstick at all, but a purely personal one. The fact of race is an ever-present one in our South African lives, and to take an example, Elizabeth Webster in the *Expiring Frog*, though she is not writing about race, does not exclude it in the manner of those romantic writers who are determined not to bring it in. Nor certainly does Nadine Gordimer exclude it in *The Lying Days*. I do not think that Mr. Jacobson need apologise for writing about it. Race is not a plot, or a structural pattern, or an obsession; it is of the very stuff of our lives, and it is life that is the making of a story. Mr. Miller in his *Mamisa*, a story which has not received proper recognition, is writing about a closed society at a time since passed away; therefore there is no unreality in his story. But there is a great unreality in any story of white people in South Africa, which, even though it brings in non-white characters, ignores their existence as an ever-present factor in white South African life.

The extreme theory of apartheid presupposes separate worlds. But in fact they do not exist, and the whole body of English fiction in this country proves that they do not exist. Even where the estrangement and alienation is greatest, the fact of race is omnipresent. It is the English novel of South Africa that has recognised this truth; it is the English novel of South Africa that is therefore nearest and truest to South African life. This I take to be the greatest achievement of our English South African literature; not that it deals with race, but that it deals with life.

English fiction in South Africa is largely the work of British and Jewish writers, but it has one distinguished Coloured contributor, namely, Mr. Peter Abrahams, and I cannot help noting that his novels are all concerned with race. I do not regard Mr. Abrahams as a solitary, but rather as a forerunner, worthy to be placed with Olive Schreiner. Indeed it is part of my thesis that it is so far the English-speaking people of South Africa, namely the British and the Jews, and the Coloured people, who provide the true storytellers of South Africa. And there is a good reason why this should be so.

I do not give this reason with diffidence, because it is too important for that. But I intend to give it with great care, because it is highly controversial. It is, I think, a permissible even though incomplete view to take of the history of South Africa, that it is the story of the struggle between the Afrikaner and the African. I myself have no great love for this interpretation, but I still think it is permissible. If I could speak as a politician, I would say that it is a barren and hopeless view, and prevents intelligent adaptation to the challenges and problems and dangers of these times. If I could speak as an historian, I should say emphatically that it is a partial view. But speaking as a writer, I say that whatever validity this view lacks, it has the validity of great drama. And great drama always abstracts from full reality for its own dramatic purpose. In this historic struggle between Afrikaner and African, it is the Englishman, the Jew, and the Coloured man, who are, even when they are drawn into the struggle, the observers. It is also they who are better placed than either Afrikaner or African to know both Afrikaner and African. It is they who are better placed to see the real drama that history has unfolded, even when they are deeply and emotionally involved. I do not doubt the validity of the Afrikaner writers' view of Afrikaner life, nor the African writers' view of African life (although there are few examples of the latter as yet). But the validity is partial. Laurens van der Post has remarked that the Afrikaner writer is unable to see the African as a person, and it is my own opinion that the African is unable to see the Afrikaner as a person. This to my mind is a tremendous handicap in the writing of a South African story.

The name of Laurens van der Post himself could be cited as an exception to this generalisation. Such exceptions are always possible. The negligible number of them proves the validity of this generalisation.

I should like to broaden the generalisation, however. It is dramatic to see the history of South Africa as a struggle between Afrikaner and African, but it is of course essentially – in this partial view – a struggle between white and non-white. I do not suppose this broader generalisation is any more palatable than the first, yet there seems to me to be an un-

shakable case for its partial validity. I do not know how otherwise to interpret our legislation of the last eight years (and indeed legislation prior to
that also), nor how otherwise to interpret the speeches of many of our
leading politicians. I do not know how otherwise to interpret the irreconcilable opposition of the African and Indian Congresses to current
legislation, nor do I know how otherwise to interpret the emergence of
that tragic and nihilistic movement known as the Non-European Unity
Movement.[2]

Now it seems to me eminently reasonable to suppose that there are
people on both sides of this white/non-white struggle who are better able
than others to observe, to interpret, and to communicate in story their
interpretation of current events. Of the whites it is the English-speaking
South Africans, and of the non-whites it is the Coloured people, who are
in this privileged position.

I do not suppose for a moment that these racial groups have any monopoly of the writer's gifts. But they are in a better position to use them. It is
often said that the English-speaking South Africans, that is, those of
British and Jewish origins, excel in commerce because they cannot hope
to achieve distinction in government and public service. I am sure there is
truth in this; and it is for the same reason that they excel in the writing of
fiction.

As yet the Indians of South Africa, though most of them are now as at
home in the English language as in any other, have not produced any notable novels in English. I know, however, that there are many aspirant
writers, and that most of those whose work I have seen are preoccupied
with their own lot and fortunes. This makes for poignant reading but not
for good stories. Perhaps they least of all are in the position to observe the
South African scene.

As I have already said, it is life, not pattern or plot, that is the stuff of
story; there is nothing fundamental in writing about race, or in not writing
about it. But where life and race are inextricably intertwined, it follows –
as a generalisation subject to exceptions – that if one is writing about life,
one is writing about race also. This view of mine has been hotly opposed,
and has been regarded as the fruits of an obsession.

But before I attempt to justify this generalisation, I must say something
about the exceptions, for I do not want people to think that I do not really
care about the exceptions, and that I mention them only so that I can get
away with the generalisation. Is there such a thing as a universal story in
South Africa, a universal story which deals with such themes as young love
and ambition and consuming jealousy, and keeps itself free from the prob-

[2] Most of the organisations mentioned in this paragraph were banned in 1960.

lems of a society composed of many races? I must admit that in theory it could be so, but I would assert that in practice it never is. I think it is true to say that the farther the white trekker got from Cape Town, the more the black man became part of his mind, and the more the white man became part of the black man's mind. It seems to me that the 'universal story' of South Africa cannot really be universal, because it is an abstraction. I understand very well what Mr. Dan Jacobson means when he hints at this 'universal story' and apologises for his own; but he need not apologise. He *is* trying to write universal stories, but they have to be placed in a setting, and Mr. Jacobson is powerless to say what that setting shall be.

No doubt some of you are thinking about Shakespeare; he dealt with the themes of young love and ambition and consuming jealousy, and placed them in settings all his own. We must leave it an open question whether we simply lack a Shakespeare, or whether Shakespeare, were he living amongst us, would have illumined South Africa with unforgettable light.

But there are other powerful reasons for believing that if one is observing and interpreting life in South Africa, one cannot evade the theme of race. It seems to me that a brief study of the better-known South African novels in English must inevitably lead one to this view. Sarah Gertrude Millin in a way started it all with her *God's Stepchildren*. William Plomer's *Turbott Wolfe*, van der Post's *In a Province*, May and Williams's *I am Black*, carried it on. And then there came Peter Abrahams's *Mine Boy*, *Path of Thunder*, and *Wild Conquest*, my own *Cry, the Beloved Country* and *Too Late the Phalarope*, Daphne Rooke's *Grove of Fever Trees*, Doris Lessing's *The Grass is Singing*, Lanham and Mopeli-Paulus's *Blanket Boy's Moon*, Phyllis Altman's *Law of the Vultures*. And now the three books of 1956 that I have mentioned above.

The above is not a list of merit, because such a list would obviously include others of Sarah Gertrude Millin's books, and the novels by Frank Brownlee, Allister Miller, Elizabeth Webster and Nadine Gordimer. But the conclusion is inescapable that the English-writing novelist turns to race as his main theme, and by that I mean, to all the drama and conflict that is bound up with race. That has been his main inspiration, and it appears at present to be an inexhaustible source; it is life, and this kind of life is inexhaustible in a changing, growing, conflict-ridden country.

Lots of people will not like this theory, and will think it is a fad of my own, but I am satisfied that it is the truth. The English-language novelists of South Africa have interpreted our country to us and to the world, and have made a workmanlike job of it too.

This in fact has been our novelists' social purpose, in a country abounding with social purposes. There is nothing wrong in a novelist's having any other social purpose as well, but the moment his pen is in his hand, he must obey the rules of storytelling and not those of morality. I myself, having a religious view of the universe, believe that the rules of storytelling and the rules of morality are fundamentally at one. But woe betide the novelist who gets them mixed up. One might risk the epigram here, that the novelist may have social purpose, but the novel may not; even though holes could be picked in this, it comes near to the truth.

This picture of a novelist settling down with high purpose to interpret his country to others is quite incomplete, and conveys little of the excitement and joy of writing. To me the real excitement lies in the communicating, and I can only suppose that to some people one of the supreme joys of life is to communicate, and, what is more, to *succeed* in communicating. I have no doubt that ambition and the desire for recognition also enter into the picture, but there is undoubtedly a *pure* joy in communicating, and communicating successfully. Any person who has watched the great teacher at work, and has perhaps been lucky enough to sit under one, knows this to be true. The whole personality is absorbed in the task, and to see this happening is a rare, almost solemn, experience. It is not merely earnestness, it is successful earnestness; the one may be touching, but the other is downright enthralling.

Suppose that I am fired with the purpose of interpreting my country to the world. This purpose in itself is quite insufficient. When I start writing, the joy of communicating must overwhelm me.

It will I think be clear to my audience that I have a strong sense of the social function of the novel. I use words like interpret and communicate, and do not dwell, as for example John Steinbeck does, on the joy of creating life, event, and character. But I am very conscious of their importance, and what is more, I am very conscious that when the pen is in the hand, they are of *supreme* importance. When one is writing the story, it is the rules of storytelling that one must obey. When one is writing about life, it is the experience of life that must not be flouted. When one has created characters, they are no longer puppets, but if truly created, they take on a life of their own. If I place great emphasis on the process of communicating, I do not forget that the novelist has chosen the story as his particular medium of communication. For me, communication includes creation. It is the communication that is creative.

Is it not possible to maintain that a novelist may derive all his joy from creation and may be indifferent to communication, and all that communication implies, namely, recognition, praise, sales and royalties? If there is such a novelist, I have not met him as yet. Many would-be writers seek help and advice from me, and one takes for granted that the joy of writing is twin-sister to the desire to have that writing read. I think it was Caruso who said that it was not singing that gave him pleasure, but being heard.

I do not presume to suppose that Professor Partridge shares my views on the social function of the novel, but am I not right in supposing that there are implications even in the title which he suggested to me, 'The South African Novel in English – what it has done, and what it can do'? Why should a novel do anything at all? In any event, it is significant to me that most of those novels in English which are still remembered, were written by people who had a strong social purpose and who had a strong view that the novel has a social function; but in addition to that, they knew what a novel was and that it had rules of its own that must be obeyed.

What can the novel still do? This is a utilitarian question with a vengeance. But there is one obvious and immediate answer to it, namely, that the novel can go on doing what it has already done, interpreting our country to ourselves and to the world, from the peculiar vantagepoint that an English-speaking novelist enjoys. But could the novel in English do anything to advance the cause of racial harmony in South Africa? This question was put to me very strongly by a friend who had read the first part of this paper, and who found it disquieting, particularly because of its acceptance of the partial validity of the view that the history of South Africa was in a way the story of the conflict between Afrikaner and African, with the English-speaking and Coloured peoples as observers.

I approach the question of the novel and the cause of racial harmony with the greatest diffidence. One thing is clear to me, it is no part of the social function of the novel to render a direct service of this kind. Nor has one even a right to expect that a faithful and truthful interpretation of life in our country would necessarily lead even indirectly to this desirable end. Indeed it will often happen that such an interpretation will cause anger and dissension; the truth is not necessarily a peacemaker. Therefore, apart from those novelists who have such a direct purpose, and who will, if they are wise, obey the rules of storytelling in carrying it out, we need not look in this direction.

And it is absolutely right that we should not, for to do so would be to debase the novel, however noble the aim. The novel is not there to have any noble aim except the very noble aim of being a novel. It is the novelist who may have the noble aim; but when his pen is in his hand, he must obey the rules. And it is a matter of utmost importance that this should be so. It is a matter of utmost importance to the democratic society, and let us make no mistake about it, the novel is a product that cannot be manufactured otherwise than in a democratic society. Now today we are wit-

nessing, in other countries as well as our own, a marked tendency to arrange all values in a hierarchy of values, to arrange all authority in a hierarchy of authorities – in other words, to 'pyramidalise' life (if you will
excuse such a shocking word that expresses so well a shocking idea). When
you pyramidalise life, you are making sure that there is no such thing left
as an absolute value, or a fundamental freedom, or a basic right. Some of
you will again think I am talking politics, but I am trying desperately to
talk about life. I am trying to show how important it is that the novel
should not become the tool of the noblest aim that ever was, because then
it also will have succumbed to the process of pyramidalisation.

Now in spite of these difficulties, I am sure that the novel in English can
contribute to the cause of racial understanding, but it is going to do so in a
way of its own, a way that I can only descibe as astringent, antiscorbutic
and antiseptic. It will illuminate the road, but it will not lead the way with
a lamp. It will expose the crevasse, but not provide the bridge. It will lance
the boil, but not purify the blood. It cannot be expected to do more than
this; and if we expect it to do more, we are asking too much.

I do not know if any of you were fortunate enough to read a book called
Trial by Sasswood, written by Esther Warner, an American woman sta-
tioned on the West Coast of Africa. It was an entrancing story of a white
woman who made a journey with her African employees to their tribal
home, where one of them, accused of theft, was to undergo the ordeal of
plunging his arm into boiling oil in order to prove his innocence. What a
book it was, recording the most illuminating conversations between
American and African. Here the writer, having great gifts, was able to set
down how she appeared in African eyes, and how her African friends appeared in hers. One gained a new insight into the possibilities of such relations.

This seeing of oneself through the eyes of others is of incalculable value.
Not only oneself, but one's beliefs, customs, prejudices, and conventions
also. Nothing is more likely to lead to a deeper understanding of ourselves
and others, and also of ourselves in relation to others, and of others in
relation to ourselves. Nothing is more likely to lead to a clearer understanding of what our country is.

However, the consequences of such revelation must be soberly weighed.
For one thing, the revelation encounters tremendous resistance. It is, I
think, indisputable that the novels of English writers in South Africa, if
they are not ignored by Afrikaner readers, leave them with a bitter taste.
Even my own *Cry, the Beloved Country*, which Oliver Walker regards as
South Africa seen through a stained-glass window, is found painful by
Jan Burger.

But this is the job that has to be done, this painful laying bare of the truth, in the form of storytelling whose rules must be faithfully obeyed. We have made a good beginning, and I am full of confidence that, in respect of fiction, the great achievements of our English South African literature still lie ahead.

To all young writers, to all aspirant writers of any age, I say, go ahead.

[1959, the fiftieth anniversary of the Suid-Afrikaanse Akademie, which was celebrated by Afrikaans language festivals of which the theme and the slogan were 'The Wonder of Afrikaans'. *English Studies in Africa*, September 1959.]

Some Thoughts on the Contemporary Novel in Afrikaans

It is the general conclusion in English-speaking literary circles that the Afrikaans novel is in a decline. Why should this be so? The question is doubly worth asking in this year of the celebration of the 'Wonder of Afrikaans'. One thing is certain, the blame cannot be laid at the door of Afrikaans. The Afrikaner novelist has to hand a nutty, fluent, resourceful, and vigorous language, that can communicate any thought, convey any emotion, say anything that one wishes to say about our exciting, turbulent, anxious life. What has the Afrikaner poet that the Afrikaner novelist has not?

If there is nothing lacking in the language, where does the trouble lie? Surely not in the lack of those talents and skills that writers are said to command. One could hardly suppose that the Afrikaans-speaking people are less capable than the English-speaking of producing writers. The tools are there, the skills are there. Is there a psychological blockage of some sort? The repressed fear of hostile literary criticism is said to be a powerful inhibitory factor. Is it not possible that the fear of hostile social criticism is equally inhibitory? And is that not perhaps the greatest contributory cause of the decline of the Afrikaans novel?

One approaches this question with some diffidence, for in a country so full of sensitivity, the critic is likely to be accused of a political, even a racial, motive for his criticism. What is more, I have up till now steadfastly refused to criticise the work of fellow novelists, because I believe that such criticism is inevitably made valueless by the importing of the most discreditable personal motives. However, I have this justification, that I am in the main not concerned to judge individual novelists; it is the failure of the group that I am endeavouring to understand.

It is deep in the Afrikaner's soul to cherish 'one's own'. It would be hard to name a racial group in the entire world where the 'own' is so fiercely cherished. It is one's own that is holy, it is only one's own that can really be known; or should one rather not say, it is only by knowing one's own that one is able to enter into the life of mankind? Assimilation is permissible only when one is assimilating, not when one is being assimilated. Smuts's theory of Holism, the creation of greater and greater wholes, is anathema. The church must be one's own, the school must be one's own. Afrikaans religion and culture and education and politics are closely interwoven. The Afrikaner's highest religious values and his highest group values are synthesised in Christian–Nationalism.

And now, by the grace of Providence, one's 'own' has come into its own. After struggle, defeat and humiliation, the Afrikaner has achieved untrammelled power. This 'own', so long cherished in powerlessness, must be entrenched in power. Because this 'own' is good for one's own, and because it must be preserved in its purity, one must also entrench the 'own' of others. Custom must become law, contact between one's 'own' and others' 'own' must be reduced to what is essential for their separate continuance. It must be the function of literature, the duty of politics and education, to enrich and strengthen this 'ownness'. Even religion must make its contribution; but the church is credited with some kind of autonomy, though this is never claimed in any extreme and uncompromising way.

What difficult problems this poses for the Afrikaner novelist! Dare he claim some kind of autonomy for his own art? One thing is certain, he will not do so publicly and provocatively. But will he be able to do it in the privacy of that room where he writes? I do not merely mean: will he be brave enough to do it? I mean also: will he be psychologically capable of it?

Would he not rather turn, if he is so gifted, to poetry? Because poetry has a secret language, not open to inspection. At least not yet.

All storytellers agree that storytelling has stern rules. They have been formulated by different people in different ways; but it is generally agreed that one cannot disobey them without destroying, or at least flawing, the story. For one thing, if one tells a story, that must be one's primary purpose. A novelist, as man, may have other purposes, but they must always be secondary, even when noble. He may wish to expose a social evil, to recall the world to religion, to immortalise a hero, to sing his people. But where one of his secondary purposes interferes with his purpose of telling a story, it must be ruthlessly struck down. The secondary purpose may even precede the first, but once the story is chosen, the telling of it becomes the primary and controlling duty. This seems to suggest that there is something *absolute* in the demands of this particular art, and this in fact is the belief of most storytellers.

There is yet another sense in which these demands are absolute; it is what we may call a moral sense. There is a widely accepted descriptive definition of the novelist's craft (due to Arnold Bennett, if I remember aright) to the effect that the novelist observes life, that he is excited by it, that he wishes to communicate what he sees (and perhaps his excitement also) to others, and that he chooses the story as his vehicle. In other words he has assumed an obligation towards the truth which makes a second absolute demand on him.

This 'truth' is of course the truth of life as he sees it, conveyed in the form of a story, and as free as possible from any other kind of judgement. This has been described as 'holding up a mirror to society'; this metaphor is good in that it suggests the fearlessness and the objectivity of the good writer, but it is deficient in two ways. In the first place it minimises the writer's own role as digester, selector, and interpreter. In the second place, it seems to suggest that 'society' is the inevitable subject of a story. This obviously cannot be so; for if it were so, Afrikaans fiction, for example, would be robbed of a novel such as Hettie Smit's highly personal *Sy Kom met die Sekelmaan*, one of its fairest jewels.

Nevertheless, most of us would agree that while the novelist himself or herself is under no obligation to paint a picture of society, and while he may incline to the highly personal and subjective, or to the romantic, or to the historical, or to the animal story, it is strange when no kind of picture of contemporary society at all is to be found in the novel at large. And that certainly appears to be true of the Afrikaans novel of today.

Two qualifications should immediately be made of this statement. The first is that the novelist can justify his choice of a particular slice of society as the one that he knows best; that C. M. van den Heever, for example, in his *Die Held*, instead of dealing with Johannesburg in the round, was justified in confining himself to the theme of the metamorphosis of the Afrikaner in the city, and of the erosion of the values of one's 'own' under the influence of materialism and anglicisation. It is natural that the serious novelist of the present should choose to write about what he knows best, and one could criticise no novelist on that account, except of course when he becomes tedious and repetitious.

The second qualification to be made of the statement is that *all* novelists writing in South Africa today must face many difficulties in writing of South Africa at large, and in seeing life whole. Therefore, when we demand of novelists that they should tell us about our times, and interpret and illumine them, we should remember that the policy of our rulers, framed in law and complemented by custom, to give each group its 'own', and to eliminate inter-group contact wherever possible, is a confining factor of the most important kind. Whether it can be overcome is yet to be seen; but quite clearly, to take one example alone, it would be made more difficult for a white writer to create any non-white character with any degree of confidence, or to enter with any confidence into any of the non-white worlds. This difficulty is at the moment felt more by the Afrikaner writers than by others, for they face not only the mystery of the 'other' but also the hostility of the 'own'. We may be approaching the point when the writing of such novels must be left to the officials, for any other person will only make a fool of himself. We may be approaching the day of a new kind of novel altogether, which, although it may not satisfy what literary critics are left, will bear the stamp of authenticity. The masterpiece will no doubt be written by the Minister, who will have the advantage of the advice of high officials, versed in the way of thought and speech of others and 'acquainted with their reasonable wants and aspirations'.

Of course, there may be a reply to the argument that the policy of our rulers is killing the novel by dividing up life into unknowable segments; the reply may be that that is exactly what contemporary life is like, and that the novelist is therefore compelled to paint it in this curious segmented way. In that case the novelist is engaged in killing the novel too. He is abstracting Afrikaner life from the whole in which it is placed; he is discussing, often with great sincerity, the problems of city life, but they are too much his 'own' to have the universal character of literature. Who would know from his novels anything of the events that appear daily in our newspapers, and fill the minds of readers, Afrikaners as well as others, with fear and speculation?

I myself believe that it is possible, even within the limitations imposed by racial laws, which limitations are growing narrower, to write novels that are more universal in their character than those of contemporary Afrikaner novelists. Even these very limitations of the essence of our South African life, and even explicit rebellion against them, may make the stuff of a novel, and go to join the literature of protest; but clearly it is dangerous stuff to handle, for when the 'own' is replaced by the protest against the 'own' (in its extreme form, naturally), one is still struggling to obey two absolutes, though now, however, with some hope of success. A striking instance of this explicit rebellion is Jan Rabie's recent *Ons, die Afgod*. In evaluating his novel, one is torn between a desire to see the Afrikaans novel liberated from the shackles of conformity and admiration for the courage of those who attempt it, and on the other hand one's obedience to the demands of the craft. *Ons, die Afgod* suffers, I believe, from the paying of insufficient attention to these demands; yet the critic cannot confine himself to these considerations. Mr. Rabie's novel has a literary significance quite apart from this, in that it is implicitly calling for a reintegration of the Afrikaans novel and the reality in which it is placed.

I am not suggesting that there was a golden age of Afrikaans fiction, and that this came to a mysterious end; rather it was an infant that never grew up. But it was a promising child. Following a number of predecessors of largely historical interest came Jochem van Bruggen's *Ampie die Natuurkind*; this was succeeded by *Ampie die Meisiekind*, and (less satisfactorily) by *Ampie die Kind*. The first was published in 1924 and has so far not been surpassed, nor I think equalled. The story is simple and clear, the simple characters are drawn with skill, and in the case of Ampie and Annekie, with love, and the language is simple also, these three simplicities fusing in a work of art well-nigh perfect. A similar tribute must be paid to that *eenling*, Hettie Smit's *Sy Kom met die Sekelmaan*. This story of a love-lost girl is a novel without doubt, though it also has the nature of a poem. Miss Smit said of it ten years later that it was like ' *'n stout kind wat vir my uit die verte uitlag en tong uitsteek*'.[1] That may well be so; a writer is always shy of any poetic upwelling in prose (good or bad, I might add), because it is always self-revelatory. But behind that was a true artist, expressing emotion with superb skill. What happened to her? Why did she not write again?

It was a simple age, I think, and it was brought to an end by Parliament's decision to enter the Second World War by the side of Great Britain, a decision especially fateful in that it was taken so soon after the Voortrekker celebrations of 1938. I was then the principal of Diepkloof Reformatory, and most of the white members of my staff were Afrikaans-speaking. As clear as I was in my mind that Hitler was a danger to the freedom of mankind, so clear were most of them that the war had nothing to do with them, and their opposition went obviously deeper than any politics. The success of the pro-war party under Smuts cloaked the final resurgence of the 'own', which in 1948 achieved the power it had so long struggled for. So the Afrikaans novelist, his people having emerged from one kind of double loyalty, had from 1938 onwards to contend with another. He had to obey the demands of the 'own' and the demands of his craft, in a way that had never been expected of his predecessors.

C. M. van den Heever was undoubtedly the most notable of the novelists who attempted to reconcile the demands of the 'own' with the demands of the craft. His novel *Die Held* may be considered an example of this. Here he breaks away from the bucolic novel with its permissible lyricism, which belonged to the earlier untroubled age, and he attempts

[1] A naughty child who sticks out his tongue and laughs at me from a distance.

to 'hold up the mirror' to the new society. He seems to have attempted a stricter form, learned, who knows, from *Anna Karenina*, and to have advanced his story with step-by-step precision. It is a touching story for any observer of the Afrikaner scene, the progressive advancement or deterioration, depending on the point of view, of the Afrikaner who, believing fiercely in his 'own', encountered the materialistic world of the city. But the story does not take fire.

Willem van der Berg's *Reisigers na Nêrens* deals with a cognate theme. He takes a Cape Town set, and with an impressive measure of objectivity, examines their sophisticated and pathetic lives. This story also does not take fire, and his truest art lies in his treatment of the love between Jannie and Julia, his letters to her having the quality of small masterpieces. Both van den Heever and van der Berg, as many other writers have done before them, see love as the only hope in man's predicament.

In both of these novels one sees the attempt, which must have been made with courage, to examine more objectively the Afrikaner scene, and one cannot withhold one's respect for it. But even when one has accepted the Afrikaner scene to be as valid for drama as any other, one is left astonished by the fact that the most important things in the drama get left out, with a consistency that is unfailing. Who thinks to write about Afrikaner power, which is the greatest fact of our present life? Who writes about the transformation of South African society by Afrikaner power? Who writes about the Afrikaner mission to regulate and order the lives of all other people? Who writes about the resistance of other people to this power? Who sees the Afrikaner drama as a drama of Africa, or as the great question-mark that throws its shadow over us all? I shall be accused no doubt of wanting to see every Afrikaner novelist take to writing political novels slating the Government. But that is not my wish. All I want is that the Afrikaner novelist should look at South Africa, and interpret and illumine my life and times for me in his own Afrikaner way. It is not important for me that he should have some secondary purpose that I approve of; what is important for me is that he should have a primary purpose to which he is faithful, that of communicating his truth about the world we live in.

But this is what he seems to me not to be doing. Or if he is doing it, it is a truth I do not recognise. Both conclusions are most melancholy.

[This is an extract from a speech made in the United States in the autumn of 1960. The author had gone to New York in order to receive the Freedom Award for that year. On his return to South Africa in December his passport was taken from him. (It was restored to him in 1970.) *Christianity and Crisis*, New York, 26.12.1960.]

A Speech in America

We are living at the end of an age – the end of the domination of the West – and Africans are experiencing the violence of being reborn. If we are to understand what is happening there, we must see the three striking characteristics of the modern African continent:

(1) The determination of every country and every people (and this Americans can well understand) to be free from any kind of external domination whatsoever. (2) Their determination to make their countries modern so that they can abolish illiteracy, disease and poverty; so that they can train their engineers, doctors, administrators and teachers. And this is not a materialistic motive. Rather this is a spiritual motive – the determination that these new countries should walk as equals in the company of the countries of the earth. (3) The bitter resentment of the arrogant rule of the West.

The tragedy of this arrogance is that it so often leads to hostility to Christianity, hostility to missions and missionaries, hostility to Western ideas of democracy and education, hostility sometimes even to the United Nations, hostility even to a man like Dr. Ralph Bunche (and the fact that he is not a white man does not save him from this particular kind of criticism). These are things that have their seeds in this arrogance of the past. And this factor must never be underestimated.

I would say that there has definitely been a decline in the self-respect and self-assurance of the people of the West. And I would say that this was the result of several very shaking experiences. When I look back on my own lifetime, I think of how war started in 1914 and was repeated in 1939. I think of the terrible shame that one of the great nations of the West should have murdered six million Jews; I think of the dropping of two atomic bombs, of the treatment of the Negro here in the United States, and of the treatment of African people in Africa.

I think also of an experience of my own: the realisation that my own people, the white people of South Africa, would not yield one jot or tittle of their power or privilege until they were compelled to do so. And I must say that it is a sobering experience to realise that while individual man may turn and mend his ways, collective man finds it much more difficult.

However, I didn't come here tonight to speak to you about the sins of the West. I come rather to speak to you about the great opportunities to restore our self-respect and self-assurance and, at the same time, to render a service of a most magnificent kind.

In the past we have always gone to other countries and said, 'We know what you need and we're going to give it to you.' Now we have to learn a new lesson. We must say to them, 'What kind of country is it that you want to build? What kind of use do you want to make of this new freedom that you have found?' And if we understand and sympathise with these things, then we must ask them further, 'What can we do to help you to realise this modernity that you are so anxious to acquire? How can we help you to develop the resources of your country? How can we help you with the education of your children?'

Most Americans are astonished to learn how few universities there are in Africa. I just want you to realise that university education in Africa is still a rare thing and that it might even be necessary for a country such as America to find some special, fresh kind of education that would enable people to learn in two years what they might at their leisure acquire in four.

I think there is one other great contribution that the people of the United States can make to the development of these new countries of Africa, and that is to restore the great damage that has been done to her own influence and authority by the fact that the deliberate speed enjoined upon her in the matter of civil rights has been so much more deliberate than speedy. Undoubtedly one of the greatest things that you could do for us in South Africa would be to hasten the pace of the attempt to get rid of any kind of racial discrimination in your own society.

I have just been down to the state of Georgia, and I must say it is very fantastic to go into the Capitol and to see the state coat of arms and its wonderful motto: 'Wisdom, justice and moderation.' But don't think I'm pointing a finger at you because we also have a great motto in South Africa. Our motto, in the most divided country in the world, is: 'Unity is strength.'

I think it says a lot about ourselves and about human beings that we pick out these great slogans and mottoes. Although we are not just, we must pay this great homage to justice; although we are not free, we must pay this great homage to freedom. Quite a remarkable thing. But I think the thing that cannot be forgiven – any man can be forgiven for not being able to obtain the great ideals that he strives after – is to proclaim these great ideals and then to proceed in a contrary direction as so many of us do.

155

One of the reasons why it is almost impossible to speak about South Africa separately is that, while the rest of the continent of Africa is moving so firmly in the direction of liberation and independence, we in South Africa are moving in the opposite direction. There was one great mistake the British made when they gave a constitution to this new Union of South Africa, and that was that they didn't give us a bill of rights. Had they given them to us, we would not be in the deep distress that we are in today – the Nationalists would have been prevented from proceeding at the fast pace at which they have proceeded.

But one thing is quite certain, that our isolation from the rest of the world increases. I am sure there are many Afrikaners, including churchmen, who are very anxious and disturbed by the direction that their Government has taken. I just wish that they would more often exercise the prophetic role of judgement that a Christian is sometimes called upon to exercise.

Naturally I would like to have seen the white people of South Africa come to their senses and I would like to have seen them open the door of opportunity to African people, not only in work and in education but also in the highest posts that could be available to them in government and in all of society. But I have come to the conclusion that, whatever changes come, they will not come about that way. I don't suppose this is a disillusionment to American people because they must realise that if it had been left to the white people of the South to abolish practices of segregation, then who knows when they would have been abolished. You are very lucky in this country to have an additional force that you can exert – the power of the law. We cannot do that. The power of the law is against us.

Even if we do not experience a change of heart, there is still hope that we might experience a change of attitude. But this will come about only if the external pressures upon us become unendurable.

I do not exclude the possibility that one day our Government may be forced to say, 'For God's sake come and help us.' However, even if that were not to happen, if conflict and violence ensued and if the nations of Africa became more and more oppressive towards us, then it might still be necessary for the United Nations to intervene, to give us some kind of interregnum, the kind of government that would call out the best men from every race group and say to them, 'Sit down and form a government; learn to work together. We'll give you a breathing space – ten years, fifteen years – to see whether you can come to your senses.'

If that is not to be true, there is a third possibility: that we would go into an age of revolution, chaos and hatred of a kind that one hardly likes to contemplate. But that will only be if the United Nations has ceased to be the instrument of world authority. Thus you will see why people like myself in South Africa also look to the United Nations for some kind of help and support.

I call South Africa a land of fear. Well, in some ways that is true. In some ways it is a land of great courage also. It wasn't long ago that many of my friends were arrested and put into prison, and were released without the preferring of any charge whatsoever against them.[1] One of my greatest friends had taught his children the sanctity of the law, to respect the police as the arm of the law. At three o'clock one morning the police knocked on the door of his little daughter's room to say that they wanted her father; an hour later she saw her father taken away. One can just imagine the bewilderment and confusion.

When these people were released, they immediately took up the very same activities for which they had been sent to prison. While one has friends like that, there is still every reason to have hope. People ask me why I don't leave my country. And I always reply that if I saw no hope I would leave it.

And I might say that these people who went to prison didn't lose their sense of humour either, for some of them were very annoyed to think that they had gone to prison while I was still living at large outside. Now they made a plan to get me in. The plan was to take a piece of paper, tie it on a stone and to be seen throwing this stone over the walls of the prison to the street outside. And on this piece of paper was to be written: 'Paton, for God's sake, hide those revolvers.'

Although we are such a separated people, there are many white people who have the strongest possible bonds with African people; many African people have the strongest possible bonds with Indian people and Coloured people. There are still people who cross these lines.

And there is another thing which sustains us, the concern of our friends, the concern of the American Committee on Africa and its Africa Defence and Aid Fund, which I would like to commend to your attention. If it had not been for the help we have received from the Defence and Aid Fund, I do not know what we would have done.[2] Four years ago, 156 people were arrested on charges of treason, and the case is still being tried. At first 60 were allowed to go, and then another 60, and finally 30 have been on trial for a period of over four years. And so far this trial has cost us something like $300,000. I have no doubt that one of the intentions

[1] A reference to the arbitrary imprisonments that took place during the State of Emergency earlier in 1960.
[2] The South African Defence and Aid Fund was banned by the Government in 1966.

of the Government is to keep people tied up in trials of this kind. But I tell you that we couldn't have given them the defence that we did if it had not been for the generosity of our friends here and in other countries. I would like to give my thanks to all those who helped the Defence Fund of the American Committee.

I would like to say a word about the witness or lack of witness of the churches in South Africa. And you know that the Church has a prophetic role which it must exercise if it is to be true to itself. There are times when the most creative thing to do is to protest. We have been very fortunate in having men like the Bishop of Johannesburg, who was deported from our country some weeks ago.[3] The reason he was deported was because his principles did not allow him to accept the principles of apartheid. We also have in the Archbishop of Cape Town, in the bishops of the Roman Catholic Church, and the leaders of other English-speaking churches a great deal to be thankful for.

Christians often imagine that the danger to Christianity and true religion is communism or something of that nature. The greatest danger to Christianity in Africa is pseudo-Christianity. And the marks of pseudo-Christianity are easy to recognise: it always prefers stability to change; it always prefers order to freedom; it always prefers the law to justice; and it always prefers what it considers realism to love. We as Christians should be rejoicing in the liberation of the people of Africa; yet so many of us are afraid to do so.

Seeing that this meeting is being held in a church, I would like to conclude with a few thoughts on the law of love. I think that ultimately if one wants to be a good man, one must live by the law of love no matter what the cost of it may be. If it means that suffering is the price that must be paid for it, then you must suffer. One simply lives by the law of love whatever the consequences may be. And if that is not the meaning of faith, then I don't know what is.

One must never identify suffering with love, nor must one seek suffering. One who seeks suffering is not loving, he is merely sick. But a person who shrinks from suffering when that is the price that must be paid is sick too. But, of course, there is so much more than suffering in love, for it is in loving that we are nearest to God; in loving we are most nearly like him.

I cannot think of any more important thing that you Americans can do than that you discharge this love and its responsibilities for your fellow men in Africa, who only now are beginning to look to a future where they will enjoy many of the bounties and blessings that you have enjoyed for so long.

[3] Bishop Ambrose Reeves.

[Durban, 5.12.1961. Not previously published. Chief Albert Luthuli, President of the African National Congress, was in 1959 banned and restricted to Groutville. In 1961 he was awarded the Nobel Peace Prize.]

Praise Song for Luthuli

You there, Luthuli, they thought your world was small
They thought you lived in Groutville
Now they discover
It is the world you live in.

You there, Luthuli, they thought your name was small
Luthuli of Groutville
Now they discover
Your name is everywhere.

You there, Luthuli, they thought that you were chained
Like a backyard dog
Now they discover
They are in prison, but you are free.

You there, Luthuli, they took your name of Chief
You were not worthy
Now they discover
You are more Chief than ever.

Go well, Luthuli, may your days be long
Your country cannot spare you
Win for us also, Luthuli
The prize of Peace.

[1961. *South African Outlook*, December 1971.]

Chess in Yugoslavia

The Passport Office. A table at which sits the Investigator. *On the one side of the table is a white chair, a brown chair over which is a cloth with design of a mosque, a yellow chair over which is a cloth on which is printed 'Daar kom die Alabama' and on the other side, three black chairs, with labels 'Zulu', 'Xhosa' and 'Basuto'. The producer should decide whether these labels need to be read by the audience, they might be distracting.*

A knock at the door.

INVESTIGATOR: Come in. Kom binne.

(*Enter Mr. Peter Boovalingam, who has a beautiful English voice*)

BOOVALINGAM: Good-morning. (*He puts an official form on the table*)

INV. (*Not looking up*) Good-morning, sir. (*He looks up*) Oh! Good-morning. Sit down. (*P.B. is about to sit on the white chair*) No, not on that chair. The one with a mosque.

P. B. Why with the mosque? I'm not a Muslim.

INV. Look, we got no time for small differences here. You can take it or leave it. (*P.B. sits*) Peter Boo-va-ling-am, eh? Now what do you want to do in India, Mr. Boovalingam?

P. B. I don't want go to to India, sir. If you look at the form, you'll see where I want to go.

INV. (*Turns over the form, and looks at the bottom of the reverse side. His eyes threaten to pop out of his head. He looks with interest at P.B. Then he sees humour in the situation. He chuckles, then he laughs, then he laughs again. Then he grows serious and speaks a little menacingly*)

You're not trying to play the fool are you? You're not trying to play the fool with the Government?

P. B. (*Rather coldly*) I certainly am not.

INV. You really want to do this?

P. B. Yes.

INV. (*He is overcome by incredulous laughter. He lifts up the phone. He speaks to Fanie*) Fanie, this chap Boovalingam. You read it, eh?

Ja, ja, ja. (*He chokes*) Ja, ja. Chess, eh? Chess! (*He chokes*) In Yugoslavia! Ja, ja. In Yugoslavia. Gits,[1] man, gits! (*Puts down the phone*) You're serious, Mr. Boovalingam. You want to go to Yugoslavia to play chess?

P. B. Yes.

INV. Gits, man, it's difficult. Why can't you go to India to play? Or – let me be honest with you – and you be honest with me – because if we are honest with each other we'll build up a fine country, eh? – tell me, why can't you play chess right here?

P. B. I do play right here. And now I want to play in Yugoslavia.

INV. Gits, man, you don't know what you're asking. Why didn't you ask something easier? (*He is torn in two*) You know, I do what I can for the Indian people. Sometimes I get their passports through in as few as six months. But they make it easy for me. They ask to see temples, and study Yoga, and see grandparents, and buy goods. But not to play chess in Yugoslavia. (*Earnestly*) And why chess, Mr. Boovalingam? Why pick on a European game? Haven't you got any Asiatic games?

P. B. (*Coldly*) Chess, is, as you call it, an Asiatic game.

INV. I'm sorry. I didn't know. (*Earnestly*) It isn't just the chess, Mr. Boovalingam. It's the chess in Yugoslavia. (*He muses for a minute, quite stuck*) Let's see your passport. (*He takes the passport. Almost absent-mindedly he holds the binding upwards and out drops a fiver. Mr. Boovalingam is not looking. The official looks at the fiver, looks at the not-looking Mr. B. He picks up the fiver and looks at it again*) I'll try, Mr. Boovalingam. I'll try with the help of my resources. (*He puts the fiver in his pocket*) But it may need more resources than are at present available.

P. B. I understand perfectly. Perhaps more resources will become available. (*He gets up*) Good-afternoon, sir. (*He goes*)

INV. Good-afternoon, Mr. Boovalingam. (*A knock at the door*) Come in. Kom binne.

(*Enter Mr. Jordan Ubani*)

J.U. Good-afternoon. (*He puts his form on the table*)

INV. Jordaan Ubani, eh? That's a fine name, Mnumzane[2] Ubani. Jordaan! Jordaan!

J.U. (*Rather coldly*) The name is Jordan. (*He sits on one of the black chairs*)

INV. (*Jumping up excitedly*) Mnu.[2] Ubani, what is your tribe?

[1] An Afrikaans expletive.
[2] A special way of addressing Africans – an artificial alternative to 'Mr.' – adopted for a few years by the Government in a vain attempt to impose the 'philosophy' of apartheid on everyday language.

J.U. (*Nobly*) My tribe is humanity.

INV. Yes, of course, of course, but I mean what language do you talk at home?

J.U. English.

INV. English! Gits, man, gits! But what I mean is, are you a Zulu?

J.U. I am a Zulu.

INV. Then please, Mnu. Ubani, do not sit in that chair. (*He motions Mr. Ubani to another black chair, on which, with raised eyebrows, Mr. Ubani sits*) Now, let me examine your application. (*He returns to his chair and takes up Mr. Ubani's application. He examines it curiously until he comes to the bottom of the reverse side. What emotions register on his face – consternation, disbelief, wrath, etc. He looks at Mr. Ubani, who looks back at him confidently and innocently. He says 'Gits' more than once, then he picks up the phone and speaks to Fanie. This time his voice is grave and low.*) Fanie, this chap . . . ja, ja. You read it, eh? What's on, eh? We may have found out something big. Gits, man, gits. Promotion, eh? (*He dreams*) Pretoria, eh? (*He dreams*) Gits, man, to see the old Union Buildings! (*Puts down the phone; after a pause he speaks*) Mnu. Ubani, why do you play chess?

J.U. (*Brightly and confidently*) I like it. It teaches one, you know, strategy. How to deploy one's forces. How to strike at the crucial moment! You know, you know. You keep your wits about you! You bide your time! You suffer assaults! (*The Investigator is listening spellbound*) You develop your secret plans you know! You prepare to exterminate your enemy! (*In his excitement his eyes flash, he rises; the Investigator shrinks back, he is a little apprehensive*) You suffer humiliations! Your men are treated like pawns! But you forget nothing! You strike here, you strike there, you strike everywhere! (*He crashes his fist down on the Investigator's table*) And all by non-violence!

INV. Gits, man, gits!

J.U. You abolish your enemy's knights!

INV. (*Recovering*) We don't care about knights!

J.U. You sweep off the bishops!

INV. We don't care about bishops!

J.U. You finish off the queen!

INV. We don't care about the queen!

J.U. The king is cornered, phelile, kaput!

INV. (*Standing and clapping*) Bravo! Bravo! (*They smile at each other embarrassedly, all emotions spent. Mr. Ubani sits on the wrong chair*)

INV. Mnumzane!

J.U. Yes.

INV. You are on the wrong chair! Ag, man, sit where you like. Mnu., your passport asseblief. (*He takes the passport, and holds it up as before, but nothing falls out. He laughs*) I always shake the passport, Mnumzane. Sometimes things fall out. (*He pauses*) Even money.

J.U. (*Cheerfully*) Money, eh? Not out of my passport! My wealth is ideas, not money.

INV. Humph! Well, Mnu., come back tomorrow. Good-afternoon.

J.U. Good-afternoon. (*He rises but, before he can go, a knock at the door*)

INV. Come in. Kom binne.

(*Enter Professor Leo Kupansky, a gentle scholar, with beautiful manners*)

PROF. (*Bowing*) Good-afternoon. I am Professor Leo Kupansky, Mr. Investigator. (*Hands over his paper, and holds out his hand to Mr. Ubani*) My dear friend Jordan. (*They clasp hands*)

J.U. Ah, Leo. It is good to see you. How is Elizabeth?

PROF. Fine. And how is Julia?

J.U. Fine, fine. And how is my little girlfriend Priscilla?

PROF. Fine, fine. You are dining with us on Thursday?

J.U. Certainly, certainly. And we shall finish the game.

PROF. Your queen is in a dangerous position.

J.U. Oh, I am guarding her. I shall make any sacrifice to keep the queen.

PROF. And your bishops. They are in a ticklish situation.

J.U. Oh, I am supporting them. What would we do without our bishops?

PROF. And don't be too sure about your knights.

J.U. Leo, I would do anything to preserve the knights.

INV. Mnu., I must speak privately to the Professor.

J.U. Certainly. I must go. (*Turns warmly to the Professor*) Leo, my love to Elizabeth and my little girlfriend. Don't forget, there is always a bed for you at Elangeni. You know, I have a new chess set. Not whites versus blacks, but whites versus reds.

INV. Pragtig, pragtig. That's as it should be.

J.U. Goodbye, Mr. Investigator. And do your best for me, eh? (*Meaningfully*) I want to play chess in Yugoslavia. (*He goes*)

PROF. Goodbye, Jordan, my friend.

INV. Sit down, Professor. Here. (*He indicates the white chair*)

PROF. Very interesting, Mr. Investigator. A white chair, a chair with a mosque, a chair with 'Daar kom die Alabama', and these three black chairs. (*He looks at the chairs*) Zulu, Basuto and Xhosa. How wonderful!

INV. (*Delighted*) You like it, Professor?

PROF. I think it's wonderful! I don't know where you get the time for it, with things moving so fast.

INV. (*Excited*) It will spread, Professor. To Zambia, the Congo, Kenya, even Ghana maybe.

PROF. (*Sitting in the white chair*) Maybe, maybe. It's wonderful, wonderful! I mean, one really wonders at it. It's fantastic.

INV. (*Confidentially*) Tell me, Professor, what's all this that's going on in Yugoslavia?

PROF. (*Very precise*) Well, Tito is certainly a clever man. He has reached an equilibrium between Russia and the West. But he's Marxist, make no mistake about that. Now in regard to . . .

INV. Professor, I don't mean that. I mean what's all this about chess in Yugoslavia?

PROF. Oh, that! (*He laughs graciously, he would not hurt a fly*) Well, the Durban International Chess Club is sending a team to represent South Africa in the World Tournament that is being held in Yugoslavia. They have selected Mr. Boovalingam, Mr. Ubani – you know, Mnu. – and myself. We want to go and play chess in Yugoslavia.

INV. But what are you really going to do there, Professor?

PROF. (*Meaningfully*) Mr. Investigator, we are going to play chess.

INV. And I take it Mr. Boovalingam is representing the Indian Club, Mnu. Ubani the Bantu Club, and you, Professor, the European Club?

PROF. No, Mr. Investigator. We have only one club.

INV. You mean, you have no separate clubs?

PROF. (*Smiling graciously*) No, no separate clubs. Only chess.

INV. Gits, man, gits.

PROF. What did you say?

INV. I said, gits, man, gits. May I have your passport, Professor? (*The Professor hands him the passport. The Investigator looks as though he will hold it upside down, but changes his mind*)

INV. Who is Elizabeth?

PROF. She is my wife, Mr. Investigator.

INV. And he sends love to her?

PROF. Certainly, he loves her.

INV. Gits, man, gits! (*He pulls a book towards him, and looks up the names Boovalingam, Kupanksy and Ubani*) Your names are not in this book, Professor. (*Gloomily*) That means I must decide myself.

PROF. Fine, fine. That will save delay.

INV. Gits!

PROF. (*Rising*) Well, I'll be getting along. I hope this will soon be settled.

INV. (*Gloomily*) I hope. Goodbye, Professor. (*The professor goes*) Gits.

164

(*The phone rings, he lifts it up*) Ja, ja, Fanie. What! (*He is in transports*) I'm promoted. To Pretoria! Gits! Tomorrow! (*He laughs uproariously*) You're taking my place. (*He laughs more uproariously*) What am I laughing at? You know why I'm laughing, Fanie. I'm laughing because you will have to decide about Chess in Yugoslavia.

[This was written in 1962, at a time when it seemed likely that the author would be issued with a 'banning order'. Not previously published.]

Under Threat of Arrest

I don't know if I shall be given house arrest. It still hangs over my head. But I would certainly not change my course to avoid it. I have lived a law-abiding life. I spent thirteen years of my life as the principal of a reformatory which was trying to help boys who had broken the law. I am still astonished to think that at the age of 60 I might find myself, not facing some trifling penalty, but facing the whole power and anger of the State.

Some of those now under house arrest were tried for treason. Their trial dragged on for four long years. Then the judges suddenly decided, without listening to further argument, that the charges could not be proved. Now the Minister of Justice is sentencing people who were once freed by the highest courts in the land. Who can have respect for that kind of justice?

The Minister has declared that Liberalism is more dangerous than Communism. Communism kills, he says, but Liberalism leads one into ambush in order to be killed. What the Minister means is that anyone who opposes the Government is – wittingly or unwittingly – furthering the aims of Communism. Anyone who advocates change is preparing the way for Communism. I am not prepared to stop advocating change. I am not prepared to stop working for the abolition of the colour bar. I am not prepared to stop working for a government in which all may participate, regardless of race. I am not prepared to stop working for these things just because change is dangerous. I believe the denial of change to be much more dangerous.

If I am put under house arrest, I will know why. It will be because I have advocated the principles of that very Christian civilisation that the Minister of Justice claims to defend. I want to share civilisation, the Minister wants to wall it round with guns and tanks and threats and un-just laws. That is the difference between us. And if I am put under house arrest it will be because I chose to stay different.

[1964. *Bolt*, University of Natal, Durban, November 1972.]

The Hero of Currie Road

Mr. Thomson was a gentle little man who belonged to the All-Races Party, which believed in equal opportunity for all people. Mr. Thomson was much liked by many people, but was disliked by many also, some because they thought he was plotting a revolution, some because they thought he would be useless at it anyway.

Mr. Thomson's white neighbours definitely thought he was crazy. This was not entirely because he belonged to the All-Races Party. They thought he was crazy before he joined the Party. He always wore an overcoat, summer and winter, and as everyone knows, Durban in summer is no place for an overcoat. His favourite walk was up Currie Road and Grant's Grove to Musgrave Road, down Musgrave Road and Berea Road, and back along Currie Road. He would stop to admire a jacaranda or a flamboyant tree, whether in season for the blossom, or out of season for the shape. To admire the tree he would stand against someone's hedge or wall, so as not to discommode the passers-by, and would think nothing of putting his head on one side for several minutes, or of turning his back on the tree and looking at it over his shoulder.

It must be said that Mr. Thomson was well-known in the part of Durban where he lived. This was not only because he took his favourite walk at least twice a day, nor because he stopped, sometimes for ten minutes, to admire a jacaranda, but also because he said good-morning and good-afternoon to all the people whom he passed. Some of them were surprised when he did this, not having seen him before. Others were amused, because they also thought he was crazy. But there were some, especially the old Indian men and women, who would respond warmly to his salutation.

Mrs. Thomson never accompanied Mr. Thomson on these walks. She had a big birthmark that had plagued her for over sixty years, and she had no intention of letting it plague her any longer. Although she never went out with Mr. Thomson, she was a strong supporter of the All-Races Party.

Mr. Thomson was also well-known in Durban in an anonymous way. He wrote letters under the name of Thos. Bilby to the morning paper and Wm. Breckenridge to the evening paper. These letters always dealt with civil liberty, the rule of law, and the cruelty and folly of apartheid. Mr. Thomson's great enemies on the left were Cossack in the morning, and Demi-Tass in the afternoon, and these enemies sneered at him for thinking that noble ideals would save South Africa without a revolution. He was also attacked from the right by White South African, Voortrekker Boy, Shaka, and Mr. J. K. Pillay, for various reasons. It was in the interludes between the battles that he would sally forth, take his walk, admire the trees, greet people right and left, and then return to the fray.

Mr. Thomson became famous on September 7th. He and Mrs. Thomson were reading in bed when an African scoundrel entered the room with a revolver, and ordered them to put up their hands. Mrs. Thomson, a firm believer in the equal rights of the races, refused to do this. The African scoundrel knocked her senseless with his revolver, whereupon Mr. Thomson jumped on his back with the firm intention of taking unprecedented steps. Mr. Thomson did not use any racial adjective, but merely said, 'You devil.' Mr. Thomson was quite unable at his age and weight to sustain any struggle. It was quite impossible for his weak hands to encompass and hold the scoundrel's neck. He was in fact exhausted in a few seconds, and would have fared badly had the revolver not gone off and sent a bullet into the left breast of the scoundrel, who fell down with a groan. When Mrs. Thomson came to, neighbours had broken into the house, the scoundrel was bleeding and crying on the floor, and Mr. Thomson was being sick into the chamberpot.

'This will be a lesson to you not to stick up for these black murderers,' said one of the neighbours.

Mr. Thomson stopped being sick for a moment.

'I have never stuck up for a murderer in my life,' he said. Then he was sick again.

Mrs. Thomson covered up her birthmark with the blanket and shouted at the neighbour,

'I'll thank you to get out of my house.'

Not everyone would have become famous after such an experience. But Mr. Thomson did. His heroism was extolled in both the morning and the evening papers. His declaration that his faith in the All-Races Party was unshaken, received front-page notice. 'Morally reprehensible but politically irrelevant,' was his summing up of the incident. His attitude was applauded by Mr. Thos. Bilby in the morning paper, and Mr. Wm. Breckenridge in the evening.

His daily walks became triumphal. White people who had never greeted him before shook his hand. Some of those non-White people who had taken him to be crazy treated him with a new respect. He was photographed by the evening paper talking to an old Indian gentleman, Mr. Chetty, in his fruit-shop at the corner of Currie and Berea Roads. Both he and the old Indian gentleman were holding their hats in their hands and addressing each other with old-world courtesy.

All this explains how Mr. Thomson came to be invited to address the Annual Meeting of the South African Congress.

It was mainly on the strength of his remark, 'Morally reprehensible but politically irrelevant.' He wore his overcoat as usual, and looked a fragile figure on the platform, flanked by two giant politicians, Mr. Andrew Kanyile the Chairman, and Mr. George Mapumulo the Secretary, both of whom had been called masterpieces in bronze by visiting journalists. This was the first occasion on which the All-Races Party had been invited to sit on the platform at a meeting of the more militant Congress. It was quite a thing for Mr. Thomson to do, because many members of the Congress had been named by the Government as Communists. But Mr. Thomson was not likely to be deterred by so small a matter.

He received an ovation on standing up, and delivered a stirring speech to the Congress on the evils of racial discrimination, and the responsibility of social conditions for much crime. However, his speech was not received with unanimous approval. Indeed there were very audible murmurs when Mr. Thomson asserted that an important cause of crime was unsatisfactory personal relationships in childhood, and that these were unrelated to the type of social organisation.

Being that kind of person, Mr. Thomson did not notice these murmurs, but he was a trifle astonished when a party of younger delegates left their seats while he was speaking, not for the purpose of hurrying to some other engagement, but merely for that of lounging around the entrance doors, where they kept up a distracting number of loud conversations. As soon as the address was finished they returned to their places.

Now a strange thing happened. Mr. Phumula of Inanda was called upon to thank the speaker for his address. While smiling at Mr. Thomson with the greatest affability, he was able to suggest with an adroitness almost amounting to genius that Mr. Thomson's theories of crime were utterly nonsensical, and that the only tenable thing was that crime was caused directly by capitalism, laissez-faire, exploitation of the worker, and the war in Korea. These remarks were greeted with loud applause by the party of young delegates, who had now changed from supercilious loungers into earnest reformers. Mr. Phumula went on to inquire whether the Mau–Mau resistance had been caused by dominating fathers, jealous mothers, and gifted elder brothers. These killings of white people were natural acts of zealots who were determined to free their country from capitalism, laissez-faire, exploitation and the war in Korea. He declared that the hearts of true democrats went out to the Mau–Mau in Kenya.

It must be said that Mr. Phumula's remarks created a difficult situation in the meeting. Some of the delegates applauded, but the great majority sat passive and unhappy. If one had been able to observe carefully, one would have noted that Mr. Thomson had many admirers, several of whom looked openly disgusted. But there was no time to observe such things; the whole atmosphere of the meeting was tense and unhappy.

Beneath Mr. Thomson's gentle overcoat there was boiling up a great passion, much the same as that which had made him launch his frail form on to the powerful back of the scoundrel who had struck down his wife. Being however a democrat, even if not quite the same kind as Mr. Phumula, he looked questioningly at the Chairman. Mr. Phumula sat down and the Chairman rose to his feet.

His face was beaming also, and his remarks were conciliatory. He joined Mr. Phumula in thanking Mr. Thomson for his address. It was wonderful to him how Mr. Phumula, who had certain views on crime, could sincerely thank Mr. Thomson, who had somewhat differing views. The fact that there were these differing views showed what a complex problem Mr. Thomson had chosen for his fine address.

'Thank you, Mr. Thomson, thank you.'

'Mr. Chairman, I ask permission to say a very few words.'

It was quite clear that the Chairman was embarrassed. He wanted to say no but could hardly do so. His face beamed but his eyes were not smiling.

'Mr. Thomson would like to say goodbye to us,' he told the meeting.

'It is not exactly to say goodbye,' said Mr. Thomson 'It is just to say that I, and the Party I have the honour to belong to, utterly condemn murder and violence, whether it be committed by Mau–Mau in Kenya, or the British in . . .'

The rest of Mr. Thomson's remarks were lost. Some of the delegates booed loudly, even though the majority, which included Mr. Thomson's admirers, kept silent. He looked at the Chairman, and the Chairman looked at him. The Chairman's face was still beaming in spite of the commotion, but in his eyes Mr. Thomson could see anger that he had been put into this position.

One thing was clear to Mr. Thomson. There was an overwhelming wish that he should leave the meeting immediately. He bowed to the

Chairman and, accompanied by the Secretary, came down from the platform. As he passed down the aisle, a few people stood up in their places and bowed to him. Those who had booed him now paid him no attention whatsoever; they had already wiped him out of their lives. It made Mr. Thomson feel unhappy.

Outside in the street Mr. Mapumulo said, 'We must get a car for you.'

'I should like to walk,' said Mr. Thomson, and said goodbye to the Secretary and shook hands with him.

He walked away from the meeting sick at heart. The crowds of people, the Indian shopkeepers and the women in their saris, the African girls walking more gaily and freely than they would have done in the white quarter, the rich smells of the spices from Kajee's warehouse, the windows of goldsmith and silversmith and silk merchant, the white women looking for bargains, the whole surging, colourful cosmopolitan scene, the meeting-place of three continents, failed for once to excite him. It seemed a montrous jest of God, this juxtaposition of such different, such utterly different people, people so blind to the vision of harmony and peace, Africans praising Mau–Mau, Indians praising Nehru, Afrikaners praising the Prime Minister, Zulus praising Shaka, the English praising Rhodes. How could he have been so stupid as to suppose that out of all this could come a country of happiness and peace? In an agonising flash of illumination, he saw how overwhelming was the Government's case, that there would never be any peace until the whole country was re-fashioned and re-ordered, every man to his own place, every people to its own territory, its own jobs, its own shops, its own doctors, its own customs and happiness.

How he had liked taunting the Government under the names of Thos. Bilby and Wm. Breckenridge! He felt ashamed to think that he at his age could have persisted with such a futility. He had asked the Government whether there would be four, five, six different parliaments, all separate and equal? Or one Parliament above the other Parliaments? Or just one Parliament, a white-supremacy Parliament? He had then gone on to show that racial domination was unstable. Was it? Would it be any more unstable than a dream state granting equality to Mau–Mau praisers, Verwoerd praisers, Shaka praisers, Rhodes praisers? He felt ashamed of his puerilities. He looked in at a shop window and suddenly saw himself as an ineffectual old man, wearing an overcoat, member of a fragmentary Party, husband of a wife obsessed by a blemish, writer of lightweight letters that no one read, or if they read them forgot them, except other ineffectual cranks like Cossack and Demi-Tass and Voortrekker Boy.

He found his way to the Esplanade and sat down on a bench, one of a dozen benches all marked for 'Whites Only'. It was against his principles to sit there, but his principles, like himself, were tired. He must have sat there for an hour, all through his lunchtime, and he must have at last fallen into a doze, for he was awakened by the small Indian newsboys crying the name of the afternoon paper. He bought one, and his eye fell at once on the headlines:

Currie Road Hero Booed at Congress

He had no heart to read on. The words 'Currie Road Hero', so distasteful to him, were exceptionally painful to him in his abject condition. He was aware that elsewhere in the paper there might be a fighting letter from Wm. Breckenridge. He was ashamed to think that this might be so. He was ashamed to think that it should be recorded that he had been booed at the Congress he had so often defended. What would Voortrekker Boy and Mr. J. K. Pillay have to say about that? He dreaded returning to his home, to the wife to whom he had always talked so boldly. But most of all he was distressed about South Africa, about the new South Africa that he wrote about so confidently, that it was in reality his own private dream, that in reality friend booed friend while enemies mocked at them. How the Government must laugh at them!

He picked himself up wearily, leaving the paper on the bench. He walked to the bus-stop, hoping to see nobody he knew. He did not want to meet anyone who would say I'm glad or I'm sad that you were booed at the Congress.

When he got home his wife looked straight at him, which she seldom did because of the blemish. She could see at once that he was tired out and dejected.

'Sit down,' she said, 'have you had any lunch?'

'No,' he said . 'I don't wany any.'

'Where did you spend your lunchtime?' she asked.

'Excuse me, my dear,' he said, 'I don't want to answer questions.'

She made him sit down and she put on the kettle.

'You mustn't worry about a few hotheads,' she said.

He made no answer. She brought him tea and a plate of small light sandwiches that he liked.

'I don't want to eat,' he said.

He drank his tea, and didn't eat the sandwiches, although he really wanted to. Then he was silent for a very long time.

'You know what you said once,' he asked, 'about going to Australia?'

'I said it,' she said, 'but I didn't mean it.'

'I didn't agree,' he said, 'but I agree now.'

She remembered that he didn't agree. That was a mild way of putting it. He had chastised her with his tongue for about ten minutes.

'It's a few hotheads,' she said.

He was too tired to tell her it wasn't a few hotheads. It was the crowd in the street, and the smells from the spice shop, and the African girls carefree in the Indian quarter, and the white women looking for bargains, and the seats for 'Whites Only' on the Esplanade. It was the whole thing, the whole total impossibility of fighting the Government because white people wanted the Government, the whole crass stupidity of an All-Races Party. He did not tell her this, but the hopelessness of his silence spoke to her. She got up and went into her room, and for the first time in five years dressed herself to go out in the daytime. In spite of his depression he was moved to comment.

'You're going out,' he said.

'I've stayed in long enough,' she said. She looked as though she had more to say, then she didn't say it, then she did.

'It was a silly thing to do,' she said. 'I'm not doing it any more.'

She had not been gone long when there was a knock at the door. It was Mr. Chetty with a basket of fruit. Mr. Thomson greeted him warmly, not only because it was hospitable, but because it warmed him to see Mr. Chetty.

'I brought a little fruit for you,' said Mr. Chetty deprecatingly. He was a humble man and always spoke in this manner.

'That's very good of you, Mr. Chetty.'

'It's only a little,' said Mr. Chetty.

'Sit down, my friend. Would you like a cup of tea?'

Mr. Chetty sat down on the edge of the chair to show that he did not presume. He was too old to change.

'I have come to apologise that they booed you at the Congress, Mr. Thomson.'

'A few hotheads,' said Mr. Thomson.

'We have Indian hotheads too,' said Mr. Chetty, 'but God has His time.'

He chatted away politely. He drank his tea, and answered questions about his family, and they ate up Mr. Thomson's sandwiches.

'They all know you, Mr. Thomson,' he said. 'They know you are a friend of ours.'

'I feel so useless,' said Mr. Thomson.

'We are all useless,' said Mr. Chetty, 'but God is not useless.'

He rose to go, and asked politely if he might have his basket. Then he went.

When Mrs. Thomson opened the front door, she heard the typewriter going. A smile broke out on her face, making the blemish look quite unimportant. She knew what it was; it was Mr. Thos. Bilby or Mr. Wm. Breckenridge knocking the daylights out of Cossack, Demi-Tass, Voortrekker Boy, and the rest of that misguided company.

[1966. *Sunday Tribune*, Durban, 6.11.1966. Originally published in *Die Welt*, Germany.]

Interview with Himself

INTERVIEWER: Ah, Mr. Paton! Thank you for agreeing to let me interview you. Let me tell you, I have a high opinion of your work. Do you also?

PATON: Some of it. When I read past work, I say to myself, that was good and that was not. I am glad to say that, in general, the better was published and the worse not.

I: When did you last read *Cry, the Beloved Country*?

P: Not since 1948, the year it was published.

I: Why is that?

P: I can't quite answer you. One reason, I think, is that I have lived twenty years since that time and, though the book still speaks to many people, it could not speak to me now. Another reason is that I am now too old for that kind of emotion, which is the same reason given by the English poet A. E. Housman when he, although he was in his prime, published a volume called *Last Poems*.

I: And your second novel, *Too Late the Phalarope*?

P: I think the answer is the same.

I: Then what past work can you read again?

P: Many articles which I wrote in the past, on all kinds of subjects, crime, racial discrimination, civil liberty, the rule of law. Many of these I could not improve; however, they would not usually be called works of art. There are, however, two poems both of which deeply satisfied me when I wrote them. One is 'To a Small Boy who Died at Diepkloof Reformatory', which was published by Professor Rolf Italiaander, I think in the annual publication of the Free Academy of Hamburg, of which I am a proud member, having received the literary award in 1961. The other poem is 'Meditation for a Young Boy Confirmed', which to this day can arouse in me the same emotion with which I wrote it. There is another book I can read again, and that is *Debbie Go Home*. If someone writes to me about one of the stories, I go back and read it, most often with enjoyment.

I: How do you rank yourself as a writer?

P: I don't think about it.

I: Is that true? Now I could tell you . . .

P: (*Hastily*) Yes, I'm sure you could. No, it isn't true, but it's more true than false. My greatest pleasure is to write something that I know is good, and I think to myself, that was good, but I don't think to myself, Jones and Smith and Brown could never have written anything as good as that.

I: Is that completely true? Now don't get angry. Think carefully.

P: (*Thinking carefully*) No, it isn't completely true. There is one exception. If I wrote a book on a certain theme, and later someone else wrote another, then if a critic were to say that the second book was superior, that would hurt my pride. But I wouldn't think about it long.

I: Are you sensitive to criticism?

P: Yes, I am. Especially at the time of publication. I've met writers who say they don't care what the critics say, but I don't believe it.

I: Could they break your heart?

P: Yes, if they all damned me. But I've never had such an experience.

I: Are you apprehensive when a new book is coming out?

P: Yes, I am. I want to go out and buy the newspaper and I don't want to go out. When my life of Hofmeyr was published in October 1964 I was afraid to buy the *Sunday Times*, which is South Africa's biggest newspaper. But the review was magnificent, and tremendous too, because it occupied the whole front page of the magazine section, and more after that.

I: How many times did you read it?

P: You know, don't you?

I: Yes, I know.

P: Then don't ask foolish questions.

I: Are you vain?

P: Yes, but not peacock-vain. My vanity is like an iceberg.

I: You mean enormous?

P: No, I mean mostly concealed.

I: I've heard you say you're not a true writer. What do you mean by that?

P: It probably is not a good way of putting it. I don't mean I am not a lover of writing. Yet I have never done what other writers have done. I have never made it my life's work, I have never put it above every other obligation. I have envied those who did so, and who went to live in Cuba, and Hand's Cove, and the Big Sur, and the solitude of Cornwall and such delectable places.

I: You got caught up in politics, didn't you?

P: Yes, I did.

I: Why did you do a silly thing like that?

P: Duty, plain simple duty, the kind of duty that makes you feel bad when you do it, and worse when you don't.

I: Don't you like politics?

P: No.

I: Then you would rather have been like the man in Cuba?

P: No.

I: Why not?

P: Because I would then have been false to myself. I have these two mutually antagonistic characteristics in me, the desire to write and the desire to do.

I: Which is the stronger?

P: The second obviously. But when I'm actually writing, I resent the second.

I: What is it like, being like that?

P: Not very satisfactory.

I: Do you resent being like that?

P: No, I accept it. I'll tell you something. When I left my job as principal of Diepkloof Reformatory, I fancied it possible that I would never wear a formal suit of clothes again. I'd be free of all the old obligations that I had served so long, and, if I might say so, so faithfully.

I: But it didn't work out, did it? You had to get up there on that public platform again, didn't you? You ruined yourself, didn't you?

P: (*With surprising mildness*) No, I didn't. Whatever reasons I had for getting up there, one of the reasons was that I had to get up there because I had something to say. You knew that, didn't you?

I: Don't ask me. I'm only an interviewer. Do you know that some people say that your fictional writing, your biographical writing, even your poems, were really just getting up there again, making a kind of propaganda? What do you say to that?

P: It's nonsense. I told you I was two men. But when I pick up that pen to write a story, the second man is dead. I have an utter respect for the craft of writing. When I pick up that pen I am utterly obedient to the rules of the craft. I believe that if I break those rules my story is lost. I may have other purposes, but I know that the moment one of those purposes, however lofty, becomes dominant, I have destroyed my work.

I: Then why do some people say you're a propagandist?

P: Because they don't like the themes, of course. They don't want to see their country as it is. So they dislike the stories and call them propaganda. Such people aren't true critics. They would condemn the most perfect story in the world if its theme was unpalatable.

I: Do you know, I find myself believing you.

P: And I'll tell you something else. There's another way to destroy one's work, and that is to run away from the themes altogether, so that your stories bear no relation to life as it is. Some of our South African writers are like that. They do in fact have a secondary purpose that dominates the primary purpose of writing, and that secondary purpose is to avoid the disapproval of the State or the Volk.

I: Do you find life hard in South Africa?

P: Any person of my kind finds life hard. But some of my friends have paid a much heavier price than I for holding the views they do. Their movements and actions have been rigorously restricted, not by a court of law, but by a Minister of Justice who has been placed above the law. Also I have another advantage not enjoyed by many. When a writer writes about a tragic and frustrating situation, the tragedy and the frustration are lightened by the creative act of writing about it.

I: Why don't you leave South Africa?

P: Why? So that you can leave too?

I: Well, thank you, Mr. Paton, for this interview.

P: What are you sighing for?

I: I was thinking, you are now getting rid of me, but I can't get rid of you.

[1966? *More Tales of South Africa*, ed. C. M. Booysen, Timmins, 1967].

The Quarry

Everywhere the city was driving back nature, to the south and the west and the north. Only the east was safe, for there lay the ocean. Skyscrapers stood on the places where elephants had crashed through the forest. Hippopotamus Pool was a city square full of the smells of buses, Lions' River ran down a straight concrete channel into the Bay.

Only Mitchell's Quarry had resisted the march of the city. It was a stony scar cut out of the side of Pigeon Hill, and though it was ugly it was a piece of nature. The large green pigeons had long since gone, but small birds and animals still clung to it, and lived in the trees and grass that ran down each side of the scar. Frogs and very small fish lived in the pools. Children were attracted there, for it was the only bit of wildness in the city.

It was Johnny Day's favourite place. Sometimes he sat by the pools for hours, watching the fish. Sometimes he climbed up through the trees, and sat on the very edge of the quarry, in the cool exciting wind from the dancing ocean. He more than once wondered whether anyone could climb down, but Tom Hesketh, who was sixteen and very manly, told him it was impossible, and had never been done, and never would be done unless one came down on a rope. One could climb up from the bottom and Tom had done it once with two of his friends.

'Which way did you take, Tom?'

'I'm not telling you,' said Tom, 'it's not for kids. Can't you see the notice?'

The notice said, NO CLIMBING, BY ORDER, only whose order it was, no one knew.

'And I'm not doing it again,' said Tom, 'because when I was halfway up, all I wanted to do was to come down again, and I couldn't.'

Sitting by one of the pools, Johnny looked at the quarry face, wondering which way Tom had taken. All he knew was that Tom had begun by the noticeboard NO CLIMBING, BY ORDER, and that is where he would begin too, on the day after Christmas Day. He would climb in a direction half-right, where it seemed there was a track of footholds made for just such a purpose. Halfway up the quarry face the track seemed to peter out, but another track bearing half-left could be seen some feet higher. All that he must do was to find the way from one to the other.

On the morning of the day after Christmas Day Johnny arrived at the quarry and found nobody there. Confident of success he took off his jacket and cap, and laid them on a stone under the noticeboard. He was wearing sandshoes, because that was what Tom Hesketh had worn. He looked up at the quarry face which was roughly a perpendicular plane. He placed his right foot in a niche that seemed to have been made for it. He drew his left foot up and now stood about a foot above the level floor and the pools. The climb had begun, and the feeling of the climber was not nervousness but pure ambition, strong in one so young, for he was only twelve.

It certainly seemed that the track had been cut deliberately, perhaps to enable the quarry workers to climb the face. There was always a place for the foot, and the rock face inclined away from him a few degrees from the perpendicular, so that he had a feeling of security. There was no need so far for skill or ingenuity, for the method was simple – a hold with the hands, right foot up, left foot up, an inching forward on the same small ledge if possible, a searching for another hold with the hands and another small ledge for the right foot. He was about twenty feet up, and could see that he could return safely, if it was necessary. He looked down, and this gave him a feeling of exhilaration. He looked up, but decided not to do it again, because it seemed to reveal his own insignificance against the vast wall of the quarry, and above that the vast emptiness of the sky. From now on he would confine his attention to the handhold, the foothold and the rock face that so obligingly allowed him to lean against it.

The track continued as before for a short distance and he was at a height of about thirty feet when he reached a place where the rock face became suddenly perpendicular for a length of some three feet, so that he would not be able to lean against it. He wondered if he could take a step direct from safety to safety, but knew that the step would be too big for him. His only hope was a good hold for hands and feet. He was the slightest bit nervous, because he knew something else too, that if he decided to take the next two steps it would be twice as hard to return.

Tom Hesketh had said to him, 'If you're frightened to take the next step, don't take it, just climb down, if you can. If you can't climb down, then you've got to take the next step, that's all. And I can tell you, kid, it's dangerous getting frightened up there.'

Well, he might be a bit nervous but he wasn't climbing down. He could see the trail clearly, and it looked easy except for this one next step. There was a place for the hands and a place for the right foot, just as good as any he had used so far.

Someone shouted at him from below. It was a big Indian man who was shouting with some Indian boys.

'Come down, sonny,' shouted the big Indian man.

Johnny shook his head. Without looking he pointed at the sky.

The big Indian man shook his head too.

'No, no,' he shouted. 'It's too dangerous, sonny. Come down.'

Again Johnny shook his head, and pointed up. The Indian man tried warnings.

'Last year,' he shouted, 'an Indian boy was killed here. He was climbing the same way you are climbing now.' This wasn't true. There never had been such an Indian boy, but the Indian man believed that if the end was good, one shouldn't worry too much about the means. When the warnings failed, he invoked divine aid.

'God sent me here,' he shouted, 'to tell you to come down. He is telling you now to come down. He does not mean for you to be up there. If you don't come down, He will be plenty angry.' He added a clever afterthought. 'Just like He was angry with that Indian boy.'

'Don't let anything take your mind off your hands and feet,' said Tom, 'or off the rock face. Don't think of the height, or of the spectators. Don't look at birds or ships on the sea. Just think of the climb.'

That is what Johnny did. To the despair of the big Indian man, and the admiration of the Indian boys, he addressed himself to the task of finding a place for his right hand and a place for his right foot, and when he had found them, he took the dangerous step. It was done. The ledge was generous, and he brought up his left foot. Tom's instruction was immediately forgotten, and he looked down at the growing crowd of Indian men and women and boys and girls, and African men from the factory near the quarry.

The big Indian man shouted at him again to come down, and it was this very shouting that brought Tom's instruction back to Johnny's mind, so that the louder and more desperate the warnings and the threats, the less he paid attention to them. He took his next step with confidence, and the trail before him was now straightforward and easy for at least seven steps. Then it stopped dead. He braced himself to look up, and there, about ten or twelve feet above him, he could see the second trail that ran half-left, and would take him to the top. He could see almost at once that he could go no further in a half-right direction, that he would have to climb straight up. He could also see toeholds for the first five feet, for that was his own height. It would all depend whether there were handholds also, and that he would have to tell by feeling for them, partly because he was apprehensive about looking up, and partly because the rock face seemed to be nearer the perpendicular when one thought of climbing it perpendicularly.

These thoughts and speculations took him some minutes, so that the crowd below knew that he was facing some kind of crisis. He was nearly fifty feet up, about one-third of the height of the quarry face. There were now a hundred people watching him, talking to each other, but not loudly, because they were subdued by contemplation of the dangers that lay ahead. The boys were filled with admiration and awe, and the women with tender feeling and care. It was a white boy, it is true, but there in the danger and excitement of his journey up the quarry face he had become one of their own. The boys wished him luck and the women shook their heads, unable to be indifferent to either his naughtiness or his plight.

Johnny lifted his right foot to make the first step of the ascent, and this action put the big Indian man into a panic.

'Sonny,' he cried, 'true's God, don't go up any more. You'll die, sonny, and no one here wants you to die. Sonny, I ask you to come down.' He went down on his knees on the quarry floor, and said, 'I pray God to make you come down. I pray God not to be angry with you.' The women there, both Indian and African, seeing him kneeling there, cried out, 'Shame,' but not because they thought his action was shameful, they were merely saying how sad the whole thing was.

The Indian man was now struck by a new idea, and he shouted, 'Sonny, what's your address?' Johnny heard him but he tried to pay no attention, needing it all for the dangerous piece ahead. However, the question disturbed him slightly, and he brought his right foot down again, causing the crowd to give a composite groan, with many meanings. The Indian man took it as a reprieve, and shouted, 'Sonny, I pray to God, give me your address.'

It was now clear to all but his would-be rescuer that the small boy intended to continue the climb. His small exploratory movements showed that he meant to go up, not down. Again he placed his right foot, but this time he pulled himself up, causing the Indian man to rise from his knees and to collapse groaning on to a rock with his hands covering his eyes. So was silenced his vocal opposition to the climb, but the rest were quiet too, speaking in low voices, even whispers, as Johnny placed his hands and his foot, and pulled himself up, two feet now above the safety of the sloping trail. Then again the hands exploring, the right foot testing, the body bracing, the small boy like a fly on a cinema screen, except that he was no intruder, rather the creator of a drama never before witnessed in this city, of a crowd of every colour and class and tongue, bound all of them together for these moments by unbreakable bonds, to a small white boy climbing a quarry face made of a stone that knew nothing of admiration or anxiety or pity. And again a step, and again the low talking, and again the exploring hands and the testing foot, and again the bracing of the body. And down below silence, and silent prayers, and silent apprehension. The Indian man took his hands from his eyes, and watched despairingly; it was clear he was in an agony of care and pity over this child of an alien race, many of whose members had shown neither care nor pity for himself or his people. And up above again the winning of another step, again the murmur from below, from a crowd growing every moment, swollen by people streaming over the waste ground between the quarry and the tarred road. There they stood, shoulder to shoulder, ruler and ruled, richer and poorer, white and black and yellow and brown, with their eyes fixed on a small piece of whiteness halfway up the quarry face, and those of them who knew a thing or two knew that the boy was in a position of considerable danger.

Fortunately Johnny himself did not know it. He was surprised that his right hand searching above his head had found another generous ledge, at least nine inches wide. Once he had reached it, he would be able to rest, even perhaps to look upward to plan the last piece of climbing that would enable him to reach the half-left trail. Therefore he set out to reach it, alternately terrifying and gratifying the watching crowd below.

The crowd did not realise the achievement when at last Johnny's feet were both planted on the nine-inch ledge. He himself decided not only to rest, but to allow his attention to be diverted from the climb. The ledge was so wide that he could turn himself about for the first time, stand with his back to the quarry face, and look down on the hundreds of people below. Some of them clapped and cheered him, some of them looked at him out of troubled eyes. The big Indian man stood up from the rock onto which he had collapsed, and called out, in a less assured voice than hitherto, for the small boy to come down, but after another man had spoken quietly to him, he desisted and it was generally understood that the second man had told him that the small boy had reached a point of no return, and it were better to leave him alone, and to pray rather for his salvation.

For three minutes, four minutes, it must have been, Johnny stood with his back to the quarry face. After acknowledging the crowd's cheers, he had cut them off from attention, and stood there reassembling his small boy's powers. Everything was silent when again he turned his face to the quarry wall. The foothold was there, the handhold for the left hand was there, but of handhold for the right hand there was no sign whatsoever. At first he could not believe it, but when he tried again he knew there was no doubt of it. Had the handhold been perpendicularly above the toehold he might have done it, but it was at least a foot to the left of his body line. No one could pull himself up from such a position.

A growl went up from the crowd, of defeat and frustration, and from the more knowledgeable, of sharpened anxiety. Again the questing hands, again the finding of nothing. The small boy, leaving his two arms in this upstretched position, put his face to the face of the quarry, almost as if he were weeping or praying, which indeed is what some thought he was doing. He brought down his arms and caused the crowd to groan and shudder as his left foot explored the rock below him, trying to find the foothold he had used to reach the ledge.

In complete silence they watched him put his foot on it, but after a moment he withdrew and again laid his face against the face of the quarry. It was then clear that his ambition to climb had gone, and in its place was the frightenedness of a small boy. Again he turned himself round so that he faced the crowd, who could see clearly his loneliness and despair. His movements, so splendidly co-ordinated until now, gave alarming signs of randomness, and for one terrible moment it seemed that he might panic and fall.

This was the signal for a young African man of about twenty to take charge.

'Hi, sonny,' he shouted, waving with outstretched arm to the small boy, 'don't be frightened. Thomas Ndhlovu is coming.'

On his way to the starting-point by the noticeboard, Thomas spoke to a white man who seemed to be senior to the others.

'Get the police, master, or the fire brigade. I go up to stay with the small boy.'

Then he started his climb, amid a new noise of laughs, cheers, approval, and advice. Thomas soon showed himself to be vigorous and unskilled, and his friends below, who had been so anxious about the first climber, made jokes about the second. As for Thomas himself, whenever he had brought off what he thought a piece of good climbing, he would turn to the crowd and raise his clenched fist, to be greeted by cheers and laughter. Every few steps he would shout at the small boy, urging him to be of good heart, because one Thomas Ndhlovu was coming. The small boy himself had recovered from his panic and watched absorbedly the progress of his saviour. What had been a tense and terrifying affair had become a kind of festival. Jests and laughter had replaced groans and sighs, and Thomas, with intention somewhat foolish, climbed flamboyantly and wildly, shouting encouragement in English to the small boy and exchanging banter in Zulu with his friends on the ground. It was only when he reached the end of the first trail, and began to inspect the sharp perpendicular ascent that the crowd again fell silent.

Thomas however would not tolerate this new respect. Turning round he shouted something at his friends that caused much laughter. He too made the exploratory motions of hands and it was very clear that he was caricaturing the small boy's motions. Nevertheless the laughter died away as he began the ascent and the atmosphere was tense, without being fearful. When at last he placed his foot on the nine-inch ledge, rulers and ruled, richer and poorer, joined in an ovation of shouting and clapping, which was doubled and redoubled when he too turned to face the crowd. He smiled down at the small white boy and put his hand on his shoulder, as if to assure him that no one fell from a ledge when Thomas Ndhlovu was on it.

'Now be quiet,' he said, 'some time the police come, and the fire brigade, and you go home to your mother.'

The small boy said, 'Thanks a million,' and Thomas said, 'What your mother say?'

'I won't tell my mother,' said Johnny.

Thomas laughed uproariously, and pointed at the crowd below, where newspapermen were taking photographs and interviewing spectators.

'Tomorrow,' said Thomas, 'big picture in paper, you and me. Your mother open paper, she say, what you doing there with that native boy?'

He thought this very funny, and for a time occupied himself with it. Then he asked, 'What's your name, sonny?'

'Johnny Day.'

'Johnny Day, eh? Very good name. My name Thomas Ndhlovu.'

'Very good name too,' said Johnny.

'Police coming,' said Thomas pointing. 'When police coming other times, Thomas running. Now police coming, Thomas staying.'

The arrival of the police was greeted with great good humour, for here was an occasion on which their arrival was welcome. Words in Zulu were shouted at them, compliments tinged with satire, for the crowd was feeling happy and free. The policemen grasped the whole situation immediately. Two of them, armed with ropes, set off up through the trees that grew at the side of the quarry and in a few minutes had reached the upper edge, where they took up a position directly above the man and the boy.

Instructions were shouted and a rope was lowered to Thomas, who, once he had the cradle-like end in his hand, laughed with uproarious delight. To the end of this rope was attached another which Thomas threw to the policemen below. More instructions were shouted and Thomas soon had the small boy in the cradle. The policemen above lowered the cradle down the quarry wall. The policemen below held it away from the stony face. In one minute Johnny was on the quarry floor, lost to sight in a swirling multi-coloured mass, shouting their joy and congratulation. This celebration was still in progress as Thomas Ndhlovu landed on the quarry floor, when it transferred itself to him. Everybody, white, yellow, brown, black, wanted to shake hands with him, to thank him for his splendid act, to ask God to bless him. The Indian man, now fully restored, was one of the most enthusiastic of these participators.

'Come, sonny,' said the senior white man. 'Tell me where you live and I'll take you home.'

'I must thank Thomas first,' said Johnny.

The senior white man looked at the tumultuous scene. 'How are you going to do that?' he said.

'I'll wait,' said Johnny.

But he did not need to wait. The policemen cleared a way through the mob of congratulators, and there, under the eyes of authority, Johnny Day put out his hand and thanked Thomas Ndhlovu again for the act which, for all we know, saved his life. This second evidence of gratitude was extremely pleasurable to Thomas and, moved to great heights by it, he led the small white boy to the noticeboard which said, NO CLIMBING, BY ORDER. What he said, no one heard, for it was lost in an outburst of catcalls, laughter, jeering and cheering.

[1966? *South African Outlook*, October 1970.]

Sunlight in Trebizond Street

Today the Lieutenant said to me, *I'm going to do you a favour*. I don't answer him. I don't want his favours. *I'm not supposed to do it*, he said. *If I were caught I'd be in trouble*. He looks at me as though he wanted me to say something, and I could have said, *that'd break my heart*, but I don't say it. I don't speak unless I think it will pay me. That's my one fast rule.

Don't you want me to do you a favour? he asks. *I don't care*, I said, *if you do me a favour or you don't. But if you want to do it, that's your own affair*.

You're a stubborn devil, aren't you? I don't answer that, but I watch him. I have been watching Caspar for a long time, and I have come to the conclusion that he has a grudging respect for me. If the major knew his job, he'd take Caspar away, give me someone more exciting, more dangerous.

Don't you want to get out? I don't answer. There are two kinds of questions I don't answer, and he knows it. One is the kind he needs the answers to. The other is the kind to which he knows the answers already. Of course I want to get out, away from those hard staring eyes, whose look you can bear only if your own are hard and staring too. And I want to eat some tasty food, and drink some wine, in some place with soft music and hidden lights. And I want . . . but I do not think of that. I have made a rule.

How many days have you been here? I don't answer that, because I don't know any more. And I don't want Caspar to know that I don't. When they took away the first bible, it was 81. By an effort of will that exhausted me, I counted up to 105. And I was right, up to 100 at any rate, for on that day they came to inform me, with almost a kind of ceremony, that duly empowered under Act so-and-so, Section so-and-so, they were going to keep me another 100, and would release me when I 'answered satisfactorily'. That shook me, though I tried to hide it from them. But I lost my head a little, and called out quite loudly, 'Hooray for the rule of law.' It was foolish. It achieved exactly nothing. After 105 I nearly went to pieces. The next morning I couldn't remember if it were 106 or 107. After that you can't remember any more. You lose your certitude. You're like a blind man who falls over a stool in the well-known house. There's no birthday, no trip to town, no letter from abroad, by which to remember. If you try going back, it's like going back to look for something you dropped yesterday in the desert, or in the forest, or in the water of the lake. Something is gone from you that you'll never find again.

It took me several days to convince myself that it didn't matter all that much. Only one thing mattered, and that was to give them no access to my private self. Our heroic model was B.B.B. He would not speak, or cry out, or stand up, or do anything they told him to do. He would not even look at them, if such a thing is possible. Solitude did not affect him, for he could withdraw into a solitude of his own, a kind of state of suspended being. He died in one such solitude. Some say he withdrew too far and could not come back. Others say he was tortured to death, that in the end the pain stabbed its way into the solitude. No one knows.

So far they haven't touched me. And if they touched me, what would I do? Pain might open the door to that private self. It's my fear of that that keeps me from being arrogant. I have a kind of superstition that pride gets punished sooner than anything else. It's a relic of my lost religion.

You're thinking deep, said Caspar, *I'll come tomorrow. I expect to bring you interesting news.*

*   *   *

Caspar said to me, *Rafael Swartz has been taken in*. It's all I can do to hide from him that for the first time I stand before him in my private and naked self. I dare not pull the clothes round me, for he would know what he had done. Why doesn't he bring instruments, to measure the sudden uncontrollable kick of the heart, and the sudden tensing of the muscles of the face, and the contraction of the pupils? Or does he think he can tell without them? He doesn't appear to be watching me closely. Perhaps he puts down the bait carelessly, confident that the prey will come. But does he not know that the prey is already a thousand times aware? I am still standing naked, but I try to look as though I am wearing clothes.

Rafael Swartz. Is he brave? Will he keep them waiting 1,000 days, till in anger they let him go? Or will he break as soon as one of them casually picks up the poker that has been left carelessly in the coals?

He's a rat, says Caspar. *He has already ratted on you.* I say foolishly, *How can he rat on me? I'm here already.*

You're here, Caspar agreed. He said complainingly, *But you don't tell us anything. Swartz is going to tell us things that you won't tell. Things you don't want us to know. Tell me, doctor, who's the boss?*

I don't answer him. I begin to feel my clothes stealing back on me. I could now look at Caspar confidently, but that I mustn't do. I must wait till I can do it casually.

I don't know when I'll see you again, he said, quite like conversation. *I'll be spending time with Swartz. I expect to have interesting talks with him. And if there's anything I think you ought to know, I'll be right back. Goodbye, doctor.*

He stops at the door. *There's one thing you might like to know. Swartz thinks you brought him in.*

He looks at me. *He thinks that,* he says, *because we told him so.*

*   *   *

John Forrester always said to me when parting, *Have courage.* Have I any courage? Have I any more courage than Rafael Swartz? And who am I to know the extent of his courage? Perhaps they are lying to me. Perhaps when they told him I had brought him in, he laughed at them and said, *It's an old trick but you can't catch an old dog with it.*

Don't believe them, Rafael. And I shan't believe them either. Have courage, Rafael, and I shall have courage too.

*   *   *

Caspar doesn't come. It's five days now. At least I think it's five. I can't even be sure of that now. Have courage, Rafael.

*   *   *

It must be ten days now. I am not myself. My stomach is upset. I go to and fro the whole day, and it leaves me weak and drained. But though my body is listless, my imagination works incessantly. What is happening there, in some other room like this, perhaps in this building too? I know it is useless imagining it, but I go on with it. I've stopped saying, *Have courage, Rafael,* on the grounds that if he has lost his courage, it's too late, and if he hasn't lost his courage, it's superfluous. But I'm afraid. It's coming too close.

*   *   *

Who's your boss? asks Caspar, and of course I don't reply. He talks about Rafael Swartz and Lofty Coombe and Helen Columbus, desultory talk, with now and then desultory questions. The talk and the questions are quite pointless. Is the lieutenant a fool or is he not?

He says to me, *You're a dark horse, aren't you, doctor? Leading a double life, and we didn't know.*

I am full of fear. It's coming too close. I can see John Forrester now, white-haired and benevolent, what they call a man of distinction, the most miraculous blend of tenderness and steel that any of us will ever know. He smiles at me as though to say, *Keep up your courage, we're thinking of you every minute of the day.*

What does Caspar mean, my double life? Of course I led a double life, that's why I'm here. Does he mean some other double life? And how would they know? Could Rafael have known?

Can't you get away, my love? I'm afraid for you, I'm afraid for us all. What did I tell you? I can't remember. I swore an oath to tell no one. But with you I can't remember. And I swore an oath that there would never be any woman at all. That was my crime.

When I first came here, I allowed myself to remember you once a day, for about one minute. But now I am thinking of you more and more. Not just love, fear too. Did I tell you who we were?

Love, why don't you go? Tell them you didn't know I was a revolutionary. Tell them anything, but go.

As for myself, my opinion of myself is unspeakable. I thought I was superior, that I could love a woman, and still be remote and unknowable. We take up this work like children. We plot and plan and are full of secrets. Everything is secret except our secrecy.

*   *   *

What is happening now? Today the major comes with the lieutenant, and the mere sight of him sets my heart pounding. The major's not like Caspar. He does not treat me as superior or inferior. He says *Sit down*, and I sit. He says to me, *So you still won't co-operate.* Such is my foolish state that I say to him, *Why should I co-operate? There's no law which says I must co-operate. In fact the law allows for my not co-operating, and gives you the power to detain me until I do.*

The major speaks to me quite evenly. He says, *Yes, I can detain you, but I can do more than that, I can break you. I can send you out of here an old broken man, going about with your head down, mumbling to yourself, like Samuelson.*

He talks to me as though I were an old man already. *You wouldn't like that, doctor. You like being looked up to by others. You like to pity others, it gives you a boost, but it would be hell to be pitied by them. In Fordsville they thought the sun shone out your eyes. Our name stinks down there because we took you away.*

We can break you, doctor, he said. *We don't need to give you shock treatment, or hang you up by the feet, or put a vice on your testicles. There are many other ways. But it isn't convenient. We don't want you drooling round Fordsville.* He adds sardonically, *It would spoil our image.*

He looks at me judicially, but there's a hard note in his voice. *It's inconvenient, but there may be no other way. And if there's no other way, we'll break you. Now listen carefully. I'm going to ask you a question.*

He keeps quiet for a minute, perhaps longer. He wants me to think over his threat earnestly. He says, *Who's your boss?*

After five minutes he stands up. He turns to Caspar. *All right, lieutenant, you can go ahead.*

*   *   *

What can Caspar go ahead with? Torture? for me? or for Rafael Swartz? My mind shies away from the possibility that it might be for you. But what did he mean by the double life? Their cleverness, which might some other time have filled me with admiration, fills me now with despair. They drop a fear into your mind, and then they go away. They're busy with other things, intent on their job of breaking, but you sit alone for days and think about the last thing they said. Ah, I am filled with fear for you. There are 3,000 million people in the world, and I can't get one of them to go to you and say, *Get out, this day, this very minute.*

*   *   *

Barbara Trevelyan, says Caspar, *it's a smart name. You covered it up well, doctor, so we're angry at you. But there's someone angrier than us. Didn't you promise on oath to have no friendship outside the People's League, more especially with a woman? What is your boss going to say?*

Yes, I promised. But I couldn't go on living like that, cut off from all love, from all persons, from all endearment. I wanted to mean something to somebody, a live person, not a cause. I am filled with shame, not so much that I broke my promise, but because I couldn't make an island where there was only our love, only you and me. But the world had to come in, and the great plan for the transformation of the world, and forbidden knowledge, dangerous knowledge, and . . . I don't like to say it, perhaps boasting came in too, dangerous boasting. My head aches with pain, and I try to remember what I told you.

You are having your last chance today, says Caspar. *If you don't talk today, you won't need to talk anymore. Take your choice. Do you want her to tell us, or will you?*

I don't know. If I talk, then what was the use of these 100 days? Some will go to prison, some may die. If I don't tell, if I let her tell, then they will suffer just the same. And the shame will be just as terrible.

It doesn't matter, says Caspar, *if you tell or she tells. They'll kill you either way. Because we're going to let you go.*

He launches another bolt at me. *You see, doctor, she doesn't believe in the cause, she believes only in you. Tomorrow she won't even do that. Because we're going to tell her that you brought her in.*

Now he is watching me closely. Something is moving on my face. Is it an insect? or a drop of sweat? Don't tell them, my love. Listen my love, I am sending a message to you. Don't tell them, my love.

Do you remember what Rafael Swartz used to boast at those meetings in the good old days, that he'd follow you to hell? Well, he'd better start soon, hadn't he? Because that's where you are now.

He takes off his watch and puts it on the table. *I give you five minutes,* he said, *and they're the last you'll ever get. Who's your boss?* He puts his hands on the table too, and rests his forehead on them. Tired he is, tired with breaking men. He lifts his head and puts on his watch and stands up. There is a look on his face I haven't seen before, hating and vicious.

You're all the same, aren't you? Subversion most of the time, and women in between. Marriage, children, family, that's for the birds, that's for our decadent society. You want to be free, don't you? You paint FREEDOM all over the damn town. Well you'll be free soon, and by God it'll be the end of you.

*   *   *

Lofty and Helen and Le Grange. And now Rafael. Is there anyone they can't break? Does one grow stronger or weaker as the days go by? I say a prayer for you tonight, to whatever God may be . . .

Did I say Rafael's name? I'm sorry, Rafael, I'm not myself today. Have courage, Rafael. Don't believe what they say. And I shan't believe either.

*   *   *

5 days? 7 days? More? I can't remember. I hardly sleep now. I think of you and wonder what they are doing to you. I try to remember what I told you. Did I tell you I was deep in? Did I tell you how deep? Did I tell you any of their names? It's a useless question, because I don't know the answer to it. If the answer came suddenly into my mind, I wouldn't know it for what it was.

Ah, never believe that I brought you in. It's an old trick, the cruellest trick of the cruellest profession in the world. Have courage, my love. Look at them out of your grey honest eyes and tell them you don't know anything at all, that you were just a woman in love.

*   *   *

Caspar says to me, *You're free.* What am I supposed to do? Should my face light up with joy? It might have done, only a few days ago. *Do you know why we're letting you go?* Is there point in not answering? I shake my head.

Because we've found your boss, that's why. When he sees I am wary, not knowing whether to believe or disbelieve, he says, *John Forrester's the name. He doesn't know what to believe either, especially when we told him*

192

you had brought him in. Doctor, don't come back here any more. You're not made for this game. You've only lasted this long because of orders received. Don't ask me why. Come, I'll take you home.

* * *

Outside in the crowded street the sun is shining. The sunlight falls on the sooty trees in Trebizond Street, and the black leaves dance in the breeze. The city is full of noise and life, and laughter too, as though no one cared what might go on behind those barricaded walls. There is an illusion of freedom in the air.

[This is an extract from the speech made by the author at the last public meeting of the Liberal Party, which was held in Durban in May, 1968. *Sunday Tribune*, Durban, 12.5.1968.]

Words to the Security Police

I should like first to take this opportunity of saying a few words to the members of the security police. These words will not be insulting, they will merely be truthful. I do not know if this is my farewell to the security police or whether we shall meet again. I used to pretend – I suppose it was my duty to pretend – that it was nothing to me to be watched by you, and to be followed by you, and to have my telephone conversations listened to by you, and to have some of my letters – I do not say all of them – read by you, and to have my house searched by you, and to have you sitting in a car outside my house so that all my neighbours could see what kind of person I was. But I was only pretending. After fifty years of a life blameless in the eyes of the law, it was painful suddenly to become the object of the attention of the security police of my own country, to fly to Johannesburg to find you waiting for me at the airport, to fly to Cape Town and find you there too. I am by nature a private rather than a public man, and this attention was painful to me.

Though this is a sad occasion for the Liberal Party of South Africa, it is of course a triumphant occasion for you, for you have carried out successfully the task allotted to you. You have advised the Minister to restrict the freedom of many of our leading members.[1] I shall mention only two of these. I shall mention the name of Miss Heather Morkill in Pietermaritzburg and Mrs. Jean Hill in Durban, who are people I can only describe as good, brave and honourable women, and it is a sick country and a sick government that must restrict the freedom of people who are good and brave and honourable.

The person who smashed my car window at the Hogsback[2] did not have his freedom restricted. But of course there may be a good reason for that, namely that his identity was never discovered. And there may be a bad reason for it too, namely that his identity was never revealed.

My relationship with you has had its happier moments. Once when we

[1] Altogether 44 members of the Liberal Party were issued with banning orders.
[2] Near Alice, Cape Province.

were holding a meeting at my house you came and parked in the street outside. And I went out and said to you, 'You are welcome to come and park in the garden, and you will be able better to see what is going on,' to which you replied, 'Mr. Paton, are we embarrassing you?' And I said, 'Yes you are.' And you said, 'Well, we'll go and park somewhere else.' And I said, 'Thank you.'

There was one funny moment too. When you came in 1966 to search my house, you came into the writing-room, and one of you said to the others, *'God, man, die boeke!'* And there was another high point too. You asked me to take you to my study, where there were still more books and papers, and I did so, and I said to you, 'Gentlemen, you may take my word or not, but I tell you that this is where I do my literary work when I do any literary work, and that there are no political papers here,' whereupon you took my word and did not search my study. Thus was never discovered my fiendish plot to blow up Parliament, and all the parliamentarians except the ones I fancied. I hope of course that these revelations of mine will not get any of you into trouble.

But there were other things not quite so happy or funny. Why did one of our leading members have to be arrested at a funeral? Why did a train have to be stopped in the middle of the veld, and one of our members arrested in full view of all the passengers, when you had seen him openly moving about on the platform at the previous station? Why did an old mother have to be visited, and warned that she would be destitute if her son persisted in being a member of the Liberal Party?

I hope you do not mind my addressing you thus. I have no wish to treat you discourteously. But for fifteen years you have been, not exactly our comrades, but closer to us than brothers. You will say to me, *'We have a job to do,'* and I shall say to you, *'Thank God I don't have to do it.'*

PART FOUR

Since 1968

With the disappearance of the Liberal Party Alan Paton has returned to 'private life'. But he has continued to be involved in the life of society in a variety of ways: he has been chairman of the editorial board of the liberal journal *Reality*, and he has written and spoken out on many important issues. *Kontakion for You Departed* (in the U.S.A., *For You Departed*), partly a tribute to his first wife, who died in 1967, was published in 1969. *Apartheid and the Archbishop*, a biography of Geoffrey Clayton, Archbishop of Cape Town, appeared in 1973. In 1970 Alan Paton was allowed to possess a passport once again, and since then he has visited Europe and North America.

[An address given on the sixth annual Day of Affirmation of Academic and Human Freedom, at the University of the Witwatersrand, Johannesburg, in June 1968. *Rand Daily Mail*, 7.6.1968.]

Why we must go on dreaming

December 10, 1968, will be the 20th anniversary of the adoption by the General Assembly of the United Nations of the Universal Declaration of Human Rights, and this year 1968 is designated International Human Rights Year.

This Universal Declaration was an affirmation by a majority of the nations of the world of the belief that man has certain inalienable rights, that he is not a man if he does not possess them, that he cannot live with dignity or purpose without them.

It is an affirmation of the belief that he has rights even as against the State, that he may not be enslaved or tortured, that he may not be arbitrarily arrested or detained or exiled. And that, if he is charged with the breaking of any law, he shall be entitled to a fair and public hearing in a court of law, and that it is only a court of law that shall have power to punish him, to lay hands on his property or his person, and to restrict his freedom.

The Universal Declaration also affirms that anyone who works, anyone who is ready to work, has a right to be given work, to choose the kind of work for which he is fitted, to be paid fair wages, to form protective unions, to be given leisure, shelter, and the necessary social services, to be given security in unemployment, sickness, disability and old age.

All have a right to education, and elementary education shall be free and compulsory. Higher education shall be accessible to all on the basis of merit. All education shall be directed to the strengthening of respect for human rights.

None of these rights shall be enjoyed or exercised at the expense of the rights of others, and it shall be the duty of the State to devise a just order in which its citizens may be able to exercise their rights and discharge their responsibilities to their communities.

This Declaration of Human Rights was the second time in the history of Man that the nations of the world sat down and dreamed a dream.

Listen to the words of General Smuts: 'We the peoples of the United

Nations determined to save succeeding generations from the scourge of war, which twice in our lifetime has brought untold sorrow to mankind, and to reaffirm faith in fundamental human rights, in the dignity and the worth of the human person, in the equal rights of men and women and of nations large and small, and to establish conditions under which justice and respect for the obligations arising from treaties and other sources of international law can be maintained . . . .'

And what has become of the United Nations? It is a common pastime to sneer at its organisations and its ineffectiveness, and a common error to forget the reasons for this ineffectiveness.

The United Nations Organisation is ineffective – not primarily because its member governments want it to be ineffective, but because it is a dream.

And one of the questions I want to discuss here tonight is whether there is any point in dreaming at all.

General Smuts started his Preamble with the words 'We the peoples of the United Nations' and ended it with the words 'accordingly, our respective Governments . . .', and we ought to know, and we must know, and especially as university people we must know, that what peoples dream and what governments do are not necessarily the same thing.

The first twenty years of this dream have not seen faith reaffirmed in fundamental human rights, or in the dignity and the worth of the human person, except on occasions such as these.

Is it worth while holding these days of affirmation when fundamental human rights, and the dignity and the worth of the human person, which are among the deepest hungers of the peoples of the world, are on the retreat in the face of the inexorable advances of our respective Governments?

Is it worth while affirming and re-affirming? – That is what we are considering tonight. The important question is not whether the dream is to be fulfilled, the important question is whether we should go on dreaming it.

It was part of the intention of the Preamble that armed force should not be used save in the common interest. In whose common interest is the war in Vietnam? To many of us the war in Vietnam is so terrible that there cannot be any justification for continuing it.

Here in our own country it requires no action by any court of law for a man or woman to be deprived of freedom to associate, to move about, to speak, to write, to publish, even to eat and drink with friends.

Year after year our Government takes to itself greater and greater power, and each time it does so, the rights of its citizens are diminished – and not only the rights of its citizens, but the rights of its institutions also, including this great University of the Witwatersrand, which each year affirms an ideal which it is no longer lawful to practise.

And here again we face the question which this night is demanding an answer from us: is there any point in affirming an ideal which it is no longer lawful to practise? Is there any point in affirming a belief which has no apparent relation to what is called contemporary reality?

What are the alternatives to the affirmation of an ideal that appears to be unrealisable? There are two alternatives – one is to give in, the other is to despair.

If any man was entitled to despair, it was Bertrand Russell during the First World War of 1914 to 1918, when the bright youth of Britain, France and Germany were exterminating one another, when 100,000 lives of promise were sacrificed to gain a few yards of mud, and another 100,000 sacrificed to win a few yards back again.

And the consequence of this sacrifice, this dying, this struggle to the death, this unspeakable heroism, was to give to Europe twenty years later the unspeakable horrors of Dachau, Belsen and Auschwitz.

Russell had to live through Dachau and Belsen and Auschwitz and Hiroshima; he lived to see the signing of the Charter that was to reaffirm faith in fundamental human rights and he lived to see the erosion of those rights.

He lived to see the use of armed force – which may be used only in the common interest – threaten not a small nation abroad, but a large nation at home, threaten its confidence and its pursuit of happiness, and its sweet American dream.

Yet if he had been here tonight, he would have affirmed what we have come here to affirm – and how then can we believe that there is no purpose, no use, no value, in affirming an ideal which can certainly not at this time be realised, and in dreaming a dream which can certainly not at this time be fulfilled?

For if we were to cease affirming, we would be ceasing to perform a task that man has performed from his very beginnings; we would by an act of apostasy have made of man the very creature that in our moments of despair we believe him to be.

Let us examine a little more closely the view – attractive to some of us in periods of frustration – that to affirm an ideal that cannot at this time be realised, is in fact to be doctrinaire, incapable of adaptation, inflexible, resistant to change, unable to adjust oneself to contemporary reality.

The holders of this view would argue that it is unrealistic to uphold the principle of the open university when the declared policy of the authorities is one of closed universities – that is, of ethnic universities, open to members of one race group and closed to those of others.

It seems to me that this is the view that is doctrinaire, inflexible, and blind to the contemporary reality of the wider world.

The reason why we affirm our belief in the open university is not because we are inflexible and opposed to change, but because we believe that it is only the open university that can guide and aid and sustain our sanity in the times of tremendous change that lie ahead – not only ahead of us, but ahead of the whole continent of Africa of which we are a part, a continent whose emancipation from a colonial past we wish to help to make more real, more meaningful.

And I believe with all my heart that the only kind of university which will be able to offer that kind of help will be the open university, the principle of which we affirm tonight.

There are times when one cannot adapt oneself to contemporary reality. If the late Professor Hoernlé had lived under Hitler he would not have adapted himself to contemporary reality – he would rather have died – and he would have died too, because Hitler would certainly not have allowed him to live.

Now I shall examine another view – akin to the first – that to pit the force of an ideal or a principle against raw and sometimes ruthless political power, is quite fatuous; that the only thing to pit against political power is another political power; that you must quit your ivory tower and get down there into the arena and play the game of power.

But there are times when you cannot get down and play the game of power, because you have no steed, no armour, no lance. The only thing that you have is your belief, and the only thing you can do with your belief is to affirm it.

I venture to read to you words which are not usually used on occasions such as this, but which are relevant to our situation.

'For, behold, I create new heavens and a new earth; and the former shall not be remembered, nor come into mind.

'But be ye glad and rejoice for ever in that which I create; for, behold, I create Jerusalem a rejoicing, and her people a joy.

'And I will rejoice in Jerusalem, and joy in my people; and the voice of weeping shall be no more heard in her, nor the voice of crying . . . .

'And they shall build houses, and inhabit them; and they shall plant vineyards, and eat the fruit of them.

'They shall not build, and another inhabit; they shall not plant, and another eat; for as the days of a tree are the days of my people, and mine elect shall long enjoy the work of their hands. . . .

'The wolf and the lamb shall feed together, and the lion shall eat straw like the bullock; and dust shall be the serpent's meat. They shall not hurt nor destroy in all my holy mountain, saith the Lord.'

And was it ever fulfilled? No, but it just went on being prophesied. It was prophesied by John in Patmos, and Thomas More in England, and Karl Marx, and the Charter of the United Nations, and the Universal Declaration of Human Rights; the unattainable goal, the unfulfillable dream, the history of man's long striving for something that he has never achieved.

But if he were to stop striving for the unbelievable world in which the wolf lies down with the lamb, and in which the nations of the world abjure the use of war, they would destroy the mountain itself, and the great adventure of men would come to its end.

I should like to address some words to the supporters of NUSAS. The words I have already used were intended to be of encouragement to them, but these are especially so.

I do not expect that the future is going to be easy for you.

You have been advised by many people to drop politics and stick to your studies. This seems strange advice, coming as it often does from people responsible for giving the vote to all White South Africans when they turn 18.

It was the intention of our legislators not that our students should eschew politics, but that they should take a lively interest in them. It was because the students of the Afrikaans-language universities took a lively interest in politics that the Nationalist Government came to power.

If there is to be any change in the dangerous foreign policies of America it will be largely due to the lively interest of American students in politics, and the fact that so many of them feel so deeply that they have actually abandoned their studies to help in the electoral campaigns – and all this because of their deep love for their country and their concern for its honourable name.

I do not think it strange that South African students should sing *Die Stem van Suid-Afrika* when they are saying farewell to a man who is going into exile because he has been restricted in such a way that he can no longer pursue his chosen career, for they sing also because of their love for their country and their concern for its name.[1]

South Africa has been called a land of fear, and that is true. But it is a land of great courage also.

Politics is life, politics is living, politics is your present and your future,

[1] The official national anthem was sung by his student friends on the departure from South Africa of Dr. Bill Hoffenburg.

with politics are bound up indissolubly your ideals and your beliefs.

There is only one word of advice that I can offer you, and that is that while you have a duty to your country and your society and your fellow man, you also have a duty to yourselves, and that duty is to join in the acquisition and advancement of knowledge, and to equip yourselves for the future by paying a proper attention to your studies.

It is right and fitting that your National Union should concern itself with the affairs of its society and its people, with the pursuit of justice as you see that justice to be, with the pursuit of freedom as you see that freedom to be, with the pursuit of truth, which is another of those unattainable goals whose pursuit nevertheless gives meaning and direction to our lives.

In those pursuits you are under no obligation to believe as others believe, or as others would wish you to believe.

No State, no Government, no Church, no Party, has any right to tell you what you must believe, just as you have no right to tell others what they should believe.

But you have a right to try to persuade others, just as they have a right not to listen to your persuasion.

It is these pursuits that make us fully human, that give us that dignity and worth of the human person which is spoken of in the Charter of the United Nations.

May you continue to pursue these things, within all the limits and restrictions that may be imposed upon you, for while you continue to do this, many others will be encouraged to continue also.

[An extract from a speech made at the twentieth annual meeting of the Civil Rights League, in Cape Town in October 1968. *South African Outlook*, November 1968.]

Civil Rights and Present Wrongs

The thesis that there can be no freedom without duty and obedience to the laws has a strong appeal for the authoritarian personality who on the whole is contemptuous of Civil Rights Leagues and of this Universal Declaration. This thesis however appeals to him in one set of circumstances only, namely, if it is he who has made the laws, and thus it loses its cogency for those of us who do not worship authority for its own sake. There is a second point to note also, that while there can be no freedom without duty and obedience to the laws, mere obedience to the laws does not constitute freedom except in one other set of circumstances, namely, when the laws enshrine and are consistent with those freedoms that we have so far assumed to be essential to the good and human life.

Are these freedoms really essential to the good life? This question may well now be asked because in so many countries of the world many of them have been abrogated. If for example the right to life is acknowledged to be a valid right, then the right not to take life is equally valid. But all over the world millions of young men are being conscripted and trained to take life. Generals in the armies of what are often called the 'developed countries' exhort their men to kill, and to kill fast, and to kill without mercy, the enemy wherever he is to be found. The conscience of the United States has been so powerfully troubled by the war in Vietnam that eminent citizens, including Dr. Benjamin Spock and the Revd. William Coffin, the Chaplain of Yale University, have gone to prison for counselling young men to refuse the draft, for the reason that the United States is persistently and implacably destroying the very countryside and people that she is fighting to defend. In Russia some of the bravest and best writers have been sent to prison for daring to write what they think. In Britain, though you can write more or less what you like, you cannot enter the country if you are an Indian British subject from Kenya. In our own country, if you are black and you go to work in a city, you have no right to take your wife and children with you, and if you do, they may be sent back home at any time, and if you visit them, you may lose your work in the city.

Is it essential for the freedom and happiness and enjoyment of human life that men and women should have privacy, and be spared degradation, and take an active interest in the affairs of their country, and think deeply about its well-being, and make common cause with those who think as they do? To most of us who are here it is essential. That is what it means to us to be human. And the strange thing is this, that this is also what it means to my rulers; to each one of them these freedoms are essential if he is to be a man. But there the likeness between us ends, for while it is essential for him to have these freedoms, he does not think it is essential for others, he certainly does not think it is essential for those who oppose him and cannot accept his ideals and cannot accept his authority.

Why should this be so? I can think of only one answer. My ruler attaches no importance to the freedom of the individual as such; for him the individual derives his whole significance from his membership of the group, and he has no other significance. If the individual should cherish values other than the values of the group, then my ruler regards him as a lost soul, lost in a profound sense, loose, rootless, promiscuous, an abject creature, signifying nothing, owning nothing, belonging to nothing. So persons like Leo Marquard, Uys Krige, Beyers Naudé[1] – whom all of us here regard as persons of substance and integrity and meaning and what is more, persons with a concern for the health of society, not mere individualists – are for my ruler persons of no account.

This losing of one's personality in the group personality – and let me be just – this finding of one's personality in the group personality, which way of life is so strongly believed in in this Christian country, is not specifically a Christian way of life at all. The emphasis of the gospel lies on man's relationship with God and his neighbour, and man derives his significance from his being a creature, and not merely a creature, but a creature on whom great value is set by his Creator. Nowhere does the gospel teach us that a Jew or a Roman or a Samaritan derives his significance from being a Jew or a Roman or a Samaritan. He derives his significance from being a man created in the image of his Creator. His greatest duty is not towards his group, but towards his neighbour. It disturbs my ruler to find that his doctrine of the individual and the group which is not only his doctrine but is his supreme doctrine, to the overlordship of which all other doctrines are subject – it disturbs my ruler that this is

[1] All three are Afrikaners: Marquard was one of the founders of the National Union of South African Students; Krige is a writer in both Afrikaans and English, who has been an outspoken opponent of authoritarianism; Naudé is the founder and National Director of the Christian Institute of Southern Africa, a body dedicated to the study and the implementation of the social aspects of the teachings of Christianity.

not taught in the gospel. So what does my ruler do? He takes the boldest step imaginable. He fuses his supreme doctrine with the gospel, and invents a creed and a way of life called Christian–groupism, Christian–Nationalism. Therefore a man to be really a man, and to enjoy that freedom that the gospel offers him, must first and foremost and last be a group-man.

Thus man's personal and intimate responses to things that have nothing to do with the group, his responses to art and music and beauty, his flights of imagination, his painting and writing and poetry, are things to be regarded with the greatest suspicion, especially when the one who responds, the one who imagines, the one who writes, does not use his gifts in the service of the group, and sometimes believes perversely that art and music and poetry exist in some kind of absolute right of their own. Therefore my ruler will never be a patron of the arts, except for the purpose of controlling them. He will never give a prize for writing, unless it is patriotic writing. As for imagination, he will regard it as a pastime of the devil, and a certain sign that the one who employs it is, wittingly or unwittingly, furthering the aims of Communism.

In this climate, civil rights do not burgeon, and we must not expect them to do so. The whole concept of civil rights, the idea that man, individual human man, father, husband, lover, artist, writer, has rights that are beyond the control of the group, is not only alien, but also disgusting, to the authoritarian personality. When the authoritarian group also has the monopoly of political power, when it in fact becomes to all intents and purposes the State, then civil rights are benefits bestowed by the State, they are held only at the pleasure of the State, they can be abridged, even abolished, if that is the will of the State.

That is the situation in South Africa today. It does not make one popular to say so. There are two kinds of people who will resent it. One is the totalitarian group which is in power, which is so far identified with the State that it never feels its own security to be endangered, and which indeed would consent to almost any curtailment of its own liberties because it has security, or should I say, it has what it believes to be security. I can well remember the frenzy which could be aroused in the '30s by the mere shouting of the word '*Vryheid*', just as I can remember the anger which could be aroused in the '50s by the shouting of the word 'Freedom', and the contempt aroused in the '60s by the word '*Uhuru*'. The second group of persons who are hostile to any open advocacy of civil rights is composed of those who used to believe, how deeply or shallowly one can but guess, in civil liberty, until they realised that the price of expressing such beliefs was growing higher and higher, until it became so high that they were not prepared to pay it any longer, and then went through the sad experience of resenting, even hating, those of their ex-comrades who were prepared to go on paying.

I suppose I should bring some evidence other than my own that in this country the power of the State is omnipresent, and I realise of course that it is easy to bring evidence for, and equally easy to bring evidence against. But one particular piece of evidence for this view is given so concisely and clearly that I thought it worth bringing forward. It is the evidence of some of the members of a group of 40 German economics students who have just completed a two-month period of working for South African firms. They belong to a non-political organisation known as the International Association of Students of Economics and Commerce, which draws its members from 300 universities. This is their evidence. They did not claim to have a thorough insight into the complexities of our problems, but they felt that this did not preclude them from commenting on the unmistakable isolation which seemed to have penetrated almost every sphere of South African life. They declared that in any country in which the State tended to dominate all spheres of life, the central authority was forced to concentrate ideology on a few basic principles or ideas, and never moved outside of them, and this resulted in sterility of thought. New ideas thus immediately became suspect, and the inevitable result was physical and mental isolation from the rest of the world community. They reported that South Africans liked being told how wonderful they were and on meeting foreigners they soon badgered them into passing an opinion on the country. Our Durban morning paper reported, 'Several of the students were absolutely flabbergasted when paid "routine" visits by the security police.' I conclude with this trenchant observation of theirs: 'The overriding influence and all-pervading presence of the State in South Africa creates an atmosphere reminiscent of that of' – and don't shudder – 'the Communist countries of Eastern Europe.'

That is what happens when there is one overriding doctrine to which all other doctrines are subject, when there is an authoritarian attitude towards the liberties of men and women. It does not matter whether this happens in a Communist or an anti-Communist country, the result is the same, a shrinking of human liberty, a merciless system of punishments often without recourse to any court of law, an abject fear of authority and the State, a lowering of voices in conversation, a cynicism towards life that passes for wit but which is in fact a surrender of one's independence, and on the part of the chosen, a rigid conformity, so that in a photograph of our rulers it is hard to distinguish one from the other –

they dress the same, they look the same, they think the same. Yet this conformity is not dull – it is not characterless – it is merciless, and it is particularly merciless to those who assert their individuality in the presence of the power and majesty of the State.

It is characteristic of the authoritarian personality that it is not given to mercy. It is suspicious of words like mercy, love, kindness, but it loves words like power, order, and of course authority. These immortal lines of Shakespeare would never win him a prize from the authoritarian state.

> The quality of mercy is not strained,
> It droppeth as the gentle rain from heaven
> Upon the place beneath: it is twice blessed;
> It blesseth him that gives and him that takes:
> 'Tis mightiest in the mightiest; it becomes
> The throned monarch better than his crown . . .
> It is enthroned in the hearts of kings,
> It is an attribute to God himself,
> And earthly power doth then show likest God's
> When mercy seasons justice.

Are we not perhaps merciful after all? Are we not perhaps the most merciful people in all the world? Is it not the work of our enemies, perhaps, that we are not seen to be merciful? Could we not show it then, to Helen Joseph[2] maybe? Or to Robert Sobukwe?[3] Or to those men who come out of prison after committing one political offence, only to be sent back again for having committed another political offence which is substantially the same as the one for which they have already been punished? Could we not be more merciful than to take people away from their homes and put them into tents? Could we not be more merciful to those thousands of husbands and fathers who are kept separated from their wives and children, and to those thousands of wives and children who are kept separated from their husbands and fathers, so that our factories can keep manufacturing those goods that make this country one of the richest in the world? Could we not do what other countries have done, and what we hope more countries are going to do in the future, and that is to appoint a high official who will see to it that the

[2] Mrs. Joseph was under house-arrest for nine years.

[3] As President of the Pan-African Congress (which was shortly afterwards banned) Mr. Sobukwe early in 1960 organised a large demonstration against the pass laws. For this he was sentenced to three years' imprisonment, then kept in prison for a further six years (an amendment to the Suppression of Communism Act made this legal), then 'freed' and placed under house-arrest. The 'banning order' was renewed in May 1974.

State in some circumstances tempers the power of the State, and corrects manifest injustices, and is merciful to the poor and the misguided and the young zealot and the hot-blooded rebel, even to those burning and tormented revolutionaries who are contemptuous of mercy? And would not these things make our country more righteous so that we could more richly deserve the tributes that we like to pay to ourselves? For the greatest disadvantage of self-satisfaction is that it prevents one from ever becoming any better.

There is another characteristic of the authoritarian society, whether it be Communist or non-Communist, and that is that it inevitably destroys the rule of law, for it is distasteful and intolerable to the authoritarian society to have any institution that is higher than itself and independent of itself. We congratulate ourselves on the independence of the courts and the independence of the judiciary, but this independence is manifestly not tolerable in the case of political offences which are not readily definable in terms of law. In other words, the authoritarian state decides – in view of the unprecedented emergency that has arisen, which unprecedented emergency will for ever go on arising, and indeed will never end, for it bears no relation to external reality, it arises only because the authoritarian state cannot function except in a state of unprecedented emergency – this authoritarian state decides to abrogate the the rule of law. The authoritarian state cannot afford to be merciful, for it is for ever subject to the relentless attacks of the wit and liveliness and courage and impudence of those of its citizens who will not go down on their knees or their bellies to worship it; therefore this wit and liveliness and courage and impudence must be curbed, and all the salt and savour and beauty must be taken out of life, and because my ruler cannot do this by ordinary legal process, because my ruler would make a fool of himself by trying to do it by legal process, he labels this wit and liveliness and courage and impudence with a new name and calls them the furthering, wittingly or unwittingly, of the aims of Communism, and gives to himself – by law – powers which have no relation to law, powers to inflict punishment on those who are not trying to overthrow the State by violence, but who are trying to change the Government by reason and persuasion. It is this wit and liveliness and courage and impudence, it is all these riches of personality and individuality, that the Declaration of Human Rights is intended to preserve and protect, and that is what makes it unacceptable to the authoritarian state.

There is no human right more important than the right to live under the rule of law. It is the right among other rights, if one is charged with any offence, to be brought before a court of law, to hear the charges and to put forward one's defence, and to have one's guilt or innocence decided by a magistrate or judge who shall have no interest other than the interest of justice. It is one of the noblest and most majestic conceptions that man has ever achieved, which takes into full account the interest of both person and society, and if it is tampered with, the life of both person and society is impoverished, and immeasurably impoverished, because life becomes uncertain and arbitrary and full of care. The moment that Parliament entrusts to any man, however wise and benevolent and noble, the power to punish and to punish with extreme severity, without recourse to any court of law, one of his fellow citizens because he is *deemed* to be committing an offence, at that moment the rule of law is destroyed. And this is what has happened to us. . . .

[An article written for the American journal, *The National Catholic Reporter*, Kansas City, 19.2.1969.]

The Problem of Suffering

The 'problem of suffering' has exercised the minds of men for centuries, especially the minds of those who want to believe that God is father as well as creator. Why does he permit pain and suffering to exist? Why didn't he make the world good and kind and peaceful? Why didn't he make men who would not hurt or destroy in all that holy mountain? Was the world worth making, and is life worth living, with its Vietnam and its Nigeria, its cancer and arthritis, its decay of personal meaning and privacy, and the hopeless gloom of lonely and disillusioned old age?

These aren't easy questions to answer. I certainly hate to be asked them at a party. How is one to explain how evil got into the universe if one doesn't believe in the devil? Is one to believe that God the Saviour came to Bethlehem to make reparation for the cruelty of God the Creator? Or is one to believe that suffering, like man himself, is a product of a blind evolutionary process that produces orderliness by accident?

I can't accept any of these answers, but I can't produce others. My intellect cannot cope with the problem of suffering, nor can it accept the speculations of other intellects, which I feel are speculating out of their range and capacity. These are questions that cannot be answered in an article or a book, but only in a life.

I have a friend who has had both her breasts removed, and has now developed cancer in the spine, but her conversation is one of continual thanks to God and her friends and her neighbours and her woman servant. What is it that she knows? What has she found out? She has certainly not found out the answers to these difficult questions, but she has certainly found a meaning for her life.

In some way she has taken her suffering and made it her instrument, the use of which has given her this continual thankfulness, and has given her friends a shining example of faith and courage and love. I don't think she did it by an act of will. I think that's the way she was heading. She was predisposed, when she was struck down, to accept her affliction as an instrument.

This kind of victory seems to presuppose this kind of predisposition, but one should not be dogmatic about that, because the sudden or gradual onslaught of an affliction causes profound changes in the personality. At one extreme the doubters begin to believe and the careless begin to be careful. At the other extreme are those who go from believing to not-believing, and from not-believing to not-hoping, from confidence to despair.

I know another woman, who, because her teenage daughter suddenly threw off home discipline and conventional morality, lost her own faith. What went wrong? Why was her faith, which outwardly appeared unshakable, not able to withstand this blow? Was her belief in the goodness of God contingent on her own good luck?

All who are mature, whether young or old, accept suffering as inseparable from life; even if it is not experienced, the possibility of it is always there. I myself cannot conceive of life without suffering. I cannot even conceive that life could have meaning without suffering. There would certainly be no music, no theatre, no literature, no art. I suspect that the alternative to a universe in which there is suffering, in which evil struggles with good, and cruelty with mercy, would be a universe of nothingness, where there would be neither good nor evil, no happiness, only an eternity of uninterrupted banality.

If my suspicion is true, then I vote for the universe we have, where we have our joy that has been made real by our suffering, as the silence of the night is made real by the sounds of the night. And we have our suffering there too, made real by our joy. Such a multifold universe, such a multifold life, despite all the unanswerable questions that they raise, seem more consonant with the idea of a creative and imaginative God than any garden of Eden.

If suffering is an inescapable part of life, what does one do about it? There are many ways of reacting to it, but only one that is profitable, and that is to accept it, and use it and, where possible, to prevent it, alleviate it, bring it to an end.

When Francis got down from his horse and embraced the leper, he solved the problem of suffering for himself. And what was more, he was later able to accept and use his own suffering, and to sing his way to death. He did not curse leprosy, nor did he curse God for making or allowing leprosy; he got down from his horse and kissed the leper. This act changed his whole life, and the lives of countless thousands of others. From that time onwards, lepers became for Francis what the untouchables became for Gandhi, 'Narijans', the children of God. What was loathsome and terrifying became a source of sweetness and strength. Francis wrote in his will, 'The Lord Himself led me amongst them, and I showed mercy to them, and when I left them, what had seemed bitter to me was changed into sweetness of body and soul.'

Although I have contemplated this miracle for many years, it has never ceased to fill me with wonder. For in that moment Francis shed all doubt and anxiety and uncertainty, and all grief over the unsolvable mystery of pain and evil and sorrow, and put himself and his life into God's hands to be made the instrument of God's peace, so that he might ease pain and conquer evil and give comfort and strength to the sorrowful. He was no longer one to suffer and endure, he was one to love and to do.

One must straightaway admit that one can do this only if one has the conviction that God is the father of all mankind, and that he cares for all his creatures. But this does not deny fullness of life to those who do not have this conviction, yet desire to be an instrument of some unknown but good power. Once we make ourselves the instruments of such a power, the grip of melancholy and doubt begins to loosen, even in our present restless and unhappy world.

We no longer agonise over the problem of suffering; we make of ourselves instruments for its alleviation. It is almost as though we said to God, 'Some say you are cruel, and we confess that the cruelty of the world troubles us, so that we have moments of doubt; but of your goodness we have no doubt, having seen it in the life of Jesus, therefore we put our lives in your hands, so that you may use them for the sake of others.' This is, so far as I know, the only way in which one can solve for oneself the problem of suffering.

Jesus accepted evil and suffering as being 'in the nature of things'. He said, 'It must needs be that offences come.' Paul wrote of the whole creation groaning and travailing in pain until now. I do not pretend to be able to interpret these sayings, but it is clear that both Jesus and his great disciple accepted this wound in the creation, and having accepted it, devoted their lives to the healing of it.

That is the creative act, not to ask who dealt this wound to the creation, not to accuse God of having dealt it, but to make one's life an instrument of God's peace. This act is doubly creative, in that it transforms both giver and receiver, and indeed it can be said of many of us that one of our deepest experiences of God is in this act of giving and receiving.

Up till now I have been writing of that kind of suffering which we are helpless to prevent. If it afflicts others, then we can become the bearers of comfort and strength, if not of healing. If it afflicts ourselves, we may

213

by our acceptance of it, also become the bearers of comfort and strength to others.

There is also the kind of suffering that we bring on ourselves through acts of negligence and indulgence, and it is closely akin to the first, and must be accepted in the same way if it is to be creative. But there is a different kind of suffering altogether, when we suffer at the hands of authority or society or our neighbours, because of what we do and say and believe for reasons of conscience. This is a kind of suffering that can be – though it is not always so – highly creative. Some of us believe that society cannot be made whole without it. This suffering compounded with joy is the gospel, so that men and women take with willingness a road that may lead them to death and the cross.

It seems to me that there is a growing eagerness among Christians to rediscover the gospel, and a growing readiness to accept the compound of suffering and joy, and a growing comprehension that the gospel story is as relevant to life today as it has ever been. If it appears irrelevant, that is because it has been so heavily overlaid by pieties, observances and prohibitions that no one can get at it any more. God has been locked into the church, into its dogmas and doctrines, and the sense of his omnipresence has been lost.

Man has always been torn between saving himself and giving himself, and Christian man has never found it easy to believe that it is only by giving himself that he can save himself. He finds it hard, even bitter, to accept that being saved is only a consequence, and that it is the consequence of having given. He used to ask the question, and with great urgency, 'Am I saved?' whereas the real question should have been 'Am I giving?'

In my own country of South Africa, it is a matter of great importance to a white South African to be saved, to be safe, to be secure, to have some future in a country in which he is so heavily outnumbered. This desire to be saved, to be secure, is a dominant desire, and the majority of white Christians simply cannot believe that one achieves security by giving. Yet they desire to remain Christians, therefore they create a pseudo-gospel which enables them to save themselves and give themselves simultaneously. One of our foremost statesmen put it categorically, that the prime duty of a Christian is to look after himself, because if Christians don't look after themselves, what will become of Christianity?

When I write that there is a growing eagerness amongst Christians to rediscover the gospel, I do not mean that this applies to all Christians; and because it does not apply to all Christians, it follows that there is developing a new cleavage in the church, not along denominational lines, but between those who are rediscovering the gospel and those who believe, either that there is nothing to rediscover, or that it is subversive and communistic or just plain heretical to want to rediscover it. This cleavage is apparent in all denominations, so that a new and odd and exciting kind of ecumenicity is appearing.

This rediscovering of the gospel is dangerous in South Africa, for the authorities don't want it rediscovered. They want it to stay as it is, because they want the country to stay as it is. Apartheid and the gospel are more or less the same thing, and anyone who doesn't believe in apartheid is really not believing in the gospel. What is more, anyone who disbelieves strongly enough, anyone who exposes the cruelties of apartheid, anyone who is too active or too vocal in his opposition to apartheid, will be dealt with severely. His right to move about and communicate and seek employment will be drastically restricted, usually for a period of five years. And if at the end of that time he is not prepared to change radically his manner of opposition, these restrictions will be reimposed, usually for a further five years.

I write with authority about this, not because it has happened to me (I have suffered only in respect of my passport), but because it has happened to many of my friends. Their trouble was that they took too seriously the injunction to 'seek judgement'. They understood clearly that to seek judgement was to invite suffering, and they decided to go on seeking judgement. Not one of them would have changed his or her course to avoid suffering.

This is suffering at its most creative. It changed no laws, it softened no customs, but it made the country a better place to live in. What was a land of fear, they had made a land of courage also. Not only did they help and encourage others, but they acquired a strength that could withstand all the assaults of the enemy. To put it in religious language, they made themselves instruments of the divine creativity.

It is interesting to note that as one writes about these matters, one writes only incidentally about suffering. And that is as it should be. One is not really writing about suffering, one is writing about living, about loving, about giving. One is writing about the discovery that you cannot – I don't know if this is true of all societies – live and love and give without suffering. But your purpose is to live and love and give, and if suffering is part of the price to be paid, then you pay it. One does not seek suffering, one seeks judgement.

To me one of the most stirring stories of martyrdom is that of Hugh

Latimer, who knew well that support for the Reformation might lead him to death. Shortly after Mary, daughter of Henry VIII, came to the throne, he was summoned to appear at Westminster, and though he could have escaped, he obeyed joyfully. On 16 October 1555, he and Ridley were led to the stake at Oxford. He greeted Ridley with the words, 'Be of good comfort, Master Ridley, and play the man; we shall this day light such a candle by God's grace in England as I trust shall never be put out.'

He then 'received the flame (as it were) embracing it. After he had stroked his face with his hands, and (as it were) bathed them a little in the fire, he soon died (as it appeared) with very little pain or none.' He died thus without fear; he had had a life to live, and if the price for living it was to be burned alive, then of course one must be burned alive.

The world is now passing through a phase – which one hopes will soon end – where the state takes to itself greater and greater powers over the lives of its citizens. In some countries (mine is one) it has taken to itself the power to punish without recourse to the courts of law. In some countries (mine is one) a citizen can be held incommunicado for an indefinite period (or a fixed period that can be repeated indefinitely), and will only be released when his answers to questions are 'satisfactory' to the authorities.

In my country, if an African man goes to work in a 'white' area (and there is very little work in any other kind of area), then he may not take his wife and family with him. One could quote a thousand more examples of the power and indifference of the state, but the question I am asking is this: 'What does a Christian do, what does a good citizen do, who is seeking judgement, relieving the oppressed, helping the fatherless, pleading for the widow? Does he, in spite of the anger of the state, in spite very often of the anger of his neighbours, stand up for the right, and speak it and live it?'

There is only one answer for the Christian who has come, often reluctantly, often fearfully, to the belief that the Cross is not just for Good Friday. He must do it if he can. Quite apart from what he does for himself, which is considerable, he kindles hope in the breasts of many people, who see in him a living proof that the world was worth making, and is worth living in after all. Fortunate is society when those who love it are alive to its faults, and ready to spend their lives in its service. Because that is what living really means.

No one ever brought greater suffering on the world than Hitler. He shook man's faith in the goodness of life and of man. Yet what evil he inflicted with his absolute power was atoned for by men and women without power at all, who died rather than yield to him, and who left us the imperishable legacy of their letters written just before death.[1]

They changed no laws, they did not prevent the world from plunging into disaster, yet they restored man's faith in the goodness of life and of man. You cannot be more creative than that.

[1] Published in *Dying We Live*, Harvill Press.

[Botha's Hill, 1970? Not previously published.]

The Perfidy of Maatland

The twenty-one students rose when the Principal entered their common-room, and sat when he was seated. Some looked at him and some looked at the walls and the floor. Their looks told him nothing. They were neither hostile nor friendly. But he sensed that they were fully aware of him, and would hear every word and catch every meaning. They were as vigilant as he, and he, clad in the robes of authority, was conscious of the power of their impotence.

'I have called you together', he said, 'to ask your help and advice. You are all leading students, and you will understand that a Principal cannot allow a repetition of last night's events. I have no wish to punish. I wish only to find out why you paint such slogans on the walls, so that I may try, in so far as I am able, to make it unnecessary for you to paint them again. Speak freely, for only I am here, and what you say to me is for my ears alone.'

But no one spoke, no one offered to help and advise him. They sat looking at whatever they had looked at before, without noise or shuffling, making the meeting more silent than any other he had ever spoken to.

'Will no one speak?' he asked.

But no one spoke.

'May I ask why you will not speak?'

A young man rose, dark and slender.

'Principal, you asked twenty of us to meet you here. But there are twenty-one. I am the twenty-first. I am not on your list, and I must leave if you order me to do so. If I were on your list, I would not speak either. Why do we not speak? Because the last one of us who rose to speak when he was invited, and told the truth as he was asked to do, sits now in a small village many miles from here, and he may not leave it. He was our cleverest student, and was about to take his degree, but it would appear that there will never be a degree for him. However, if you wish me to speak, I shall do so.'

'Will no one else speak?' asked the Principal. But no one answered.

'If none of you will speak, then I shall ask this young man to speak for you, but you must understand that I assume you wish him to do so.'

'Principal,' said the young man, 'that is what they wish.'

'Then you may speak.'

'Principal, you must not be offended by me. I do not come here to offend you. But you will no doubt wish to ask me questions. Are you willing that I should question you also?'

The Principal smiled. 'You may do so, but I may not always answer you. Nor would I expect you always to answer me.'

'Then let me ask you, Principal, why is it these twenty who are asked to meet you? You have been here only a week. How do you know which students to ask? We have no Students' Council. It is too dangerous to be a member of the Students' Council. Who told you that these were the twenty to ask?'

A hard question indeed, the kind to make outraged authority rear up and strike. No one had ever asked him such a question in his life. His own students at Maatland would never have done so. They would have asked, *Professor, what does the professor think about this?* At public meetings people said, *Thank you, professor, for your message,* or even, *Professor, you are God's gift to our people.* Then of his own doing he had left it all behind to come to this troubled and tempestuous place. *We've had too much trouble there,* the Minister had said. *It doesn't do us any good. That's why I want you to go there. What we need is a man from Maatland.* So he had left the town of the oaks and the mountains and the historic houses, where the Minister and he had been young men together, and he had come to this dry and barren place. And at his installation, a bare twenty-four hours ago, he had promised that in ten years' time they would take all courses, in the Arts and the Sciences, in Theology and in Medicine, in their own language. Then to be called at four in the morning by his Disciplinary Officer, who was also his Vice-Principal, to see the mocking slogan VERNACULAR DEGREES – HA! HA!, and the insulting one MAASDORP, HUISTOE! painted above his own office.

He smiled at the young man. 'I am not willing to tell you who told me that these are the twenty leading students. Just as I would not expect you to tell me who painted the slogans.'

'Principal, we think we know who told you. Is it important to you to know what we think?'

Was it important? Or was this the time to say, *No, I wish only to find out why you paint such slogans on the wall?* He had always taught his students to fear no knowledge. How could he say, *No, it is not important?*

'Yes, I wish to know.'

'You see, Principal, we have no Students' Council. Whenever anything went wrong here, it was the members of the Students' Council who suffered. This clever student of whom I told you was not insolent. He was brought up to be mannerly and respectful, but he was also taught to respect himself and to speak the truth about all matters on which he was asked to speak or on which he felt a duty to speak. I should know this, for the parents who taught him these things were the ones who taught me also.' The young man's voice rose a little, as though he felt suddenly some little pain.

'There is nothing in our village, Principal, no money, no work, no great property, no rich people, only people like my parents, whose one desire is to see their children educated. Do you understand how they feel, Principal, when their clever son must humble himself and plough the fields, and may not move from the valley where they live, because when he was invited he stood up and spoke the truth?'

He added, with an irony seemingly wistful and gentle, but wounding to the one who heard it, 'That is what he thought a university was, a place where you learned and spoke the truth.'

'Everyone in that valley knows, Principal, even the most unlearned, that this young man was sent home, not because he did not work, not because he stole or murdered or raped, but because he stood up and spoke things that all of them know to be true. That gives great pain, Principal, to know that one of your young men is punished, and so heavily punished, because he speaks what he thinks to be true.'

He said with some pride, 'He was the best speaker of us all, not humble, not arrogant, but clear and beautiful in thought, with words simple when they needed to be simple, and not so simple when they needed to be otherwise, and every word true.'

Maasdorp sat impassively, but inwardly strange emotions were stirring in him, strange and embarrassingly powerful, because they were compounded with some element that could cause the voice to tremble if one did not master it. He was experiencing something hitherto unknown to him, a pride in a young man who though of his own country, was not of his own race or colour.

He said slowly and carefully, 'You speak well also.'

The young man answered him proudly. 'We inherited it from my father. When he spoke in council, no one could take his eyes from that face or his ears from that sound.' And then again the irony, 'He spoke in the vernacular, Principal, not being able to speak in any other language.'

Yet though the young man was ironic, he was clearly in some kind of distress, so that Maasdorp said to him quietly, 'You were going to tell me something.'

'I was going to tell you, Principal, that we believe that the list of twenty names was supplied to you by the Disciplinary Officer, and that this list was given to him by the security police, or compiled by him together with them. Over each of these twenty students hangs the sword that struck off my brother's head. I tell you these things because you are new. We do not know who runs this place, you the Principal, or your Disciplinary Officer and the police. But so long as we think it is your Disciplinary Officer and the police, we shall not speak, and some of us will paint words on the walls, because only in that way can we communicate at all.'

The young man sat down, and the twenty-one students sat and looked at the walls and the floor, or at a Principal who, of his own will and choice, had torn down a barrier that no one had breached before. Again he controlled his voice carefully, and said to them, 'Are you against university education in your own language?'

The slender young man rose again. 'None of us here takes responsibility for the slogan on vernacular education. Another twenty must be found for that. But we are totally opposed to vernacular education. We want to equip ourselves and our people to enter the modern world. We believe that we shall never do so through the medium of our own language. Your people did it through Afrikaans, with the help of English where necessary, but Afrikaans is a western language, and it could be made a language of science and technology. But our language cannot be. Do not think we despise it, Principal. It speaks to us of our land and our people and our aspirations. It will make our literature and our songs, and our deepest thoughts will always be spoken in it, but we cannot make it a language of science and technology.'

He looked at the Principal very directly. 'I see that you do not believe me, or that you do not want to believe me, but if we had time and could all speak freely, we would give you good reasons for our conviction.'

'The Russians entered this modern world through Russian,' said Maasdorp patiently, 'and the Chinese are now doing it through Chinese. What do you say to that?'

'We say nothing, Principal. It is not considered safe by us to discuss anything that happens in those two countries.'

He sat down again, and the silence now contained a sharp note of mockery. Maasdorp was not a man to believe that all things could be done by an edict of authority, and he was glad of it, for he was now realising the strange power of these young men and women who could endure these things in this inscrutable silence. He was aware too that within seven days of his arrival he had made a speech that had deeply antagonised his students. Must he renounce it? The Minister's own wish? *I want to see more and more own-language education in these universities. I don't think ten years too short a time for it. And I want you there because of your own knowledge of the language and the people. You are, if I may say so, a major prophet of own-sort development.*

'I am your Principal, and I cannot bow to threats. You would not respect me if I did. My goal is own-language education, and if I fail to reach it, then I must think again.'

He could not tell from their silence whether they were outraged or despairing or did not care. He said to them very deliberately, 'This university will be administered by me, and not by any external authority. But I shall not allow insubordination.'

They turned their eyes to him, as though he had suddenly said something worthy of direct notice. The mockery of their silence was palpable. They were waiting to hear how he would deal with their insubordination. And again he felt the power of their impotence.

'I shall post notices immediately to say that these acts of last night will be condoned, but that any further act will bring severe punishment. And I appeal to you. You are students of authority. Will you use it to see that no further acts are committed?'

He looked at the slender young man. 'Will you answer?'

'How can we answer, Principal? If further acts are committed, will we then be held responsible? We are not students of authority. We are only twenty names on the list of the police, and therefore we cannot be expected to act responsibly. You cannot appoint us as a Students' Council. Only the students can do that, and they refuse to do it, because it is their representatives who are always sent home. Therefore, Principal, we cannot accept any authority.'

Maasdorp was angry, but he concealed it. He said tonelessly, 'Then I can only express the hope that these acts will cease, and that some or all of you will use your influence to prevent them. Students, good-day.'

He rose, and they rose too, and stood in impeccable silence while he walked out. As he walked to his office, he passed many students going to and from their lectures. They walked past him with all correctness, opening their ranks to give him passage, but giving him neither look nor word. He could hear the voice of Van Riet, his Vice-Principal and Disciplinary Officer, saying, *Firmness is the only thing they understand, Principal, swift, firm, strong action – and they like it, because they know where they are.*

Back in his office Van Riet said to him, 'In other words you're offering them a second chance. It won't work, Principal. I know these students. They broke Martens because he gave them a second chance. Now he shuts himself up in his house down there in Riversdale, and won't show himself in the street.'

When the Principal did not answer, Van Riet said to him, almost angrily, 'They don't want a second chance. They want to break *you*, that's all. And it's my duty, to you and the college and to our people, to see that you're not broken.'

'I know you are a man of duty,' said Maasdorp. 'But I am a man of duty too, and in the end it is my duty that I must do.'

'Naturally,' said Van Riet, if not with contempt, then with impatience for a man who could utter truisms when a nation was fighting for its life. 'Principal, Captain Smith is in my office and wishes to meet you.'

'Send him in,' said Maasdorp, 'in ten minutes.'

He had heard of Smith, a hated, feared, admired policeman. He was correct with superiors and equals, and ruthless to all enemies of authority, whether they plotted secretly or opposed openly. Unmarried, he lived alone in a house whose garden was always ablaze, so that people in passing would say, *A man who loves flowers can't be a bad man.* Without vices, he knew all the vices of others, and it was said that he knew the thoughts and intentions of all of the thousand students of Mount Jerboa. And they in their turn supposed him to be the true head of the university. The Minister had said, *The head of the security police, Captain Smith, is an extraordinary man, and you will find his help invaluable.* Then after a pause he said, *I know what is in your mind, Professor. But this is no ordinary job you are undertaking. It is my considered opinion that it can't be done without the police.*

What sort of a job was this, that could not be done without the police? This university, that was preparing a nation for its independence, why must it depend for its being on the police? Had he come here merely to teach, and to leave discipline in the hands of others? He did not delude himself. His predecessors had all worked closely with the police. But Martens, the poor creature who shut himself up in his Riversdale house, had not been able to endure it any longer. It was not only the students that had broken him, it was the police also. In their battle Martens had been the main casualty.

'Principal,' said Smith, 'firstly I am here to meet you. Your writings and speeches are well known to us, and I am glad to welcome you to Mount Jerboa.'

'Thank you, Captain. I hope our relations will be good.'

'I hope so also. Principal, my superiors take this matter of the slogans very seriously. I understand you have decided to take no action on this occasion.'

'That is so, Captain.'

'It could be argued that you are not empowered in law to do so, but I am not going to raise that matter. However, if the offence is repeated, then the police must take action. But it would be better for all concerned if we took it together.'

'You know as well as I do', said Maasdorp, 'that I am trying a new approach. I admit I am trying to do what my predecessors were unable to do. I am trying to administer this university without threats, particularly the threat of expulsion. I want to administer it without any help from the police, except of course when a criminal offence is committed. I have nothing against the police, Captain, but just as you would not want me in your police offices, just so do I not want you in my university.'

'The painting of slogans is a criminal offence, Principal. Let me make it clear to you. I do not have to be called in. I can come in, not only when an offence has been committed, but when I believe that an offence may be committed.'

'I understand you well, Captain. But let me make one thing clear to you also. You reported the painting of the slogans to Dr. Van Riet at four in the morning. In future you will make such reports to me. Dr. Van Riet is the Disciplinary Officer, and his task is to recommend what action should be taken against offending students. He is not an administrative officer.'

'I shall do that, Principal. I was merely following your predecessor's arrangements. He did not like the police either, but his solution was different from yours. You want to see them yourself, he did not want to see them at all.'

'I must ask you not to say I do not like the police. I don't want them to help me to administer the university, that's all.'

'I beg your pardon, Principal. May I say one last thing to you?'

'Certainly.'

'I was also at a university, Principal, and I know what you are talking about. But this is not Maatland, it is Mount Jerboa. Neither you nor anyone else could run this place without the police. These students don't trust you, and in the end you won't trust them.'

No sooner had the captain gone than the telegram arrived. STRONGLY DISAPPROVE YOUR ACTION IN THE MATTER OF SLOGANS. KINDLY CALL EMERGENCY COUNCIL FOR SATURDAY. VAN ONSELEN, CHAIRMAN.

So the Chairman of the University Council, who lived two hundred miles away, had already heard of his private meeting. Though he had known a lot about Mount Jerboa before he came, he had not been prepared for the web of intelligence that was spun about himself. It was his first experience of such a world. Who could have done it but Van Riet? He suddenly felt sick at heart. His great aim had been to gain the confidence of his students, but how would he ever do it under the surveillance of Van Riet? His Vice-Principal's reputation was well known, as a merciless and humourless ruler of young men and women. He had been the punitive officer of the last three principals, and he had resolved the endemic crises of Mount Jerboa with firm decision, resulting in the expulsion of the best and brightest and most vital students, who would never again find entrance to any other institution.

With sudden clarity Maasdorp realised that such actions were unforgivable whatever the provocation. He remembered with pain the young man punished for life for speaking the truth. His despondency left him. He would call the emergency council, and tell them that he would never consent to any diminution of his authority.

'You'll be appointed without question,' said the Minister. 'Own-language education in ten years, and absolute co-operation with the security police. Professor, I wish you luck,' he said with emotion. 'Our people have always been like that. When one fails, there is always another to make it good. The West is lost, Professor. But one day when it wants to find itself, it will come to us, to you, Professor, and to Mount Jerboa, to learn the way.'

Something was troubling the Minister. All was not well with him. He had what is known as *a nail in the soul*. Behind the glow there was anger and pain.

'Do you know, Professor, that Maatland has taken Maasdorp back? Yes, you're right, it *is* a scandal. It's a slap in the face of the nation.'

The Minister sat brooding, the professor forgotten. In the Minister's eyes was a look blended of frustration and pain.

'Do you see what I mean about Mount Jerboa? Maatland has failed us, but Mount Jerboa has come to our aid. Professor, you must make it a shining example of our civilising mission. Don't think nothing will be done, Professor. Notice will be taken. I am discussing it with my colleagues. You are not to repeat this, but some of them think Maatland is too big to touch. But it will be touched, Professor.'

The Minister sat there, lost in angry thoughts. 'Be assured, Minister,' said the professor soothingly, 'we shall not fail you at Mount Jerboa. You are a busy man, and I must go.'

He rose, and the Minister rose. They shook hands, and the Minister brought himself to attention. He said, 'We shall be watching you with approbation.'

At the door of the enormous room the professor turned to smile, but the Minister had already retreated into his angry thoughts.

The Principal put down the telegram with satisfaction. STRONGLY APPROVE YOUR FIRM ACTION. VAN ONSELEN, CHAIRMAN.

It was a good beginning.

[Botha's Hill, 1970. The Imam Haron, a Moslem leader who had been arrested under the Terrorism Act, died in prison in mysterious circumstances in September 1969.]

Death of a Priest

Most Honourable I knock at your door
I knock there by day and by night
My knuckles are raw with blood
I hope it does not offend you
To have these marks on your door.

I know you are there Most Honourable
I know that you hear my knocking
But you do not answer me
Pity my impotence I cannot reach your power
I cannot bring you my tale of sorrow
You may die and never know
What you have done or you may fall
And leave no chance of its undoing.

Most Honourable the sorrow is not my own
It is of a man who has no hands to knock
No voice to cry. A sorrow so deep
That if you had it for your own
You would cry out in unbelieving anguish
That such a thing could be.

Most Honourable do not bestir yourself
The man is dead
He fell down the stairs and died
And all his wounds can be explained
Except the holes in his hands and feet
And the long deep thrust in his side.

[An address to the annual meeting of the Associated Alumni of Harvard University in June 1971. The author had gone to Harvard to receive an honorary doctorate. *Harvard Bulletin*, 5.7.1971.]

Our Two Countries

I first visited the United States in 1946, and was overwhelmed by it, by its size and its competence, and its extraordinary mood of optimism and confidence; the mood of doubt and anxiety was then rarely encountered. I left it with a multitude of impressions, of which one was easily the greatest and most easily remembered. That was the way in which the founders of your society had dared to set down in black and white a charter for the future, which was to be subscribed to then and there, which was to be amendable only in ways which were purposely made difficult, and which was not only to limit the power of the law-makers, but which was to subject their laws to the scrutiny of the highest court of the land. That there were defects in this fundamental constitution I have no doubt, but they did not obscure for me the majesty of the conception. And it was a natural consequence of your colonial history that the liberties of men should have been protected against the attacks of overweening authority.

The position in my own country is quite different. Parliament is sovereign, and this sovereignty has enabled it to embark on a programme of racial legislation the like and scope of which have never before been seen in the history of man. If one supports these laws, one calls them laws of racial differentiation, laws for the preservation of racial identity, laws ensuring the peaceful and harmonious social and cultural and political development of all the different racial groups in the country, laws enabling them to move side by side but separately to their own individual and autonomous destinies. If one does not support these laws, one calls them laws of racial discrimination, and one regards the ideal of separate autonomous development as unrealisable, particularly in a country whose economy has brought together the people of all its races, even though their status within that economy is decided by ideological rather than by economic considerations. What is more, one does not believe it possible to implement such laws without inflicting hardship and suffering on voteless and voiceless people.

228

At this point there is something that I should make quite clear. When I am honoured by your University, and am invited to address its alumni, I have one overriding obligation, and that is to speak that truth which is the object of pursuit of every university which deserves the name. That is what I am trying to do now, and I am trying to do it as a university man should, soberly and clearly, without offensiveness. I might have chosen some safer subject, but I would much rather speak on a subject which is related to our lives and our aspirations. And this brings me to another issue that vitally concerns our two countries.

To what does one give one's highest loyalty? A religious person – which I myself am, though of no great quality – could claim that his highest loyalty is given to God, which is a just claim and a safe claim only when it is made humbly. A person who claims to have no religion could justly claim that his highest loyalty is to the truth, and that also is a safe claim only when it is made humbly. But in what way can one's highest loyalty be given to one's country? Surely only in one way, and that is when one wishes with all one's heart, and tries with all one's powers, to make it a better country, to make it more just and more tolerant and more merciful, and if it is powerful, more wise in the use of its power. I should add that I am stating a very high ideal, because it is seldom that one wishes a thing with all one's heart or tries to do it with all one's might, even though there are sometimes external observers who imagine one to be doing just that. But when loyalty to one's country means loyalty to some party or some government or some policy, or even to that mythical power known as the State, there are many people in both your country and mine who find it difficult, and sometimes impossible, to give that kind of loyalty. I would find it difficult to say what love of South Africa means to me. It certainly means a love of the place where I was born, a love of the physical land, of mountain and river and plain, a love of its infinite variety, a love of its peoples and especially of those who have suffered for the things that they believe in. South Africa is often called a land of fear, and so it is. But it is also a land of great courage – and so is this. A friend of mine was once asked at a symposium, 'If you did not live in South Africa, where would you like to live?' to which he gave the totally unexpected answer, 'If I did not live in South Africa that's where I should like to live.' My own views and beliefs which are often called un-South African, were made nowhere else but there in South Africa, just as many of the views that are called un-American were made nowhere else but in America.

Now when people hold un-South African and un-American views, there is a great temptation on the part of rulers to take steps against them. I should say at once that protest in South Africa has never been as vigorous and as widespread as it is in the United States. And I should say at once that the reason for that is that one has to pay a much higher price for protest in South Africa. Therefore one is tempted to conclude that if rulers took a firmer line in the United States, protest would to some extent die away. And in order to take a firmer line, rulers would have to interfere with that charter that was subscribed to when your country achieved its independence, and would have to curtail that liberty the entrenchment of which was the firm resolve of your founders, and would have to adopt the methods of Hitler and Stalin, which methods have rightly been held in such abhorrence by Americans.

So it is – in your country as well as mine – that there comes this schism between those who believe that the maintenance of law and order is the prime obligation of any good society, and those who believe that the preservation of civil liberty is the prime obligation. And this schism is made more bewildering by the coming into being of other schisms which are related but not identical – between the rich and the poor, the old and the young, the white and the black, the rulers and the ruled. The temptation to achieve conformity by legislation is very powerful, and I hope that the American people will never yield to it, because it will mean the erosion of liberty and the rule of law, and that is what it has meant in my own country, whose parliament has sovereign power, and whose government is representative of one-eighth of the total population.

It may distress you that the blemishes of your body are so visible to the outside world. But at least you lance your boils and suppurations. It would be a tragic error of judgement if you allowed yourselves to believe that a total bandagement would restore your body to health. You at least know you are sick. We do not believe that we are. It is true, I think, to say that we do not really know what goes on beneath the all-covering mantle of our law and order.

I want to note one more difference between our country and yours. We are both countries of many races, but whereas your policy – with many halts and hesitations – has been to aim at one American society, our policy – vacillating under earlier governments but determined under the Nationalist government – is to create a multiracial society, with its African nations, which comprise 70 per cent of the total population, allotted various portions of the country which total something like 13 per cent of the total area, and the aim of the policy is to create homelands where these national groups will achieve cultural, social, economic and eventually – in ideal theory – political autonomy. To a person like myself the policy is a self-deception, a way of disposing of a problem by putting it somewhere else. The possibility of achieving economic independence, or even a healthy economic interdependence, by people whose average earnings are often one-tenth or less of the average earnings of white South Africa, seems totally remote. And it is a source of grief, frustration, and anger and hatred to many that the policy of separate development seems likely to make real economic advance improbable, if not impossible.

I was the president of the interracial Liberal Party which was made illegal in 1968, and we opposed uncompromisingly the policies of separate development, and the creation of what we would have called subservient sub-governments. Now I find myself hoping that all our people who are not white will make the fullest use of these instruments of power which are being put into their hands by the architects of separate development, no matter how feeble they may be; for the creation of these instruments has made it possible for the leaders of these sub-governments to speak with authority to an audience they could never have reached before. And it would be my hope that this would be a stage in our development towards some kind of common society. For in my view no other kind of society could ever give to black men a just share in the fruits of their labour and the earth.

I am often asked the question as to whether Americans should withdraw all investments in South Africa. I know this view is strongly held by some, and I respect it, but it is not my own. If those American enterprises in South Africa – and there are not a great many – and here I am quoting from the statement of the Polaroid Corporation entitled 'An Experiment in South Africa' – would 'improve dramatically the salaries and other benefits of their non-white employees', then I have no doubt that this would exert a moral pressure on South African employers to do the same. It is my opinion that – apart from any colour of skin or difference of race and culture – the great disparity between white and black wages leads, paradoxically enough, to an intensification of white fear, for people of other colours and races, when they also, owing to their poverty, live a totally different kind of economic life, seem more alien and more other than ever. Therefore I stand not for the withdrawal of American investment but for this dramatic improvement in salaries and benefits.

Now I have reached my end. Your tribulations are known to the whole world. Some of us in the outside world derive satisfaction from them. Some of us in South Africa believe that your troubles are due to your policies of racial integration, and such people are trying anew to prove that separate can be equal. Yet you should not be discouraged by this. The problems of racial prejudice and friction, the problems caused by man's destruction and pollution of his environment, the problem of war and of deluding oneself, after all these centuries of experience, that war can make the world better, the problem of the terrible gulf that yawns between the rich and the poor, the problem of the impersonality and meaninglessness of human life, especially in the great city, they are our problems too, even if only in miniature. It is foolish of us to gloat when you appear to fail to solve them, for are we any better, any wiser than you? Therefore you must regard yourselves as the testing-ground of the world, and of the human race. If you fail, it will not be America that fails, but all of us.

And may I say a word to the younger people of my audience? I understand well your dissatisfaction with the world that we have made. But I do not believe that one can make it any better by withdrawing from it. I understand your argument that if you take part in it, you are only prolonging its existence. I understand your argument that if you take part in it, it will corrupt you just as it has corrupted us. But it is not a very good or a very brave argument. The only way in which you can make endurable man's inhumanity to man, and man's destruction of his own environment, is to exemplify in your own lives man's humanity to man and man's reverence for the place in which he lives. It is hard a thing to do, but when was it ever easy to take upon one's shoulders the responsibility for man and his world? So good luck to you all.

['Topical Talks' 28, South African Institute of Race Relations, 1971.]

Case History of a Pinky

This title seems frivolous, but the theme itself is not. If one intends to speak about one's life and one's development, then one shies away from a pompous title. 'The Story of Myself' would be a very unsuitable title for a meeting of the Institute, whereas the 'Case History of a Pinky' is very relevant to its work and purpose. The title is half-mocking, not only of oneself, but of those who try to mock one.

What is a Pinky? It is no less than four different things, each relevant to this case history. In some countries a Pinky is called a Whitey; he is definitely not a Blackie. In 'some future time he may feel impelled to rise up and cry 'Pink is beautiful' and to call for 'Pink Power', but that time has not yet come.

A Pinky is also one who has not had the conviction or the inclination or whatever else is required to become a Red. He is despised by both the White and the Red, though he might well be the progeny of both. Our Prime Minister, for example, hates both Pink and Red, though he is trying hard to like Brown and Black. It is the Pinky who lures you into ambush, so that you may be killed by the Red. He is a nasty and cowardly fellow. Alas, one is speaking to us now.

A Pinky is also a small boat that ventures out into the open sea. It is not really equipped for such voyages. It must have some kind of bravery, or should one say more modestly, some kind of something?

And lastly – and this I did not know until my wife told me – a Pinky is a small fish, a minnow, that nibbles at the bait when you are after something big. It is too small or too smart to get caught. Otherwise one would not be speaking to us now.

This particular Pinky was born in Pietermaritzburg on the 11th day of January, 1903, eldest of the family. Some of my younger hearers will hardly believe that anyone born in 1903 is still around, still able to walk and talk, which he was not able to do then. The human race was going strong in 1903. As man does now, so did he do then. He made love and he made war, he built and he destroyed, he lifted up and he threw down. He was about to enter a century as bad as any that had gone before.

The British had waged a war in this country from which we have not yet recovered. Western man waged the most suicidal war of all history, and when it was over, he returned to his fields and sowed the seeds of the next. In 1903 Adolf Hitler was 14, unaware that he would become one of the most evil men who has ever walked upon the earth. Gandhi was 34, unaware that he would enter the ranks of the immortals. The British Empire was to fade away, giving place to two new giants who were to divide and terrify the world; now they watch with apprehension the entrance of the third.

Man's scientific and technological advance took on a speed not remotely approached in any other century. He discovered how to liberate the energy of the atom, and learned how to destroy the earth, how to poison its skies and its lands and its seas, perhaps beyond redemption, and to prepare the way for who knows what new forms of life. In 1903 we lived in a world that seemed to unseeing eyes to be safe and sure; today our children live in a world where nothing is safe, nothing is sure, where unending change is the law of life. I cannot find words strong enough to describe the arrogance and the stupidity of those who think that the shaking of the foundations of the world is our children's fault.

In 1903 Pietermaritzburg was safe and sure. The soldiers of the King marched down Pine Street to the Polo Ground, with their brave red coats and their brave bands playing, to celebrate the King's birthday. The regiments left in 1914, when the First World War broke out. Therefore what I tell you now I remember from the days when I was at the most 11 years old. What I remember is that when the soldiers were allowed to march at ease, they winked and nodded at the African girls, who, like the rest of us, had come out to see the grand sight. The White citizens disapproved strongly of this. It was something not to be done, and when done in daylight it was worse. I must record that no bolt from heaven ever struck down one of these wicked men.

Pietermaritzburg had about 30,000 people, roughly one third African, one third Indian and one third White. Although the city was founded by the Voortrekkers, and was named after Piet Retief and Gerrit Maritz, I did not hear Afrikaans spoken till I was 22. In those days the graduands of the Natal University College went to Pretoria to be capped, and it was in the station yard at Volksrust that I first heard Afrikaans. It simply never occurred to me that Greyling Street, Boom Street, Loop Street, Burger Street, were not English names.

We knew no African people except our servants. My parents were considerate employers, but they were people of their day and age. My mother was a born Natalian, and her mother also. They were an upright family, and would never have used violence or abuse, but they would have paid the wages of the time. I wish I could tell you what they were, but it would not be fair to try to remember. My father was a Scot and came to South Africa in his late twenties. He learned Hollands, which was then one of the two official languages of the Union. He spoke Zulu enthusiastically and badly, and when we were out walking used to embarrass his children by conversing with every Black stranger.

He spoke to Indian people too. The man who sold us fruit was Sammy, and the woman Mary, but S. R. Naidoo the lawyer was Mr. Naidoo. My father did not live to see Mr. Naidoo, in his old and respected age, thrown out of his office in the centre of the town by that evil law known as the Group Areas Act. The words 'coolie' and 'kaffir' were not used in our home, but you must not think we had any great ideas about race relations. In those days such ideas were limited to prophets and prophetesses, such as W. P. Schreiner[1] and Olive,[2] John Tengo Jabavu,[3] Dr. Abdurahman,[4] and the Revd. John Dube, who founded *Ilange lase Natal* in 1903. Mohandas Gandhi had founded the Natal Indian Congress even earlier, but after he returned to India in 1913 it went into a decline. There was no Institute of Race Relations to keep us alert and informed. In all my years at the Natal University I can remember only one debate on international or racial affairs. The African National Congress was in its infancy.

There was no NUSAS. It was largely through the work of NUSAS that the young generation of today is not as ignorant as mine was 50 years ago. Sometimes it does things that one does not approve of, sometimes it does them in ways that one does not approve of, but it stands for ideals and principles that are sound and true. It is opposed to all forms of racial discrimination, it stands for the rule of law and for the proper freedoms of the university, it does not believe in a slavish obedience to custom and convention and authority and it does all these things with courage.

May it long be able to do so.

I want to read you a passage from *Cry, the Beloved Country*:

'It is hard to be born a South African. One can be born an Afrikaner, or an English-speaking South African, or a Coloured man, or a Zulu. One can ride, as I rode when I was a boy, over green hills and into great valleys. One can see, as I saw when I was a boy, the reserves of the Bantu people and see nothing of what was happening there at all. One can hear, as I

[1] Former Prime Minister of the Cape Colony.
[2] The distinguished writer.
[3] African leader.
[4] Leader of the Cape Malays (as they were then known).

heard when I was a boy, that there are more Afrikaners than English-speaking people in South Africa, and yet know nothing, see nothing, of them at all. One can read, as I read when I was a boy, the brochures about lovely South Africa, that land of sun and beauty sheltered from the storms of the world, and feel pride in it and love for it, and yet know nothing about it at all. It is only as one grows up that one learns that there are other things here than sun and gold and oranges. It is only then that one learns of the hates and fears of our country. It is only then that one's love grows deep and passionate, as a man may love a woman who is true, false, cold, loving, cruel, and afraid.

'I was born on a farm, brought up by honourable parents, given all that a child could need or desire. They were upright and kind and law-abiding; they taught me my prayers and took me regularly to church; they had no trouble with servants, and my father was never short of labour. From them I learned all that a child should learn of honour and charity and generosity. But of South Africa I learned nothing at all.'

This describes well the kind of world in which I grew up. What two worlds could have been more different than the kind of world in which I grew up and the kind of world in which our children are growing up? I thought South Africa was a land of sun and gold and oranges. But they know that South Africa is a land of loves and fears and hatreds, of a thousand harsh and unjust laws, of aspirations, and frustrations, of protest meetings and detentions and of strange, inexplicable death. They know that there are people who can write to the newspapers and say, 'What's wrong with the detention laws? I haven't been detained, have I?', and imagine that this is a kind of logic.

I'm not suggesting that our children are a different breed from ourselves. It's the world that has suddenly opened out, like a beautiful and monstrous flower. The endless slaughter of the bright youth of Europe in 1914, the false peace, the rise of Adolf Hitler, the Second World War, the massacre of the Jews, the bombs on Hiroshima and Nagasaki, the emancipation of the Black people of the world, the breakneck speed of man's scientific and technological discoveries, the journey to the moon, the emergence of America and Russia, and now China, and the coming to power in South Africa, in this modern epoch of incessant change, of a government committed to the task of arresting change, of keeping alive policies of race and colour that everywhere else were dying, and of preventing change by forbidding it, and by punishing those who want it and preach it, and by detaining them without charge or trial, forever if need be. How then could our children be as blind and deaf as we?

But let us return to Pinky, for his emancipation was slow, and the time it took was long. I must now mention a very important determinant in his case history. I have just been reading in the magazine *Encounter* for November, an article by Ronald Hayman on the drama of Arthur Miller. And he contrasts Miller with Beckett and Pinter, in that the actions of Miller's characters have their roots in the past, whereas, says Hayman, for Beckett and Pinter the past no longer exists, and indeed, when Pinter's characters remember it, it has already undergone a chemical change during its time of storage in the abyss of memory. I believe with Miller that the roots of our character are to be found in the past, though I would admit that our memory and interpretation of the past may be faulty.

Nevertheless I think that the Christian character of his home had a great influence on Pinky. That does not mean that he became a good man. To be a Christian does not mean to be a good man, it means to want to be a good man and to try to be a good man, and sometimes to try less hard than others. If Archbishop Hurley[5] were to say, 'I am a good man,' we would all be very disappointed. If we were to ask him, 'Are you a good man?' we would expect him to say 'No'. But we might still think he was a good man. When I say that Pinky's Christian home had a great influence on him, I am not saying that he grew up to be a good man. I am going to try to tell you what I am saying. I am going to tell you something about his home.

His parents wanted very much to keep their children unspotted from the world. It can't be done, but that is what they wanted to do. They taught their children a great number of moralities that weren't really moralities, and a great number that were. Alcohol was almost never seen in their home. His father smoked but not his mother; it was considered somehow *wrong* for a woman to smoke. They played card games but never for money. They did not dance or go to the races, or play games on Sunday. They went to the cinema but not to the theatre. Their sexual ethics were strict and puritanical. The children were not allowed to go out without supervision, except to school or on some errand. Later this was relaxed but their friends had to be approved, and were in large part selected by their father.

But mixed up with these lesser moralities were greater moralities also. One did not lie or cheat or be contemptuous of people because they were Black or poor or illiterate. Justice was something that had to be done, no matter what the consequences. *Fiat justitia et pereat mundus.* Let justice be done, though the world perishes. We would have rejected – had we known it, which we did not – the cynical saying that justice is the interest of the stronger. The greatest offence was not murder or theft or adultery,

[5] Roman Catholic Archbishop of Durban.

but to be cold and indifferent, and not concerned about what happened to others, that callous quality that the English language expresses in inimitable fashion in the saying, 'I'm all right, Jack.' Cruelty and callousness were the great sins, and the worst cruelty was that which is done so that some noble end may be achieved.

Pinky was very sensitive to this teaching. But he was also sensitive to the incredible language in which these great moralities were affirmed (e.g. Isaiah 42, 1–7, 14–16). And from the same great prophet:

'The wolf and the lamb shall feed together, and the lion shall eat straw like the bullock; and dust shall be the serpent's meat. They shall not hurt nor destroy in all my Holy mountain, saith the Lord.'

The extraordinary thing about these visions is that they show no signs whatever of ever coming true, yet they sustained the Jews through centuries of isolation and repression. And it is the same vision that sustains those of our young people who sing 'We shall overcome, we shall overcome some day'. When will they overcome? When will their cause – which they believe to be the cause of right – achieve its triumph?

They also sing 'Black and White together' – it is Black and White together who are going to overcome. Do they believe that? Is it not easier to believe that White and Black will each want to overcome the other? Isn't it easier to give the whole thing up, and go to live in some other country? Yet they do sing it, and they do believe it, with all the fervour of their young hearts, and they believe it for an intellectually unacceptable reason, and that is because they hope it.

We haven't time to discuss the relation between hope and belief, and the relation of each of them to doing. The Institute of Race Relations is an example of doing inspired by hoping. It is often the vision of the unattainable that inspires us to reach the attainable. I must be honest and say that Pinky never stopped hoping. But how much of that was due to his own effort, and how much to his luck is a mystery that he cannot unravel.

Let us make one more point and then leave it. Doing is not always inspired by hoping. There are some things that have to be done whether you have hope or not. You do them because they have to be done. Such actions are by no means unknown in our own country.

In 1934 Pinky was in hospital for seventy-seven days. He had been a schoolmaster for eleven years, and when he came out of the hospital he wanted to do something new. He wanted in fact to have a reformatory. He did not want a Black reformatory, but that is what he got. It opened his eyes. For the first time in his life – he was now 32 – he saw South Africa as it was. I do not propose to tell you all about it, but during those years at Diepkloof Reformatory he began to understand the kind of world in which Black people had to live and struggle and die. I won't say that he overcame all racial fear, but I will say that he overcame all racial hatred and prejudice. He learned that it was an offence to keep talking about 'them', and about what 'they' do, and about what 'they' don't do and cannot do. He not only learned that it was offensive, he learned to feel that it was offensive. During those thirteen years at Diepkloof he had one especially deep experience, which he later described in these words:

'The emancipation of a White person from colour prejudice is very seldom a sudden conversion. It is rather the result of a number of experiences. Yet there is one experience that lives in my memory. Through it I knew that I was no longer primarily a White person. I had never been militantly White, but now I became militantly non-racial. I saw a vision, there is no other word for it.

'There was a White woman in Johannesburg called Edith Rheinallt Jones. She was not beautiful in the conventional sense. She was a woman in her fifties, heavily built, and she breathed heavily after any exertion. She had been told almost ten years before that her heart was finished, and that if she wanted to live, she had to give up her many activities, with the Institute of Race Relations, and the Wayfarers (a kind of Girl Guides for non-White children), and the Helping Hand Club (a hostel for African girls in Johannesburg), and a dozen other things, too, not to mention the running of a hospitable home where any person was welcomed.

'Edith Jones decided that although she did not want to die, she did not wish to live without the Institute and the Wayfarers and the Helping Hand Club and the dozen other things, too. Therefore she decided to carry on as usual. Her most vigorous activity was with the Wayfarers. She went out into the most remote parts of the countryside to visit little troops of schoolgirls, and to encourage and instruct the Wayfarer leaders, who were mostly schoolteachers. When she was there, she usually visited the chief and the church people and the magistrate and the health authorities as well, so that she became, in time, the best-known White woman in the whole of South Africa, and one of the best-loved too.

'I was Principal of Diepkloof Reformatory then, and Edith Jones and her husband, J. D., were great supporters of the experiments in freedom and responsibility that we were carrying out. Then came the war, and everyone was working twice as hard as before. Edith Jones asked if I, when I was free from the reformatory at week-ends, would drive her in her car to visit some of these Wayfarer troops in the country areas, and I agreed. So it was that I began to learn what this woman meant to hundreds and thousands of unknown people in the most remote parts of South Africa.

'One of these journeys remains clearly in my mind. We set out from Johannesburg early in the morning, and took the Great North Road into the land of the Bavenda people. We left the main highway at Pietersburg and took a road into a countryside where long hills lay like tawny lions in the sun. After driving deeper and deeper into the tribal place, we could take the car no farther, and we left it and walked down a steep and stony hill to the school. Edith Jones was not supposed to take walks like this, and her breathing was painful to hear, but she had no time for rest or self-pity. At last we could see the school, and the schoolmistress, too, Mrs. Takalani, a woman as large as Edith Jones, waiting for her visitor with every sign of pleasure. Already some of the Wayfarers had come for the parade and the inspection and were peeping from behind a corner of the school building to see their chief. . . .

' "Thank you for bringing her," Mrs. Takalani said to me as we were leaving, "and bring her again." . . .

'She pointed down in the direction of the invisible school. "You should have said goodbye to the school," she said, "for you will not see it again."

'And that came true. A month later, ten years after the doctor's warning, the brave heart gave in altogether.

'They had a farewell service for her in St. George's Presbyterian Church, Johannesburg. That was my deep experience. Black man, White man, Coloured man, European and African and Asian, Jew and Christian and Hindu and Moslem, all had come to honour her memory – their hates and their fears, their prides and their prejudices, all for this moment forgotten. The lump in the throat was not only for the great woman who was dead, not only because all South Africa was reconciled under the roof of this church, but also because it was unreal as a dream, and no one knew how many years must pass and how many lives be spent and how much suffering be undergone, before it all came true. And when it all came true, only those who were steeped in the past would have any understanding of the greatness of the present.

'As for me, I was overwhelmed. I was seeing a vision, which was never to leave me, illuminating the darkness of the days through which we live now.

'To speak in raw terms, there was some terrible pain in the pit of my stomach. I could not control it. I had a feeling of unspeakable sorrow and unspeakable joy. What life had failed to give so many of these people, this woman had given them – an assurance that their work was known and of good report, that they were not nameless or meaningless. And man has no hunger like this one. Had they all come, no church would have held them all; the vast, voiceless multitude of Africa, nameless and obscure, moving with painful ascent to that self-fulfilment no human being may with justice be denied, encouraged and sustained by this woman who withheld nothing from them, who gave her money, her comfort, her gifts, her home, and finally her life, not with the appearance of prodigality nor with fine-sounding words, but with a naturalness that concealed all evidence of the steep moral climb by which alone such eminence is attained.

'In that church one was able to see, beyond any possibility of doubt, that what this woman had striven for was the highest and best kind of thing to strive for in a country like South Africa. I knew then I would never again be able to think in terms of race and nationality. I was no longer a White person but a member of the human race. I came to this, as a result of many experiences, but this one I have related to you was the deepest of them all.'[6]

When Pinky wrote 'deepest' he was speaking of emotional experience. But from 1941-3 he had what one might call an equally important intellectual experience. He was a member of the Commission appointed by Geoffrey Clayton, the great Bishop of Johannesburg[7] to discover what it believed to be 'the mind of Christ for South Africa'. This Commission presented to Synod a report entitled 'The Church and the Nation', which faced the problems of Black wages and Black poverty, of racial discrimination, and the extension of the franchise. And Pinky had to face them, too, and to reject finally all the arguments for White political supremacy. It took him, therefore, forty years to do what I believe many of our young people do in a week or a month, or a year, usually their first year at university.

Yet he must now confess that if the present Bishop of Johannesburg appointed a similar commission, it would present a report very like that of 1943. The section entitled 'Economics and Industry' reads as though it had been written today. Nevertheless, this section had one weakness – it did not really face the question as to how far the wealth of White people comes, not from gold or diamonds or technological skill, but from the poverty of Black people. Or, to put it still more cruelly, from their wages.

I do not offer you this case history as something to be proud of. I can well imagine someone saying to me, 'You're taking a long time over it, aren't you?' I don't mean a long time over the case history, though that might be so. I mean a long time over the emancipation, the conversion, the coming to one's senses. Well, judged by the pace of the modern world,

[6] From *The Long View*, Praeger, 1968, pp. 54-9.

[7] The author's biography of Clayton, *Apartheid and the Archbishop*, was published in 1973.

that would be so. The only virtue of this case history is that it is true.

Pinky was born in a house with no windows, and with a door that was never opened. Inside the house it was warm and safe and secure. Then one day the door was opened, whether by chance or design or by the winds of change, who can tell, and Pinky saw with astonishment that there was an outside world, of such space and light, such flowers and trees, such freedom and such beauty. He heard a great voice crying, 'In the name of God and His servant the Minister, close that door, for the penalty of opening it is 5,000 rand, 5,000 lashes and 5,000 days and inexplicable death.' So with what fear, what excitement, what rationalisations, what reservations, one approaches the forbidden door, and touches it, and opens it a little, and looks through at that shining world, and fearfully shuts it again, till the day comes when one finally opens it and goes through and shuts it against oneself, and enters into a new country whose very dangers and anxieties and adversities become resplendent in this new and exciting light.

One's self has been remade, and one can no longer return to the self that one was before. Nor does one wish to return, except sometimes in deep depression when the dangers and anxieties seem too great, and one thinks of the warmth and safety of that windowless house. I have known people who have returned; they either keep silent, or they defend the safety and the warmth and the darkness of the windowless house with twice the passion with which they once extolled the shining world, and sometimes they begin to hate those who have gone out and never returned.

Now while it is true that one has gone from darkness into light and, to use words of Isaiah, had the twisting roads made straight, it is also true that one has gone from safety into danger. This is more true of the Afrikaner than of the rest of us. He goes out from the safety and solidarity of his own group into a universality that is feared and despised and often actively hated by the group he has left. He has in fact gone out to live on the holy mountain which exists only in the visions of prophets.

Pinky said once to Beyers Naudé, 'Don't you ever want to go back?' and Beyers Naudé said to Pinky, 'How can one ever go back?' Mr. Willem van Heerden[8] once exhorted English-speaking South Africans to be proud of their English-speakingness, and go out and become prime ministers and ambassadors and chairmen of boards, but how can you do that when you'd rather sit down and talk to Beyers Naudé? And if you sit down and talk to him, you won't become that kind of ambassador.

I must confess to you that Pinky, this poor fellow who is neither White nor Red, who is too small or too smart to get caught, once said that

[8] Journalist.

extreme nationalism was to him the extreme vulgarity. And I must say that he still adheres to this contention. The poor fellow would rather be a doorkeeper in the house of Beyers Naudé than be the head of the English-speaking Territorial Authority.

And what about Black Power? Many of us, including Pinky, are encountering it only now. Let me say first that Black Power is the inevitable consequence of White Power. The creation of the separate Territorial Authorities is not likely to impede the growth of Black Power. On the contrary, it may well advance it. Black Power is a fact of life, just as the Territorial Authorities are. It is going to have a determinative effect on our future. I have no doubt it is going to receive the close attention of BOSS[9] and the Security Police.[10] Some Black Power people will go to prison, some will go into exile, and some will give it up. The going into exile of Black Power people can have only one effect, the intensification of external pressure and of guerilla warfare.

What will our Government do about this? It is my fear that they will seek to deal with it as they have already dealt with other opposition, namely, by ruthless suppression and unceasing vigilance. I believe that General van den Bergh[11] takes far too simplistic a view of our situation. He tells us that world Communists – including those of our own who have gone into exile – are continually plotting against us, and we cannot over-estimate their implacability. But on what internal forces are such plotters relying? They are relying on all those who have been thrown out of houses, and kept out of jobs, and denied education, and been insulted and humiliated, all those in fact who rebel against the whole machinery of discrimination under which they live, against the whole order of society that is designed to keep them in subjection, against the power of authority to take almost any step it wishes against those who are critical of it and want to reform it.

Can we see any active movement on the part of authority to redress these wrongs and remove these humiliations? Pious adjurations by Cabinet Ministers are no substitute for social reforms. What kind of society is it where White children have a free and expensive education that has been made possible in large part by the work of Black people, and where the parents of Black children have to pay for what education they can get,

---

[9] Bureau of State Security.

[10] This statement has proved to be all too true. Since it was written, many upholders of 'Black Consciousness' – members of SASO (South African Students' Organisation), B.P.C. (Black Peoples' Convention) and B.C.P. (Black Community Programmes) — have been banned and/or imprisoned without being brought to trial.

[11] Head of BOSS.

and for their children's books, and for new classrooms whenever they are needed? Is this the kind of society that is made safe from within?

Many people have taken courage from the growing and openly expressed concern of so many people about the excessive powers which Parliament – which in this country appears to be both sovereign and impotent – has given to BOSS and the Security Police. Our Prime Minister has said that this concern is not spontaneous but deliberately organised; here is another simplistic view which can be used to justify the use of greater and greater force, and used to deny the need for the reform of society. 'The child cries, so strike it. The child cries again, so strike it again. The child cries yet harder, so strike it yet harder.' I think of the girl of 13 who was asked by a pressman why she had attended the big meeting in the City Hall, and she replied, 'If you must know, it's my conscience.'

I am not here to prophesy. I only reaffirm what you know already that the only sure defence against subversion, rebellion, and treason is to create a just order of society. I reaffirm that to rely on harsh laws and force of arms will bring about the end of Afrikanerdom. The future of our country – if it is to follow an evolutionary course – depends on the ability and willingness of White South Africa, and particularly the Afrikaner, to adapt itself to the new world, and to create a just order of society. One can see the concern of so many of our children. One can witness the awakening of so many of our people to the social and political poverty of their lot. All this is good. But if it is not taken note of by those in power, if their only response to it is that this is the work of plotters, then God save us all. But make no mistake about it, whatever the response of the powerful may be, these things must still be done and said.

It is time to come to an end, and to close Pinky's case history. Pinky is in a tough world. He is despised by some Whites as a renegade. He is despised by some Reds as a blunter of revolutions. He is despised by some Blacks for his powerlessness. Well, let him say what he thinks, too. He couldn't really care if he is despised by some Whites; there are others who, far from despising him, actually rather like him. He couldn't really care if he is despised by some Reds; he could take a lot of socialism, but he couldn't take any of Stalinism. He couldn't really care if he is despised by some Blacks; there are some Blacks who like him, and in any case it is a stupid wish to want all Blacks to like you.

Black Power he accepts as a fact of life, and he accepts his own part-responsibility in making it. He knows it is ambivalent, or ambi-facial, if there were such a word. The mouth of the one face is saying, 'I'm Black, and I'm proud of it, and I want to be proud of all Black things,' and

Pinky says to it, good luck to you. And the mouth of the other face is saying, 'Pinky, get to hell out of this country, while you have time.'

It would be very foolish for anyone of whatever colour to make authoritative pronouncements about Black Power. It is much too early. It is Black people, and especially younger Black people, who must resolve, if it is to be resolved, the ambivalence of Black Power and Black Consciousness. Only one thing is certain and that is that Black voices are going to be heard more loudly and more often and more compellingly and they are not going to be saying 'Ja, baas'.

Well, that's the kind of country that Pinky lives in. I have told you that Pinky is not a good man. The most I can say for him is that he tried to be better, and he tried to free himself of all those chains and fetters that are part of everyday dress in a race–caste society. In 1965 – six years ago – he wrote a piece called 'Beware of Melancholy' for *Contact*, the magazine of the Liberal Party that was made illegal in 1968. Newspapers always describe it as 'defunct', which means, according to the Oxford Dictionary, 'having ceased to live'. It is a gross misuse of words. The Liberal Party did not cease to live; it was killed, by no less a person than the Prime Minister of South Africa. These words were written in the face of impending death. They are as true today as they were in 1965. Let me quote some of them:

'All the visitors ask me – the American, the British, the Scandinavian – "What is the future?" They ask me as though I had some special knowledge. South Africans ask me, too. Experience has taught me the answer, and the answer is "I do not know." At the moment it is possible to believe that nothing will change, that Afrikaner nationalism will never consent to any change that threatens its own position of power, however remote that threat may be. In its treatment of its enemies, it is becoming quite merciless. Those who openly oppose apartheid (or separate development, to give it its sweeter name) are going to suffer more, not less. It is plain to me that the only opposition that will be allowed to continue will be an opposition that differs only in respect of the way apartheid is implemented.

'For how long will this future last? My answer is "I do not know." To me there is another question: "How long can I last?" And there is still another question: "Is it worth trying to last?"

'People answer this question in different ways. Some leave the country. Some leave politics. Some stick to their course, even if they expect certain consequences. And even this last group is diverse, for some would face *any* consequences and some would not.

'What is my own answer to this question? I must give my own answer, because I would not dare to answer it for anyone else. I think it is worth trying to last. It is worth something to me, even if it apparently achieves little.

'If someone were to ask me, "What would you and your wife do if you had young children?" I would answer, "We would have two choices: to stay here and to give our children a father and mother who put some things even above their own children's safety and happiness, or to leave and to give them a father and mother who put their children's safety and happiness above all else." Which would I choose? They are both good courses, are they not? I hope I would choose the first.

'To those who want to stay, whether out of love or duty or just plain cussedness, I direct these few words:

'Stand firm by what you believe; do not tax yourself beyond endurance, yet calculate clearly and coldly how much endurance you have; don't waste your breath and corrupt your character by cursing your rulers and the South African Broadcasting Corporation; don't become obsessed by them; keep your friendships alive and warm, especially those with people of other races; beware of melancholy and resist it actively it if assails you; and give thanks for the courage of others in this fear-ridden country.'[12]

---

[12] From *The Long View*, pp. 249–51.

[7.4.1972. Not previously published. An extract from a Graduation Address delivered at Rhodes University, Grahamstown, in April 1972. The author had just received an honorary degree.]

The Wage Gap

It is my opinion that there is more questioning, more of what is called heartsearching, more real thinking, more willingness to look at the truth about South Africa now than there has ever been before in our history. It is a white phenomenon, because other people don't need to do this heartsearching. They don't need to be willing to look at the truth because they live with it every day. It is always the rulers, the powerful, the privileged, who have to do these things. Various proposals, policies, programmes, are put before us for the future political development of our country. It would be improper of me to say which of them, if any, I think will work. But they all have two characteristics in common; they were all devised by white people, and they are all based on the assumption that an evolutionary development is possible, and that there is time for it.

Now I want to say one thing about all these policies, and I want to say it especially to you young men and women, because if the future is in any way in your hands, you will have to do something about it. Not one of these evolutionary policies has a hope of working while there is this gross disparity between white income and black income. It has been estimated by the research officer in economics at the Institute of Commonwealth Studies at Oxford that 68 per cent of our population, i.e. the African people, receive 20 per cent of all income, and that 19 per cent of the population, i.e. the white people, receive 74 per cent of all income. Therefore each white person receives four units of income, and each black person two-sevenths of a unit of income, and that means that white income per capita is fourteen times black income per capita.

This is shocking, not only because we like to call ourselves a Christian country, but because it is dangerous. It is dangerous not only for the reason put forward by one of our Ministers, that it could cause such utter frustration and such unconquerable resentment that the result could be violence and murder. It is dangerous for another reason, and that is that it is easier to transcend differences of race and colour, as we are beginning to see on the sports field, for example, than it is to bridge that tremendous gulf that separates the white earner from the black earner. It is impossible to find any common goal, any common loyalty, any common love of country, in a multiracial nation where one racial group has a per capita income fourteen times as high as another. Racial fear, racial prejudice, racial resentment, are intensified in such a situation, and on both sides. Individual men may surmount these barriers of race, colour, and standard of living, collective men never.

I am not expressing any expectation that you, the Rhodes graduates of 1972, and those who went before you and those who will come after you, are going to make all crooked things straight, and bring the prisoner out of the prison, and those that sit in darkness out of the prison-house. But most of you will become employers of domestic labour, and some of you employers of agricultural and industrial labour, and some of you influential in the professions, the church, the university, and politics. And this thing must weigh upon your minds and your consciences, and you must speak about it, and not stop speaking about it, and do about it what is in your power to do.

Some of you will no doubt go into politics. Whether any of you will ever become members of a government, no one can foresee. But one thing should be clear, and that is whatever efforts are made by employers and other people of influence, it is the Government and the Government only that can do anything substantial towards lessening this indefensible disparity. It is its clear duty, through machinery that already exists, or independently of it if necessary, to lay down a minimum wage for all workers, and this minimum wage must be based on those estimates made by authoritative researchers of the wage below which it is impossible for any family to live a decent and law-abiding life. One is told that this would be a very difficult thing to do. That may be so. Why should it be easy to save our country from catastrophe? For one thing is certain, unless such a course is taken, no policy of separate development, or of race federation, or of a common society, has any hope of realisation.

This terrible income gap has had one terrible consequence, namely that every service for black people has been grossly inferior, and this is based on the totally unchristian dogma that black people should pay for their own services. This is contrary to the teaching of the Christian gospel, that the strong should care for the weak, that the rich should care for the poor, and that brother should care for brother. Quite apart from that, this dogma is based on an ignoring of the truth that white people are affluent because black people helped them to be. The wealth of white people has not been created by gold and diamonds and technological skill alone, but by the help of black labour. Or to put it more cruelly, white wealth in some measure comes from black poverty.

This great disparity in the quality of public services is to be seen nowhere so starkly as in the field of education. The education of each African child per annum cost R16,97 in 1969–70. The cost of the education of each white child was variously estimated, but was in the region of R250. The education of white children is free and compulsory, of coloured and Indian children free, but not compulsory, of African children neither free nor compulsory. My white neighbours in Botha's Hill pay sums from R6 to R10 per child per annum to a school games and library fund, and nothing more. My black neighbours pay school fees, pay for school books (by no means cheap) and pay for new school-buildings, each child in primary school costing between R20 and R25 per year. Further consequences of this disparity are the miserable salaries of African teachers, the exhausting double sessions in half the schools, the dilapidated buildings, and the final matriculation of one tenth of one per cent of the total of scholars then in school. Because of the policy of separate development, there is a reluctance to provide secondary education in those areas adjacent to white cities, commonly called the locations or the townships, and everywhere there is a shortage of accommodation.

There is evidence – slight indeed – that our rulers are sensitive to the revelation of these facts, and intend to ease in some degree the restriction placed on education expenditure from general funds. They are also sensitive to the criticism that you cannot give any real kind of autonomy to people of whose children only one tenth of one per cent reach matriculation. Changes such as these are not brought about solely by changes in the hearts of rulers. They are also brought about by the efforts of people like yourselves. It is often said – and more often today – that people like yourselves say and do these things because of a sense of guilt. That may be so. A sense of guilt is not the thing most to be ashamed of, or most to be afraid of. What is most to be ashamed of, and most to be afraid of, is a refusal to repent and to do better. Perhaps more still to be afraid of is the inability, deliberate or otherwise, to find anything to be guilty about. And we need to be afraid of that refusal and that self-deception, because they could mean the end of our time in Africa.

I am saying these things to you, not to advance any party or to pull down any government, but for the sake of our country, and because I hope that to you will be given the chance to influence the course of events, and to save us from that catastrophe which might well over-whelm us if we are indifferent, or worse still, if we deceive ourselves that all is well with us.

[A speech made at Groutville, Natal, in July 1972 on the occasion of the unveiling of the tombstone of Chief Albert Luthuli, the great leader of the African National Congress. See also p. 159. *Reality*, September 1972.]

Memorial to Luthuli

Mrs. Luthuli and those members of the family who are able to be present, I thank you for the honour of being asked to say a few words on this memorial occasion. I shall say a few words about the man whose memory we honour, and I am sure he would not mind that. But I should like to say a few words also about the work to which he gave so much of his life. I think he would like me to do that, because that work was close to his heart, and it is not yet finished. How much of it is done, no one of us knows. There are some people who think none of it is done, but that I do not believe. There are other people who think that the end of the work is near. That we do not know. We are not able to tell what the future will be. But there is one thing we are able to do, and that is to work for the future we desire.

There was a great writer in Europe called Franz Kafka. He wrote a famous book called *The Trial*. There a man from the country comes to the city to look for justice. He goes to where justice should be, to the court of law. He knocks on the door, but the doorkeeper will not open for him. There he sits, day after day, month after month, year after year. And he goes on knocking on the door. But it is never opened for him.

For the greater part of his life Luthuli knocked patiently on a door. But it was never opened to him. Yet that was the work of his life, to knock on that door. And it has been, and is, and will be, the work of many of those who are here today.

I use this figure of knocking on a door because it is simple. Also because it is found in all the literature of the world. It does not mean just standing, with your hat in your hand, waiting hopelessly for someone to open. It means work, planning, organising. It means courage, resolution, devotion. It means patience, persistence and a great strength of spirit. It means speaking, writing, persuading. It means trying to be the kind of person that Luthuli was. It means carrying on the work that Luthuli tried to do.

What is the use of spending most of your life knocking at a door that is never opened? Some people say it is of no use at all. I want to say to you today – and the Chief would wish me to say it – that this is not true. How you live your life is a thing of great importance. In a country such as ours how you live your life is a thing of great importance to many other people. If Luthuli had given it up, if he had stopped knocking on that door, we would not be here today to honour his memory.

There are two sides to this door. There is the outside on which Luthuli was knocking. There is the inside where sit the rulers, the men of power, who will not open. There is no need for me to tell you that the men of power are white. Sometimes we think that the ones who knock have no freedom. We think it is the ones inside who are free. Is that completely true? What freedom is there to live in a house or room, and to be afraid to let anyone enter?

Fourteen years ago I wrote some words for my white brother. I went to my brother and said, 'Brother, a man is knocking at the door.' My brother said, 'Is he a friend or an enemy?' I said to my brother, 'I have asked him and he says, you will not know, you cannot know, until you have opened the door. There you are, my brother, you will never know if the man outside is a friend or an enemy until you open the door. But if you do not open the door, you can be sure what he will be.'

There are already those who say that it is a waste of time to knock on the door. They say you must bring battering-rams and axes and break it down. That this will happen in the future, I cannot say. But that it may happen is nothing but the truth.

I am sorry to speak these grave words to you. But the longer they take to open the door, the harder they will find it to open. Meanwhile they have opened other doors, small doors, unimportant doors, that lead to small places, unimportant places, what one might call the servants' quarters. That isn't the door that Luthuli meant. He means the door that would let him enter as a son of the house.

He used to say – but of course the law says I cannot tell you what he used to say, although he has been gone from us these five years – so I shall tell you what he used to believe. He believed that this country – this country of South Africa, not KwaZulu or the Transkei or Vendaland – belonged to him, just as much as he believed that it belonged to you and me. Many of us remember that in 1959, when his restrictions were lifted, he went all over the country, and his leadership was accepted by many white people. So powerful was his voice, that he had to be silenced again. One thing is sure, that the day is coming when that voice will be heard again, and the voices of those who silenced him will be forgotten.

I have one last thing to say. We are living in grave times. The rule of white supremacy is coming to its end. But it is often when the rule of rulers is coming to an end that they are most cruel to those they rule. We must be prepared for that. We all know that there are South Africans who have either left their country or intend to leave it. They want the air of freedom, they want freedom for their children. Some of them have suffered, and they do not feel able to suffer any more. It is not for me to pass any judgement on them. But my closing words must be for those who cannot leave, who will not leave, who have duties to do here that they feel they must perform.

In our late Chief we have an example to follow. He was not allowed to use his great gifts in the service of his country. He was not allowed to use his great voice to speak the words of truth and honour. He was punished for his vision of a country that would be the one home of us all. Yet he persisted. And the way in which we can best honour his memory is not to come here and make speeches and listen to speeches, but to carry on his work with the same courage and devotion.

Luthuli was a Christian, and one of the best-known sayings of Jesus is 'Knock and it shall be opened unto you'. How, when, not one of us knows. But of one thing we may be certain, that time is coming.

[An address given in August 1972. Not previously published.]

A 'Hunger Supper'

This observing of a week of compassion, this eating together of a hunger supper, this sharing of a common hope, often with people whose lives are so different from our own, raises tremendous difficulties in the minds of many of us, indeed perhaps all of us. I should like to speak about them tonight. I am not here to instruct or preach. These are my difficulties too. I am talking to myself as well. That is why I accepted this invitation with much diffidence. What right have I to speak on the tremendous issues that are raised by a week of compassion and a hunger supper and the sharing of a common hope?

What is the meaning of a week of compassion? In itself, it means exactly nothing. What could be more absurd than to say, 'I have just observed a week of compassion, and next year I am going to observe another'? So therefore it must have some far deeper meaning than just itself. We are not like the passengers on a train who get off at a station called Christianity and stay there for the rest of their lives while the train goes on with its journey. We are travellers ourselves, on a journey that never ends, and the week of compassion is a resting-place on the journey, and it can have only one meaning, that we rest there to fit ourselves for the next stage of our journey. A week of compassion can have meaning only if it is a stage in a life of compassion, if it helps us to think more deeply and more seriously about what we are doing and where we are going.

The same is true of a hunger supper. It has no meaning in itself. To have a hunger supper between a good lunch and a good breakfast can have no meaning unless it has a meaning beyond itself. It is therefore in a way a sacrament. It is a sacrament in which we are partaking. In partaking of it, we are repenting and promising to amend our lives, and to use them better. No matter whether we are old or young, that is what we are doing, because this journey that we are taking does not end.

It is therefore not an absurd and meaningless thing that we are doing. We are tonight confronting, not just the poverty and hunger and incessant struggle of so many of our fellow South Africans, we are also confronting ourselves, and asking ourselves what is the use and purpose of our lives. And these two things cannot be separated from each other. If our lives have nothing to do with the poverty and hunger and incessant struggle of so many of our fellow men and women, and their children, then there is something very wrong with us. And if there is something wrong with us, this week and this supper are the opportunities to make amends and to begin to use our lives better.

What we are doing tonight is nothing less than confronting the two great commandments of our Faith, that we should love the Lord our God with all our heart and soul and mind, and our neighbours as ourselves. It is not just a hunger supper, it is a judgement also. We are judging ourselves in the light of these two great commandments. And we may not like very much what we see. We may find that there is too much luxury and selfishness, too much indifference and coldness in our lives. We may remember times when we have said, 'Well, I couldn't do anything about it, could I ?' We may remember times when the sudden intrusion of someone else's troubles into our own well-ordered lives has filled us with anger or fear. We may remember times when the tempter's voice has said to us, 'Surely you're doing enough; surely no one expects any more of you than what you are doing; surely you have a right too to a life of your own.' And perhaps we listened to it.

There is certainly one way in which your life ought to be your own. But there is another in which it can never be your own. Indeed that is part of the meaning of being a Christian, that your life is not your own, that it belongs in fact to God and your neighbour.

It is necessary for us to balance these two demands – the one that our lives should be our own, and the other that our lives should be given to others. None of us can follow the example of Francis of Assisi, who renounced the world and all possessions, and even stripped himself of all his clothes so that he could yield everything given to him by his father. Yet on the other hand we do not wish to achieve that kind of living death of those who keep everything to themselves. Lucky are those whose lives and homes are happy, and who can therefore go out and give themselves to others and get everything back again. That is what our Lord said: Give, and it shall be given unto you; good measure, pressed down and shaken together, shall men give into your bosom. For with the same measure that you mete shall it be measured to you again.

There are sad persons in this country speaking often of their servants and saying, 'Look what I did for them, look what I gave them, and look what they did to me.' One may be sure that almost always such persons never gave themselves with their gifts. They give a gift, some thing, some money, and their giving does not evoke the response that they think they deserve. But when we give ourselves with our gift, we are often overwhelmed by the response in some other person who at that moment gives himself or herself to us.

There is one last thing to speak about, and that is our common hope. All Christians have a common hope, an expectation of present good and future life, because they have been made anew. That it is possible for me, a white man, living in comparative affluence and freedom from material anxiety, to have a common hope with a black man living in comparative poverty and struggling to live, is I know true, and one has only to go down to the Church of the Holy Spirit or to meet people from that Church in a common service of worship at Hillcrest, as we did some time ago, to know that it is true. But it is a miracle. It is a miracle to go there, me the lord, the ruler, the maker of cruel laws, and to feel the warmth and love that comes from fellow Christians who have so little, who make no laws, whose only duty is to obey them. It is a miracle of Christian love and common hope, and I would be blind to doubt it.

But it raises another tremendous difficulty in our minds. One can experience this miracle in our personal lives, but can it ever be experienced in the life of our society? Can white people make common cause with people whose average wage is one-fourth, one-tenth, one-fourteenth, of the average white wage? If you will allow me to make a political observation, I do not see any hope for the Nationalist dream of separate and self-respecting homelands, or for the United Party dream of a confederation, or for the Progressive Party dream of a common society, so long as there exists this shocking disparity in income. You may experience the common hope in the Church of the Holy Spirit, but that's not enough. This hope must be found somewhere, sometime, in the larger society.

I know there are some of you on whom the realisation of black poverty is like a burden on the soul. We white people can try to be just to our servants, and try to pay them better, and give them time off and paid holidays, and a decent room and food and hot water for a bath. But what about their other life, the cost of clothes and schooling, the cost of travelling, the cost of some crisis unforeseen?

Will an affluent society ever share its wealth with a poorer? Harder still, will an affluent group ever share its wealth with a poorer? Hardest of all, will an affluent race group within a society ever share its wealth with a poorer race group within that society, especially a race group which outnumbers it? Has economic change ever been brought about by spiritual forces, or is it only brought about by economic, even military, forces?

There is one thing we cannot say, and that is, 'Well, I couldn't do anything about it, could I?' If I am right, our white society is more aware than it was of the wealth gap, and is more aware that this is dangerous to itself. All of us, members of church groups, of groups concerned with school-feeding and service of any kind, members of Black Sash and Rotary and Lions and Jaycees, teachers and writers, employers of workers both domestic and industrial and commercial, employers of government and provincial and municipal labour, must go on hammering on the question of black education, black wages, black poverty.

The more we do that, the greater our common hope will be. We shall not change the world, but we might change some part of it. Do you remember Reinhold Niebuhr's prayer, 'God grant me the serenity to accept the things I cannot change, courage to change the things I can, and the wisdom to know the difference'? If we try to achieve that, then this week of compassion, this hunger supper, this talk of common hope, will gain for us a greater meaning.

[*Sunday Tribune*, Durban, 7.1.1973.]

On Turning 70

In a few days I shall turn 70. I observe that I approach this birthday solemnly, in a way I have never approached a birthday before. I suppose it is largely because of those words:

'The days of our age are threescore years and ten, and though men be so strong that they come to fourscore years, yet is their strength then but labour and sorrow; so soon passeth it away and we are gone.'

Hazlitt's last words were, 'Well, I've had a happy life.' I hope in due season to be able to say, or even whisper, the same.

I didn't live it as well as I might have, but I don't dwell upon it because I believe in the forgiveness of sins. Nevertheless there are acts of mine that I do not like to remember. When these acts suddenly come back into memory, I sometimes find myself saying aloud, 'No. No. No.' Sometimes this astonishes some person who happens to be in my company at that moment. To him or her I give a general, not a particular, explanation. These acts were without exception mean ones.

I am a Christian, though of an inferior kind. I understand – with my intellect – the paradox of the gospel, with its cross and its resurrection, its persecution and its joy, its sword and its peace. I don't claim to have lived it out. I didn't do much suffering. Others had to do more. But if it had been required of me I would have been willing to die for my faith – not for any dogma – but for what it commands me to do about love and justice and mercy. That is why I concede that South Africa is not a second Nazi Germany, though I have called it a good imitation. Under Hitler I would have died. Under Vorster I live. Thanks to the Minister. I was lucky. Not everybody was so lucky.

I have a deep love of my own country. Am I loyal to it? The question is meaningless. What does loyalty to South Africa mean? Does it mean that I should be ready to take up arms to preserve White supremacy? I should hope to be spared such a necessity. It is my fear that if White South Africa fights another war, it will be to preserve White supremacy. I cannot think of anything else that she would fight for. If this war is fought blatantly, and not disguised as a war against communism, it will be the last war that she fights. It would probably be her last war anyway.

I repudiate absolutely the right of Afrikaner Nationalism to rule us all and decide our destinies. The belief that this is God's will I find utterly repugnant. The belief that we can be instruments of God is very strong in me, but for purposes of love, justice, and mercy, not for the purposes of kicking people about and breaking up families and destroying personality and celebrating annually the defeat of the Zulus. In 1938 I was a believer in the resurgence of Afrikanerdom. I could see good in Afrikaner Nationalism. In 1973 I can do so no longer. Its cruelties are insupportable.

I could have made better use of my life, but I did try hard to do one thing. That was to persuade White South Africa to share its power, for reasons of justice and survival.

My efforts do not appear outwardly to have been successful. There are two things to be said about that. The first is that one does not uphold love, justice and mercy in order to be successful, but because it has to be done. The second is that one has no means of measuring. One is no more than a worker in a kind of apostolic succession. All one can say is that one has had some noble predecessors, contemporaries and successors. That is why I hold in contempt those young White radicals who sneer at liberals and liberalism. Who were their mentors? If it had not been for the Jabavus, Marquards, Hoernlés, they would have been in darkness until now. One cannot measure past labours in terms of present demands. One expects Black power to sneer at White liberals. After all White power has done it for generations. But if Black power meets White power in headlong confrontation, and there are no Black liberals and White liberals around, then God help South Africa. Liberalism is more than politics. It is humanity, tolerance, and love of justice. South Africa has no future without them, least of all White South Africa.

As a man of letters I have lost much by not knowing the literatures of the European continent except in translation. When I read English writers and critics I am aware of this. But South Africa is not a cultural desert except for snobs. How can an English-speaking person live his life with Afrikaners, Coloured people, Africans, Indians, and not be enriched? It is a different kind of richness, but richness it is. Those who are impoverished are those who shrink from this diversity.

What about the future? Will White South Africa change in time to save itself and its soul? All I can say is that the pace is funereally slow. And Afrikaner Nationalism remains fundamentally fearful and chauvinist, opposed to any change that will weaken its entrenchments. The question can be simply posed. As Black power grows, will Afrikaner Nationalism parley or fight? Everything depends on that.

I am certain that while I retain my health and faculties I shall always concern myself deeply with the affairs of our country and its people and write and speak about them also. But the task of planning and doing is now for younger hands and fresher minds.

I have always read and sung with a sceptical mind those words '*Ons sal lewe, ons sal sterwe, ons vir jou, Suid-Afrika*'. Who is meant to die? I suspect the Afrikaners and the reluctant English and a few 'loyal' stooges. I don't think anyone will put on my stone 'He died for his country' but I'll settle for the words 'He tried to live for his country'.

[Botha's Hill, April 1973. *Sunday Tribune*, Durban, 6.5.1973. In April 1973 a party of South African black policemen were ambushed in the Caprivi Strip by guerillas operating from Zambia. Four were killed.]

Caprivi Lament

Makwela, Ikgopoleng, and you two Sibekos,
what were you fighting for?
Makwela, was it for your house in Springs
and your security of tenure?
Or did you fight for me and my possessions
and this big room where I write to you,
a room as big as many houses?

Sibeko of Standerton, what did you die for?
Was it for the schooling of your children?
Were you so hungry for their learning
or were you fighting for the rich grand schools
of my own children?

Sibeko of Bloemfontein, was it for those green pastures
of your own Free State country
that you poured out your young man's blood?
Was it for the sanctity of family life
and the infinitude of documents?
Or were you fighting to protect me
and my accustomed way of life?

Ikgopoleng of Lichtenburg,
was it South Africa you fought for?
Which of our nations did you die for?
Or did you die for my parliament
and its thousand immutable laws?
Did you forgive us all our trespasses
in that moment of dying?

I was not at your gravesides, brothers,
I was afraid to go there.
But I read the threnodial speeches
how you in life so unremembered
in death became immortal.

Away with your threnodial speeches, says the Lord.
Away with your solemn assemblies.
When you lift up your hands in prayer
I will hide my eyes from you.
Cease to do evil and learn to do right,
pursue justice and champion the oppressed.

I saw a new heaven and a new earth
for the first heaven and earth had passed away
and there was an end to death
and to mourning and crying and pain
for the old order had passed away.

Is that what you died for, my brothers?

Or is it true what they say
that you were led into ambush?

[*Sunday Tribune*, Durban, 13.5.1973. The Nationalist Party came to power twenty-five years earlier on 26.5.1948.]

Where are you going, Afrikaner?

Yes, where are you going? And where are you taking me? I want to know because my future, and that of my children and my children's children, is in your hands.

You've ruled us for twenty-five years. Will you rule us for another twenty-five? Will you be here at all? It depends – to a great extent – on you.

I fear for my children and for you too. I fear you may destroy all you have built with much struggle and devotion. So I take the liberty of writing these words to you.

Some of you will be angry, but it is not my intention to anger you. What I want to do is to show you what a fellow South African, who knows your language and your literature and your history as well as many of you, thinks and feels about your future.

You are spending a million rands a day on arming yourself. This is as much as you spend on education, three-fifths of which is spent on your children and mine. If you were ever foolish enough to use your power to preserve your 'traditional way of life' – because that is what you say it is for – it would be the end of both your power and your way of life. The world would at last rise up in wrath against you. Don't deceive yourself that this would be another Vietnam, and that the world doesn't want another. The war in Vietnam was a disguised war between great powers. The great powers would not lift a finger to preserve your 'traditional way of life'.

There are religious zealots among you who say, 'It was God's will to make us, and if it is His will to destroy us, then God's will be done.' That's all very well for you, but it doesn't appeal to us. We've had enough *kragdadigheid*. We'd like some commonsense.

There's one thing you don't understand. It's not just that you can't preserve your traditional way of life with a gun. The fact is you can't preserve it at all. Your traditional way of life was to be the boss. It was interrupted for a while by the British. Then you got it all back, with a few totalitarian extras. Now you have to change it yourself. If you act with wisdom and

262

justice, you may save your language and your identity. But you can't save your *baasskap*.

The homelands won't save you. Dr. Verwoerd started a process the end of which is not yet in sight. Don't make them your enemies. You dare not.

When are you going to demand that your Government lays down decent minimum wages? Our wage determinations are a disgrace to a nation that calls itself Christian.

Some of you think it clever to tell our Black people that our country is rich and the guerillas want to take it from them. Do you think they believe it? Our Black policemen on the border, what do they die for? Job Reservation? Limehill?[1] And the Nico Malan Theatre?[2]

There is another thing you do not understand. You think you can control change with the law and the gun. You think your biggest enemies are on the border, but they're here. They are poverty, frustration, unjust treatment, and hatred of being shoved about. The majority of your fellow South Africans are not itching to fight for you. You have been spectacularly successful in alienating them.

You admire power, determination, physical courage, *kragdadigheid*. Moral courage in other people you are suspicious of. You throw out your Malherbes, Marquards, Kriges, Beyers Naudés. You shy away from love, compassion, and mercy, even from the words. You suspect those who use them of being Communist tools.

You think you can educate our children to have a 'proper national consciousness'. You can't. You won't succeed with any children but your own. And there are signs that even they are beginning to question the myths on which they were brought up.

Is there a chance for you? Can you alter your course? Can you have a change of heart? I just don't know. Your banning of students, your harrying of organisations, your threats to increase the value of Afrikaner votes, seem to show you still think in terms of Afrikaner power. That is why I am anxious about you and our country. Sometimes I despair of you.

The things you have to do to prove a change of heart are not easy ones. You must show yourself willing to narrow the gap between White wealth and Black poverty. You must improve drastically the standards of Black education. You must stop protecting inferior White workers at the expense of superior Black workers. You must make spectacular changes in

[1] A bare patch of ground in northern Natal to which, early in 1968, Africans whose villages had been proclaimed 'black spots' were unceremoniously removed.

[2] A theatre in Cape Town then reserved for the exclusive use of White people; in February 1975 it was opened to all races.

the colour bar.

Above all you must plan to share political power. No one expects you to rush into universal suffrage. But you must open your minds to the idea of federation. This is one country and you'll never make nine or ten of it.

I feel a deep concern for you when I think of the magnitude of the tasks you will have to perform. They will require a wisdom and courage none of us has shown as yet, and a new kind of patriotism, more generous, more all-embracing, than your patriotism of the last twenty-five years. If you enter these second twenty-five years without the firm resolve – to which kind of resolve you are not a stranger – to perform these tasks, that will be the end of you and me.

Evolution or revolution? It depends – to a great extent – on you.

[Review of Karel Schoeman, *Na die Geliefde Land*, Human and Rousseau, 1973. For this review Alan Paton won the Pringle Award for 1973. *Sunday Tribune*, Durban, 10.6.1973.]

A Noble Piece of Afrikaans Writing

I suspect this novel is a masterpiece. I cannot make the claim outright, because my judgement is largely subjective, the reason being that the theme of the novel is one that is always present in my mind. The theme is nothing less than the death of Afrikanerdom, though the publishers say it is something else. They actually call it, among other things, a description of farm life. In that case it is the story of a kind of farm life yet unknown to us, telling not of fields and fruit and flowers, but of grief and desolation, and of longing for the days that will not come again. The reluctance of the publishers to say what the book is about is understandable. How many Afrikaners would want to read a novel about the death of Afrikanerdom?

I should make it clear that the novel is not about the actual cataclysm, the 'troubles' which destroyed the Afrikaner countryside and which drove so many Afrikaners overseas. It is about the South Africa of twenty, thirty years later. At no point does the writer tell us what happened, nor does he tell us who destroyed the Afrikaner, but we can guess. Nor does he tell us how it comes about that there are still Afrikaners living on farms like 'Moedersgift' and 'Eensgevonden' and 'Kommandodrift', without labour, without hope. Nor does he tell us why the destroyer of the Afrikaner, the destroyer who surely must have had a fierce land-hunger of his own, still allows Afrikaners to occupy what one supposes to be large tracts of land. Yet it does not matter. Indeed, if we had been told too much, we would have lost the sense of the brooding presence of this desolation. One thing we know for certain: the Afrikaner has fallen from 'on high'.

It is one of those Afrikaners whose parents went overseas, George, son of Anna Neethling, who now returns to visit the country of his birth and to see the farm 'Rietvlei' which he has inherited from his mother. The confrontation is shattering. 'Rietvlei' is deserted, the homestead and the farm-buildings have been destroyed, and the road to it is disused and overgrown.

He finds a room with the Hattinghs, and from them – by inference and indirection – learns of the poverty, the lack of hope, the hidden grief of the remnants of Afrikanerdom. From the first page one is aware that a past and present tragedy is unfolding.

Karl Kraus said there were two kinds of writers – those who are and those who aren't. With the first, content and form belong together like soul and body. With the second, they match like body and clothes.

This seems to suggest that a good writer must not be too cerebrally and clinically conscious of what he is doing, and how he is making his book. That Mr. Schoeman is such a writer I have no doubt. Or perhaps I should say that in this particular novel he shows himself to be such a writer.

I do not know whether his other works have this characteristic, of a situation that is in itself so entire, so full of many meanings, that the writer does not have to use any devices – or does not appear to have to use them – because everything, every grief, every irony, every longing for that which cannot be again, is there already in the situation that he has chosen, so that even conversations themselves seem to have some mark of inevitability. I do not know whether Mr. Schoeman is always so fortunate but I hope to find out.

There are some terrible ironies in the book, and I shall record two of them. The first is that on these desolate farms there are still pictures of the past heroes, the ministers and the senators and the members of parliament, of all those in fact whose *kragdadigheid* and patriotism led Afrikanerdom to its doom. But the owners of the pictures do not understand this and talk with pride of these illustrious forerunners who, though they called themselves Afrikaners, could never come to terms with Africa.

The second example of irony is more cruel. The farmers give George a party at 'Kommandodrift', an occasion which is superbly described. It goes on till the early hours of the morning, when suddenly the dogs that have been shut up in some farm-building break out into demented barking. It is the police, with their uniforms, holsters, and guns. The schoolmaster is struck in the face and falls bleeding to the floor. The police laugh at the spectacle. What colour the police are we are not told, but we know. They shout at the young men, who endure it in silence. Then three of them are taken off. Whether they will ever be seen again, no one knows.

The scene is starkly reminiscent of what we already know. The 90 days, the 180 days, the death in the cell, the fall from the window, the laughing at the blood. How well one learns! Hattingh says:

'I feel that we must apologise to you for what happened there, George. Or in any case, for the fact that you were dragged in. We wanted to make you welcome here, we wanted you to feel at home with us. . . .'

George in his innocence asks how the young men can be held if they have done no wrong. Hattingh says, 'They can hold us or let us go, they can kill us or let us live, they do not have to answer for anything.'

George says, 'Such a thing is not possible,' and Hattingh says, 'That's how we live.'

It is time for George to go back to Switzerland. Young Paul Hattingh clings to him and begs to be taken away. 'It's the only chance I have, the only chance I'll ever get; you must help me. Help me, help me. I tell you I'm afraid.' But George will not take him. How would the passportless boy leave the country? He gives Paul the only thing he has to give – money.

The daughter Carla is tougher. He tries to tell her that he is sorry for all the hardness of their lives, but she interrupts him. 'You do not need to say anything, rather go.' He learns from her that 'Rietvlei' was destroyed because young Afrikaners plotted a rising there. He offers to marry her, but she will not. She will not go with him to a land of ease and self-reproach. Nor will she stay on the farm, and be trapped in memories. '*Ek wil iets uitrig; ek wil lewe. . . .*'[1]

But what that means one does not know. Father and Mother, Carla and Paul, they wave him goodbye. The aeroplane goes that night. Tomorrow morning he will be home.

So ends a remarkable book. But like all true works of art, whether on screen or stage or canvas or the printed page, it lives on in the mind. And it leaves two questions with me.

It is generally conceded that most writers have two supreme aims. The one is to write, the other is to be read. If a writer believes he has written a masterpiece, his joy of achievement is enhanced when others believe it too. The more people read him, the more joyful he will be.

A writer in Afrikaans cannot expect a great circle of readers. Quite apart from that, the theme of Mr. Schoeman's novel, so poignant, so compelling, cannot be expected to arouse the same response in other breasts. In all those countries where there is a burning hatred of apartheid, and therefore of Afrikaner nationalism, the grief of this book might well be greeted with indifference or gloating or glee. So a true work of literature might well be rejected for non-literary reasons. A South African publisher could offer a small reparation to Mr. Schoeman. He could publish the book in English. Quite apart from its claim to be literature, it is a book of prophecy, and as such should be read by as many White South Africans as possible.

That brings us to the second question. What is the prophecy? Will there be a cataclysm, and will only a remnant of Afrikaners be left, powerless and lost, some still in possession of their land by who knows what kind of

[1] I want to accomplish something; I want to live.

miracle, some bowing their heads to God or Fate, the only relics of their past being the hallowed names, 'Moedersgift' and 'Rietvlei' and 'Kommandodrift'? And if there is a cataclysm, will it be because it was inevitable, or could it have been avoided by Afrikaner deeds of love and generosity and courage and wisdom? Or is it beyond reason to expect rulers to do such deeds?

Did Mr. Schoeman intend to ask us these questions or was he simply extracting the last drop of blood out of the drama of Afrikanerdom? A writer may have two purposes. The first, of course, is to tell a story. The second may be to teach a lesson. But the second must never overwhelm the first. In fact the second must never be seen at all. One must never in the reading or hearing of the story suspect that one is being taught a lesson. *Na die Geliefde Land* meets these inexorable demands.

Will we turn in time? Will the Afrikaner turn in time? Is it really only power and privilege that he loves, or is it true that he loves South Africa? Hattingh makes it clear to George that there were two kinds who stayed, those who couldn't get away, and those who decided not to get away. But the ministers and the senators and the members of parliament were not conspicuous amongst them.

And what of the three young men who were taken away by the police from the party at 'Kommandodrift'? Are they not the kith and kin of the Mandelas[1] and Sobukwes,[2] the Hugh Lewins and the Eddie Daniels,[3] the students of NUSAS and SASO? Or were they the kith and kin of the ministers and senators who ran away?

Let us leave these questions. There are too many of them. And the biggest question of all we do not know the answer to. Let us return to literature, and record our thanks to Mr. Schoeman for this noble work in the Afrikaans language. And may we be preserved from the day when it is no more spoken, except in places of grief and desolation.

But that, of course, is not a literary question.

[2] Nelson Mandela, African leader, who is serving a life sentence on Robben Island, near Cape Town. He was convicted of having plotted the overthrow of the State. For Robert Sobukwe see note on page 208.

[3] Both have been imprisoned for sabotage. The former, having served his sentence, is now in Britain; the latter is still in jail.

[June 1973. Not previously published. Mrs. Helen Suzman was the sole Progressive Party member of parliament from 1961 to 1974. In the latter year she gained six colleagues. The University of Oxford conferred on her an Honorary Doctorate.]

For Helen Suzman

I take it upon myself, Helen Suzman, to write to you on behalf of all liberals in South Africa, including the ex-Liberals, the ex-members of the Liberal Party, which did not go defunct as the newspapers like to put it, but which was killed by the Prime Minister in 1968, because he did not like the idea of people of all races thinking and working together for the good of their common country.

We decided that we could not continue as a uniracial party, because we came into being as a consequence of our refusal to accept apartheid in our political and social and personal lives. It was therefore with a great sense of loss that we faced our new situation. Some of us retired from party politics, some joined other parties, some threw themselves into good works, some left the country, some withdrew into private life.

But one thing is certain, all of us who continued to concern ourselves with the things of love and justice, the dignity of the person, the rule of law, the honour of our country, began to look more and more to you as the champion of all these things. How you continue to do it, day after day, in that hostile or at the best, indifferent house, in the face of continuous and contemptuous interruption, we do not quite understand. But we understand well why one of the great universities of the world should wish to honour you for it.

Minister Horwood, with that inimitable gift of striking at the very heart of things and missing, once at a public meeting called you a 'bonny fighter'. We do not wish to cast any aspersions on your looks. But we know your fighting is not bonny, and we have no wish to be at the wrong end of it.

I know only one word to describe you as a parliamentarian and a politician, and the word is 'tough'. This leaves out a host of other qualities, but others will no doubt write of them. But if you were not tough, you would not be able to show these other qualities. You ascribe it to your peasant origins. I have no doubt your peasant forebears would be proud of you. You have many a time lifted up the hearts of those who were cast down. You have learned well the injunction of the great prophet to relieve the oppressed, to judge the fatherless, and to plead for the widow.

May Oxford be a big day for you. I know you have said you receive this degree in a representative capacity. That's true. It's also equally true that you receive it in your own personal capacity. We haven't made a study of all your predecessors. All we know is that there never was one who was more deserving of the honour that is being done you.

Siyakubonga![1]

---

[1] A Zulu expression of praise and thanks.

[*Sunday Tribune*, Durban, 28.10.1973.]

Eight Signposts to Salvation

Does a ruling group change towards those it rules because of considerations of justice? The answer is, almost certainly, no. Does it change because of internal and external pressures? Possibly, yes.

This second answer is not wholly encouraging. If the internal and external pressures become really dangerous, it may be too late to change. The people exerting the pressures may no longer care if you change. The time has come to destroy you. But the answer is not wholly discouraging. A ruling group may consent to change while it can still influence the situation. It may realise that the way to survival no longer lies in resistance to change. It may see the clouds on the horizon and know what they mean.

There is a not very nice picture that comes often to my mind. A man lives in a house full of possessions. The poor and the angry and the dispossessed keep knocking at the door. Inside some members of his family urge him to open the door and others tell him that he must never open the door. Then comes the final imperious knock, and he knows at last that he must open. And when he opens, it is Death who is waiting for him.

And the man is me, my wife, our children; he is the White man; above all he is the Afrikaner.

But I am not writing to spread gloom. I am writing especially for those inside the house who are telling the man to open the door. I am writing for White students and priests and newspapermen and trade unionists, for the young people of the United Party and the National Party and the Progressive Party, for all those who are working for change in this implacable land.

Why on earth do they do it?

They do it because of those strange unweighable and immeasurable things like hope and faith. And I admire them for it in this faithless world where for many nothing exists that cannot be weighed and measured, a world that believes in so little.

What a strange thing, to have been away from South Africa for some months, from its threats and bannings and denial of passports, and its implacability, and then to want to get back to it again!

Some people would say: Of course, you want to get back to your White comforts and privileges. Whatever truth there is in this it's not true enough. You want to get back because it's there that your life has meaning. You want to get back to those stubborn things which are the very stuff of your life. You want to get back to the students and the priests and the newspapermen. They make you feel you are alive more than all the sights of Paris and London and even Copenhagen.

These young White people, the Young Turks,[1] the young UPs and Progs and Nats, what do they want?

Well, at least it is clear what a great many of them want. They want nothing less than a new country. They have realised that White leadership and Anglo–Afrikaner solidarity and Afrikaner supremacy don't mean anything any more. Nothing means anything at all if its architects and planners are all White.

I am no longer a party man, and I must confess my impatience with those who think that any existing political party can possibly hold the best, wisest, most practicable solution for our problems, or can possibly know the best, wisest, most practicable way towards such a solution. Some of the computer-like arguments between party and party are exasperating. The house is burning down and the would-be saviours are arguing about what colour to choose for the buckets.

I don't expect younger White people to rush into a new party. But I do expect them to drop these useless recriminations. They must not shun one another. One thing binds them together that is greater than any loyalty to any party, and that is loyalty to their country and all its people.

Are there any things they might all agree about? I believe so and here they are. But I do not dogmatise about them.

1. The days of White domination are over.

2. The days of unilateral White political decisions are over.

3. The progress of the homelands to political independence – however much may be left to be desired – is irreversible.

4. The possibility that all or most of the homelands will eventually form a Black Federation must be recognised.

5. The possibility that the Black Federation may itself offer to federate with 'White' South Africa must be recognised.

6. If it does not make this offer, or if the offer is refused, then the final extinction of 'White' South Africa will be assured.

7. The offer will not be made if 'White' South Africa is not prepared to begin the dismantling of the machinery of apartheid.

[1] *Verligte*, or enlightened, members of the United Party.

8. It is the political constitution of the future 'White' South Africa that is the supreme political question facing all White people, especially young White people. When I say 'young', I don't mean only students. I mean all who are young enough to know that we must change or die.

The problem of 'White' South Africa is that there are:

Some four million Whites.

Some two million Coloured people.

Some 750,000 Asians.

Some eight million Africans.

According to Nationalist theory these eight million Africans are 'temporary sojourners'. They really belong somewhere else. But at least six million are permanent residents, *except for the fact that no urban African has any real sense of permanence*.

Four million Whites therefore constitute a third of the population of 'White' South Africa. The days of their domination are over. They are faced with the problem – the magnitude of which cannot be exaggerated – of constructing a social order in which justice will be done to all. And they cannot construct it unilaterally. Better wages, the quality of education, the quality of housing, the preservation of family life, all are important. But they are no longer gifts to be given by Whites to Blacks.

I beg to close with three questions to all White people who understand that we change or die. Is there any future for apartheid in 'White' South Africa? Is Afrikaner–English co-operation good enough, and is Afrikaner–English–Coloured–Asian co-operation not only unattainable, but downright dangerous? Is there any place for the qualified franchise in 'White' South Africa, or is it only another of these unilateral gifts?

Change is in the air. It will come whether we White people like it or not. It won't – it cannot – be completely safe, completely sure, completely satisfying. But it will be safer and surer and more satisfying if we take our share in bringing it about in the company of all our fellow South Africans.

[Not previously published. An address given in Durban in April 1974, when the author received the Central News Agency Literary Award for 1973 for *Apartheid and the Archbishop : The Life and Times of Geoffrey Clayton, Archbishop of Cape Town*, 1973.]

Pornography and Censorship

Mr. Chairman, Ladies and Gentlemen, it is an honour for me to receive this award from the Central News Agency for 1973. It is also a pleasure and a help to receive the handsome prize that goes with it. The writing of biography is an expensive occupation, unless one's research material is all to be found in South Africa, which was not the case in the biographies of Jan Hofmeyr and Archbishop Clayton. The cost of three or four years' work, at what one may call a reasonable but not an extravagant salary, cannot be recovered. It is extremely difficult for a South African publisher of a South African biography to produce a second edition. If there is a steady annual demand for 200 copies of the second edition, which would be good, it would take him ten years to dispose of a second printing of 2,000. The selling of British biography in Britain, and American biography in the United States, is a totally different proposition.

Indeed I would not be able to write biography at all if it were not for *Cry, the Beloved Country*, which continues to sell a six-figure total every year, though one must remember that this is no longer in expensive hardcover editions, and that the royalty taxes in overseas countries are very high.

It looks as though a long war waged by authors for some kind of royalty on books borrowed from lending-libraries is coming at last to a conclusion. For the more expensive books there are fewer buyers and more borrowers, but the author has received his royalty, not on the number of borrowings, but on the number of books bought by the library. It seems likely that in Britain this practice will soon be revised. Let us hope it will be revised here also.

However, I do not wish to waste this opportunity by using it to discuss the cost of authorship. There is another much more important problem, and it affects in the first place authors and publishers, in the second place readers, and in the third place every person who thinks seriously about the well-being of his society. This is the problem of censorship, and in no country is it a more immediate problem than in our own.

The rulers of our country concern themselves greatly with two social phenomena – pornography and subversion – and I shall confine myself to a discussion of pornography. The two phenomena are not however completely separable. There are people in this country who believe that there is a dark conspiracy to take South Africa away from them, and that the conspirators use pornography and permissiveness in general to corrupt the characters of the young. There are also people in this country who believe that subversive activity and even public protest are themselves a kind of pornography, and of course they are quick to note that protesters, and especially young protesters, like to draw attention to their protests by shocking the sensibilities of their elders, and particularly of the establishment, by examples of lavatorial art.

I do not belong to either of these schools, and I try as far as possible to examine the problem objectively. Is pornography harmful? Does pornography corrupt character or is the person who is attracted by pornography already sick? I do not think the question has been answered yet, nor am I sure that it ever will be answered. It seems as though pornography can have dangerous consequences when it is combined with physical cruelty and violence. In Britain a young man committed murder soon after seeing the film 'Clockwork Orange'. In the infamous 'Moor murders' it seems that the writings of the Marquis de Sade strongly influenced the murderers but was it perhaps the already sick persons and the sick literature which combined to produce their terrible consequence?

I have highly intelligent friends of what would be called stable character who, if they had to choose between pornography and censorship, would choose pornography. They argue that there are people who need pornography, and who may well be more dangerous if they don't get it. They argue that the appetite of censorship is insatiable, and that it will not confine itself to pornography, but will extend its powers to political and philosophical ideas, to news, indeed to every kind of thinking that is not acceptable to the establishment and is critical of government, rulers, and the policies of the ruling party.

And what indeed is my own attitude to the censorship of pornography alone? I have so far failed to define for you what pornography is, but it is an extremely difficult thing to do. If I follow the Shorter Oxford and Webster dictionaries I shall have to define also the words obscene, unchaste, licentious, and lewd. What does the word *risqué* mean? Or naughty? Or bawdy? I thought 'Oh! Calcutta' disgusting in many parts, but what does the word 'disgusting' mean? It means 'disgusting to me'. There was one scene in 'Oh! Calcutta' which was beautiful. It was a dance in the nude by a man and a woman. The dance was erotic in nature. It follows then that, to me, erotic is not necessarily pornographic. This serves to show that the task of definition is almost impossible. The film 'Deep Throat' is for me sheer pornography. It has no story worth telling, but has endless scenes of incredible gyrations. Yet it has been hailed as a major breakthrough in the field of sexual art.

I have a confession to make to you. I confess that the thought entered my mind that it would cause a sensation if I were to 'streak' tonight through the banqueting hall, even though my figure is not what it used to be. But I did not pursue the thought, not because it was licentious, but because it was unthinkable. I have not the figure or the courage or the wind for such a performance. But if I had done it, the reactions would have been very mixed. I think that the reactions of my present audience would have been strongly disapproving, not because of the licentiousness, but because of the bad taste. Of those who would read about it in the newspapers, some would have found it very funny, but this group would not have included members of my family.

Consider for a moment the art form known as the novel. It is supposed to be about life. It is supposed to hold a mirror to the face of society. It is supposed to be one form of expression of the truth about life, men and women, society. Now sexual love and sexual lust, the awakening to sex, the perversions of sex, fidelity and infidelity, sex for sex's sake, are all truths of life, and of women and men, and their society. What is the novelist to do about them? Is he to ignore them, or to wrap them in cotton wool and perfume?

It is my belief that a novelist has a right and even a duty to write about anything that is essential to the work of art that he is creating. If the treatment of sex is essential to the work of art, then he must treat it. But when he uses sex, not for the sake of his creation, but for money, sales, film rights, then he is writing pornography. This is an easy statement for me to make, but it by no means disposes of the problem. Suppose that the writer is describing a sex scene, and that the sex scene is essential to his story, and suppose that he appears to find excessive enjoyment in describing it, is he becoming pornographic? Should he find intense enjoyment in describing a sex scene, in the way that he might find intense enjoyment in describing a scene of natural beauty? What kind of scale should we draw up so that up to, say, 50 points it is pure art, but after that it becomes pornography? I say these things to make it clear how difficult it is to say what is pornographic and what is not.

Who is then to decide? In Denmark there is nothing to decide about, but South Africa is not Denmark. If the matter has to be decided, it must obviously be decided by persons, by some kind of a committee or board.

Now this country being what it is, I think it has to be accepted that there will for the foreseeable future be some kind of a board. I would not fight against it. I would certainly fight for it to be widely representative, and to include publishers and booksellers. I would certainly fight against giving this board the power to decide on appeals against its own judgments. And the country being what it is, I would abide by the final decision of a judge of the Supreme Court. I have read that the Minister – or some high official – I can't quite remember – has said that the trouble with a judge is that he is too judicial. And I think – but I won't swear to this – that this high personage went on to say that the judge couldn't help it, that was why they made him a judge.

Well, I had much rather be judged by a judge who was too judicial than by a moralist who was too moralistic. The judge, whether in the criminal or the civil court, sees all the strengths and frailties of our natures, the deceits, the jealousies, the hatreds, the lies, our offences and our repentances or our lack of them, our braveries and nobilities, our jokes and our pleasures. But he also has the task of judgment, and if he is a good judge he will overcome censoriousness and vengefulness. I would much rather entrust to him the care of the health of society than to any moralist, whose standards would tend to be impossibly remote, and would tend to be decided by his own prejudices and perhaps by his desire to please authority. Don't assume me to believe all judges are wonderful, but you may assume me to believe that judges make better judges than do moralists.

If one wishes to limit the power of censors, and I have no doubt that their powers ought to be limited, then the right way to do it is not by asking for their abolition, but by demanding the final right of appeal to the Courts.

If this right is taken away then I do not see much hope for the future of South African art or literature.[1] And I would say, in view of our history, our races and our languages, that no future could be more bright.

[1] This right has been taken away by the Publications Act 1974.

[*Christian Science Monitor*, Boston, 2.4.1974.]

Roy Campbell—Man and Poet

Roy Campbell is certainly the best known of all the South African poets who wrote or write in English. That is partly because his work appears in so many anthologies – and that again is because many of his poems are very good, and because the lyrics, as distinct from the satires, are easily understood. Many South African schoolchildren, even though they may not become readers of poetry, know who Roy Campbell was and something of what he wrote.

Campbell prided himself on the fact that his lyrics were easily comprehended. It was his aim to make them so. He wrote:

> I will go stark; and let my meanings show
> Clear as a milk-white feather in a crow
> Or a black stallion on a field of snow.

These three lines tell a great deal about his poetry. It is clear. It is not subtle; in fact he does not want it to be subtle. He is a master of imagery. His lyrics are essentially poems of the senses, not of the intellect. He makes great use of colour, even though these three lines are in black and white. We shall see also that he was a lover of sound, of violent words, violent movement. His poems are full of thunder, lightning, explosions, crashings, eagles, serpents (poisonous not otherwise), hurricanes and tempests. The wild animals of Africa, the wild horses of the Camargue, the wild bulls and the bullfighters of Spain, are all to be found there. In his first published work, *The Flaming Terrapin*, published in 1924 when he was 23, he poured out a spate of words upon the world, many of them new to poetry. His poetry was remarkable for its loudness and vigour, both of which revolted many of his contemporaries.

The Flaming Terrapin brought him instant fame. Among his admirers at that time were T. S. Eliot, Lawrence of Arabia and the Sitwells. Its very lack of subtlety and intellectuality, its savagery, its absence of any feeling of sorrow that one had been born, its boastfulness and its swashbuckling, were in such contrast to the poetry of England at that time that it was greeted with both excitement and revulsion.

Six years later, in 1930, Campbell published *Adamastor*, a collection of lyrics and satires. It contains – in my opinion – half-a-dozen of the finest poems of the 20th century. I shall choose one of them, 'The Zulu Girl'.

When in the sun the hot red acres smoulder,
Down where the sweating gang its labour plies,
A girl flings down her hoe, and from her shoulder
Unslings her child tormented by the flies.

She takes him to a ring of shadow pooled
By thorn-trees: purpled with the blood of ticks,
While her sharp nails, in slow caresses ruled,
Prowl through his hair with sharp electric clicks,

His sleepy mouth, plugged by the heavy nipple,
Tugs like a puppy, grunting as he feeds:
Through his frail nerves her own deep languors ripple
Like a broad river sighing through its reeds.

Yet in that drowsy stream his flesh imbibes
An old unquenched unsmotherable heat –
The curbed ferocity of beaten tribes,
The sullen dignity of their defeat.

Her body looms above him like a hill
Within whose shade a village lies at rest,
Or the first cloud so terrible and still
That bears the coming harvest in its breast.

This poem, which reveals Campbell's deep understanding of the South African situation, and which contains in its last two lines a prophecy of doom for white South Africa, shows that the absence in his verse of what one must call (in this brief space) *intellectuality* is not correlated in any way with an absence of *intelligence*. In fact Campbell despised intellectuality; it was anaemic, and could not comprehend the thunder, the tempest, the eagle and the bull. After *Adamastor* Campbell never wrote another poem of this kind.

There is reason to believe that Campbell was at this time strongly under the influence of the revolutionary ideas of William Plomer and Laurens van der Post, whose hatred of apartheid and racialism was intense. Campbell left South Africa for England, despised England and went to the Camargue, left the Camargue for Spain, and there gave his heart to the Spanish people, the Roman Catholic Church, and finally to General Franco.

His life in Spain, in the Catholic Church, and during the Civil War, gave an entirely new content to his verse. His new loyalties were flaunted in almost every poem.

He had already made enemies with his poem 'The Georgiad', which satirised the English literary world and its figures. Now their enmity was intensified by his support for Franco.

One must not give the impression that Campbell could not write anything but violent and tempestuous poetry. There is a quality of quite another kind in the first eight lines of 'To a Pet Cobra', a stanza which is – in my opinion – superb poetry.

> With breath indrawn and every nerve alert,
> As at the brink of some profound abyss,
> I love on my bare arm, capricious flirt,
> To feel the chilly and incisive kiss
> Of your lithe tongue that forks its swift caress
> Between the folded slumber of your fangs,
> And half reveals the nacreous recess
> Where death upon those dainty hinges hangs.

And there is yet another kind of beauty in 'Mass at Dawn'.

> I dropped my sail and dried my dripping seines
> Where the white quay is chequered by cool planes
> In whose great branches, always out of sight,
> The nightingales are singing day and night.
> Though all was grey beneath the moon's grey beam,
> My boat in her new paint shone like a bride,
> And silver in my baskets shone the bream:
> My arms were tired and I was heavy-eyed,
> But when with food and drink, at morning-light,
> The children met me at the water-side,
> Never was wine so red or bread so white.

If Campbell had left it to his lyrics and even his satires to speak for him, his reputation would have been bigger than it is today. But he wrote two autobiographies, *Broken Record*, which deals with the first thirty years of his life, and *Light on a Dark Horse*, which is a rewriting of the first book, but takes us up to the beginning of the Spanish Civil War of 1936, Campbell then being 35.

In these books Campbell sees himself as the flail, the scorpion, the lash. He chastises mediocrity, poems about hunted hares and cruel men. Charlie Chaplin he hated, the tragic symbol of the decline of the West. 'Anything therefore that savoured of conscious power, privilege, authority, was virtually spat upon and derided.' Campbell totally misunderstood the real meaning of Fascism and Hitlerism, and saw true modernity working in them. This he was later to regret, but I could not go so far as to say he repented.

In 1941 Campbell returned to London to take part in the Second World War. Dylan Thomas and he were very capable air raid wardens. At the end of the year he was accepted by the army. He wrote to his wife that after so long a period of ostracism, it gave him immense pleasure to find himself so popular in the regiment. In January 1946 he was accepted by the BBC as a talks producer. He was in fact re-establishing his tarnished reputation. In 1951 he did his best to destroy it again, when he published *Light on a Dark Horse*.

In the world of ideas Campbell moved with great elan and no skill whatsoever. He called Calvin and Luther crooks, and thought his praise of Afrikanerdom would be appreciated by the Afrikaners, who were Calvinist almost to a man. He despised Jews and Quakers. He thought that the killing of bulls should be reserved for the aristocrats of mankind, the people whom he called equestrian. He despised democracy, egalitarianism and any kind of socialism. He defended the virtues of illiteracy – he whose own literacy had opened to him so many doors. His hatred of communism and the communists amounted to a mania. He boasted of his own exploits, the kind that befitted a man.

Laurie Lee wrote of him that 'behind the arrogant chest-thumper there was a humble and kindly man capable of the most sensitive acts of friendship'. I have no doubt that this was true. But the trouble was that the great majority of his detractors had never met the man, they had read only the autobiographies.

We must leave the mystery there, of how so sensitive a poet could write so foolishly, so aggressively, about the affairs of mankind. In the closing paragraph of his introduction to *Light on a Dark Horse* Campbell says he was compelled to write the book 'so as to repay my debt both to Almighty God and to my parents, for letting me loose in such a world, to plunder its miraculous literatures, and languages, and wines; to savour its sights, forms, colours, perfumes, and sounds; to see so many superb cities, oceans, lakes, forests, rivers, sierras, pampas, and plains, with their beasts, birds, trees, crops, and flowers – and above all their men and women, who are by far the most interesting of all.'

That in part redeems the book. But one cannot forget that one of his main pleasures was to hold many men and women in contempt. That was the great flaw in his nature and, like his boastful swashbuckling, was caused no doubt by a deep lack of confidence in himself.

[*Race Relations News*, Johannesburg, June 1974.]

Gatsha Buthelezi

It is an irony that Chief Buthelezi's active political life, with its opportunities and frustrations, and its almost daily publicity, is the work of the late Dr. Verwoerd. Some think Buthelezi should have taken no part in the implementation of Separate Development; in other words he should have given up his hereditary duties. Some think he should go to Zambia and join the revolution, and yet others think he should start the revolution here.

There is really only one important person involved in Buthelezi's choice of what he does with his life, and that is Buthelezi himself. He has chosen to work within the framework of Separate Development. He has made it clear that it wasn't a wholly free choice.

There are lots of people around who know what Buthelezi should be doing. They are without exception people who haven't got his gifts. Very few knew he had those gifts. It was Verwoerd who posthumously showed them to the world. But the moment the gifts are known, the moment the owner becomes a public figure, from that moment some people want to use him for purposes of their own. And if he won't be used, he is a stooge and a sell-out; underneath all those lion-skins he's still a good boy.

Make no mistake about it, Buthelezi is no man's fool. His speeches (which according to some M.P.s are written by others) show a clear, informed, and sometimes cutting mind, with a great sense of what is appropriate for whom. His address to the Durban Jewish Club showed that he understood what it is to be a Jew, especially in a world that produced a Hitler. His answer to the northern revolutionaries cannot be bettered; he said in effect, 'I have to live there and you don't.' His intelligence is high, his English excellent, his knowledge of South African history very considerable, and of world affairs extensive. He likes discussion, but the final choice is his own. Though his name is known in Africa, Europe and America, he remains humble in the true sense. He would defer to any person, black or white, whom he thought to be good and wise.

He is a Christian. I don't want to embarrass him by saying he is a good one. Let us say that he knows what it is all about. He is – or seems to be – incapable of hatred or vengefulness, nor does he indulge in scandal or sneering. I should say, leaving personal relations out of account, that his loyalties are to Christ, humanity, South Africa, and the Zulu people, in that order. This must not be thought inconsistent with his statement that his first duty is to the Zulu people. That is his job. He is a pragmatist as well as an idealist.

Though guiding the Zulu nation is his first duty, he is a non-racialist. He does not go round beating the national breast. Although he is proud of being an African and a Zulu, he would not regard Zuluness and black-ness as the highest values. He would regard it as absurd in a man to regard his whiteness as his greatest possession.

Yet here the pragmatism reveals itself. He has made calls for black unity. If the whites can stand together for common advantage, why not the blacks too? He has said, 'I do not speak for Zulus only, but for all blacks.' And again, 'Our unity as blacks is the only way of making white South Africa listen to us.'

On yet another occasion he acknowledges the existence of white fear. It is something to be taken into account. It is a political factor. Buthe-lezi is perfectly capable of encouraging white South Africa today, and warning her tomorrow. But he knows what he is doing. He knows that a frightened man may do better, but that he may also do worse.

There is another reason for his adoption of this monitory role. Black Power and Black Consciousness watch Buthelezi with a calculating eye. If he visits a black university, he could be ignored, picketed, or given an ovation. A great deal would depend on his current form or on Black Power's current policy. But he does not want to alienate Black Power, he does not want black fragmentation. It is a complex role. He must frighten white South Africa but not too much, he must be a militant black leader but not intransigent. He is sensitive to criticism that he is not militant enough, that he hobnobs with the white liberals of the Christian Institute and the Institute of Race Relations, even though the Black Power leaders think that they smell, they being too negative to stink. He does not take kindly to those who tell him what he ought to do.

There is no easy life before him. Does he have to accept KwaZulu in eight or nine pieces? It looks like it. Will he get Richard's Bay? It doesn't look like it. The future does not depend so much on what he gets, but how he uses his gifts of intelligence and persuasiveness and bluntness to knock some sense into the heads of white South Africans. Will he and his colleagues open the door to some kind of federation that will have some of the elements of a common society? Will it be a unitary society? It doesn't look like it. He will have to contend with those who demand that South Africa must be one and indivisible. Without revolution, that lies many years away.

Can he stand in mind and body the tremendous pressures under which he will have to live for years to come? There are those in Pretoria, and a few in KwaZulu, who would like to see him broken. Therefore one prays that he may be given generously the gifts of courage and wisdom. South Africa cannot afford to have him broken.

[Paper read at Koinonia, Botha's Hill, 17.9.1974. Not previously published.]

The Nature and Ground of
Christian Hope Today

I find that in the closing years of my life I am being asked to speak, and to discerning audiences too, on themes to which I have never devoted what might be called systematic thought. I have always regarded theologians and philosophers as systematic thinkers, and I have had some envy of those whose actual job it was to think systematically, and who actually got paid for it.

I have only one claim to speak to you today, and that is that I am a man of hope, that to me hope is inseparable from life. If there is one human action the contemplation of which fills me with grief, it is the act of suicide, especially when it is committed by someone who is young. For such a person presumably has been living without hope, and has presumably come to the conclusion that it is better to be dead.

I am not only a man of hope, but I have thought a great deal about hope, and especially in my more mature years. And I have thought about it in my non-systematic manner. This is not false modesty on my part. I think I have thought about hope intelligently, but not systematically. Lastly, I speak as a Christian, but as one who is afraid of dogmatic thought, and believes it has done great harm to the Church. It seems to me that ultimate reality, assuming that there is such a thing, can be comprehended only by God, and that therefore we should not pontificate about it. That is why, for example, I am unable to comprehend the doctrine of the Trinity. In fact I am a humble disciple of Francis of Assisi, who found that the only way to respond to the incomprehensibility of the Creation, and the beauty and terror of human life, was to pray to be made the instrument of God's peace. There is a wound in the Creation, and it groans and travails until now, and I don't know why; therefore I follow Francis, and ask to be given some part in the healing of it. It is the only way in which I can give meaning to my life, and indeed meaning to life upon the earth.

When young people who have no religious faith, or certainly no dogmatic faith, and would call themselves atheists or agnostics – when they sing 'We shall overcome, we shall overcome some day', what is the ground of their hope? It surely can only be some kind of faith that the universe is such that righteousness will triumph. It is a hope that has no rational basis whatsoever, and it seems to me to be related to a belief of which I am intensely sceptical, in spite of Teilhard de Chardin, namely a belief in the perfectibility of man. Here again is a matter on which we dare not dogmatise. It is a humbling thought that 1900 years after Christ, Europe could produce a Hitler. Who is right, Teilhard de Chardin or W. B. Yeats, who wrote those lines:

> . . . but now I know
> That twenty centuries of stony sleep
> Were vexed to nightmare by a rocking cradle,
> And what rough beast, its hour come round at last,
> Slouches towards Bethlehem to be born?

This belief, this faith, is surely akin to the faith of Isaiah expressed in his vision, in words that can only be described as ineffable. And although I prefer them in the old Bible I shall read them from the New, just to prove that there are some words and thoughts so ineffable that even modern language cannot destroy their ineffability.

> Then the wolf shall live with the sheep,
> and the leopard lie down with the kid;
> the calf and the young lion shall grow up together,
> and a little child shall lead them;
> the cow and the bear shall be friends,
> and their young shall lie down together.
> The lion shall eat straw like cattle;
> the infant shall play over the hole of the cobra,
> and the young child dance over the viper's nest.
> They shall not hurt or destroy in all my holy mountain;
> for as the waters fill the sea,
> so shall the land be filled with the knowledge of the Lord.

I must confess that when I read that the infant shall play over the hole of the cobra, and the young child dance over the viper's nest, I cannot help remembering the older words, 'And the sucking child shall play on the hole of the asp, and the weaned child shall put his hand on the cockatrice' den.'

The vision of Isaiah is paralleled in the New Testament by the vision of John of Patmos, who sees a new heaven and a new earth, for the first heaven and the first earth are passed away; and in the new heaven and the new earth God shall wipe every tear from their eyes, and there shall be an end of death, and to mourning and crying and pain; for the old order is passed away.

What grounds are there to hope for that holy mountain, and for the new heaven and the new earth? Can you find them in the newspapers? or in the journeys of Dr. Kissinger? or in the deliberations of Vatican Councils? The fact is that although we shall never reach the holy mountain, the whole journey of the Christian life is directed towards it. It is the vision of the unattainable that determines what we shall attain. There is no holy mountain. It exists only in the vision of the prophets. Yet the vision of it can move men and women to unparalleled deeds, and to lives devoted to what is just and holy. Therefore our hope is concerned with the Future and the Now.

But before I attempt to define the ground of hope, I want to tell you that William the Silent, who would certainly have called himself a Christian, thought that it was possible to act without hope. Now I assume that all of us would think it impossible to live without hope, but we must recognise that there are times when one must act, not because one hopes, but for the simple reason that it is one's duty. William the Silent said, 'It is not necessary to hope in order to undertake, and it is not necessary to succeed in order to persevere.'

In a country like South Africa there are many things that must be undertaken without any hope that the ventures will be successful, and there are many ventures with which one must persevere in spite of this lack of success. I am told that this is stoicism, and that stoicism is not a Christian virtue. I find that hard to believe, but do not propose to argue it. All I would like to say is that these words of William the Silent have been very much valued by me. I think that in his use of the word 'hope' he is referring to this or that particular venture, and that he is not suggesting that man can be indifferent to hope. That would surely be the ultimate stoicism, and I do not think it can be reconciled with the Christian teaching about hope.

I have one last introductory thing to say about hope. It *is* possible to cherish hope without a ground. Sometimes we describe a person as having a hopeful temperament. We say that he looks on the bright side of things. We use the quite unprovable proverb, 'Every cloud has a silver lining.' We also speak of people as having a melancholy temperament. They look on the dark side of things. For them every silver lining has a cloud. People sometimes ask me the extraordinary question, Are you an optimist or a pessimist? Yet we must acknowledge that hope, or at least hopefulness, may depend on the state of our own metabolism, on gland secretion, on physical health. All of us know that it is possible to rise one morning feeling depressed and hopeless, and on another, buoyant and full of hope, whereas there has been no change whatsoever in our circumstances. This knowledge should make us wary of pontificating about hope.

What is our Christian hope? What do I as a Christian hope for most in the world? How careful one must be here! If there are psychologists and psychiatrists in the audience, I would ask them now to recuse themselves, and cynics also. For it is the triumph of righteousness that I hope for most, and of course most of all I hope for it in my own country. One cannot separate this desire for the triumph of righteousness from one's desires for happiness, for the happiness of those one loves, for health, for recognition, for freedom from want, for other things innumerable. One's motives for pursuing righteousness may be extremely mixed; the desire to be important and well known and to be held in esteem may well be there too. One thing I have learned is that one must never yield a noble quest just because one or more of one's motives are not so noble. Can I give any proof that the hope for the triumph of righteousness is my most cherished hope? Yes, I think I could. At the age of 71 one is no longer easily moved, by a preacher or a speaker or a story or a poem, or indeed by any words. Yet the passages I read to you from Isaiah and Revelation, and the stories of the Good Samaritan and the washing of the disciples' feet, still have power to move me deeply – I think it would not be wrong to use a phrase which would be avoided by good writers – *they move me to the depth of my being*. We are contemplating some kind of perfection. It is a moral perfection conveyed in simple and what appear to be artless words, but the art of them is sublime.

Yet the vision of the triumph of righteousness is the same in its essential elements as the vision of Isaiah and of John of Patmos. You will note that in Isaiah's vision there is an end of conflict and hurt and destruction, and the Lord rules the land. In John's vision the world is made anew, and there is an end to death and sorrow and pain, and the Lord rules heaven and earth. The element of compassion is dominant, as it is in the famous passage beginning, 'Behold my servant, whom I uphold; mine elect in whom my soul delighteth,' for the Lord says, 'I will bring the blind by a way that they knew not. . . . I will make darkness light before them, and crooked things straight. These things will I do unto them and not forsake them.' So in the vision of the triumph of righteousness in one's own country, the element of compassion is very strong.

So I, with no pretensions to be an Isaiah or a John, cherish the same hope, and am sustained by it, though it appears to have no chance of realisation. From whence then its might and its power?

It is, I think, clear that its might and its power cannot come from any source but the highest and the deepest that man is capable of comprehending. The might and the power of hope must come, and can only come, from a faith that there is a Might and a Power that is above all, and that rules all, and directs all. It is a faith in the Holy Spirit, that He moves abroad in the world, that He contains all and sustains all; and the inevitable corollary of this faith is that the Holy Spirit is in us, and can use us in the achievement of His purposes. Yet this might and this power are not to be confused with any might or power of this earth; they are totally of another order. This distinction is made clear in the book of the prophet Zachariah, where it is said to Zerubbabel, 'not by might nor by power, but by my spirit, saith the Lord'. It is not the power of rulers and parliaments and armies, but the power of the Spirit; and when men and women have believed in such a power, they are able, if it is required of them, to defy rulers and parliaments and armies.

The confidence and security given by such a faith in the power of the Spirit is immense. For it can in fact put an end to fear. Aldous Huxley, who was not a Christian, writes this about faith in the power of the Spirit, though he calls it 'the loving and knowing of the divine Ground'.

'Fear cannot be got rid of by personal effort, but only by the ego's absorption in a cause greater than its own interests. Absorption in any cause will rid the mind of some of its fears; but only absorption in the loving and knowing of the divine Ground can rid it of *all* fear. For when the cause is less than the highest, the sense of fear and anxiety is transferred from the self to the cause – as when heroic self-sacrifice for a loved individual or institution is accompanied by anxiety in regard to that for which the sacrifice is made. Whereas if the sacrifice is made for God, and for others for God's sake, there can be no fear or abiding anxiety, since nothing can be a menace to the divine Ground, and even failure and disaster are to be accepted as being in accord with the divine will.'

And that of course is true; if one's ultimate faith is in the power of the Spirit, despite wars and pestilences and man's inhumanity to man, and despite what would appear to be to some a complete and utter indifference of the Creator to His Creation, if indeed there is such a being as a Creator and such a work as the Creation, then such faith is the end of fear. But that kind of faith is not only the end of fear, it is the indestructible ground of hope.

I now venture into a difficult field for a non-theologian. It would, I think, be my fault if any of my hearers imagined that for me the Christian hope is not sufficiently identified with Christ. However, the theology is for me extremely complicated. Jesus did not embark upon his mission until he had received the gift of the Holy Spirit. When after the Crucifixion he appeared to his disciples he breathed on them, saying, 'Receive the Holy Spirit.' Earlier at the Last Supper he had told them that he would ask for another to be sent to them, the Spirit of Truth who would be with them for ever; yet almost in the same sentence he says it is he himself who is coming back to them. You will remember also those words of Genesis, 'And the Spirit of God moved upon the face of the waters,' and one must remember them in conjunction with the words used by Jesus to the Jews, 'Before Abraham was, I am.' And then of course came the day of Pentecost, when the Spirit of God was poured out on the disciples.

Although the concept of the Spirit is encountered at the very beginning of the Old Testament, it begins to appear with greater and greater frequency from the beginning of the gospel according to St. John. The early Christian Church is above all the Church of the Holy Spirit. Is the Church of today the Church of the Holy Spirit? Or is it the Church of Christ crucified, resurrected, and then departed? Is it perhaps true to say that the Church of today is afraid of the Holy Spirit? Is it perhaps true to say that the South African Churches, the Dutch Reformed Churches, the Romans, the Anglicans, the Methodists, the Congregationalists, the Presbyterians, are all afraid of the Holy Spirit? I do not presume to speak for the Black Churches. I read that Dominee J. D. Vorster says that those who will not fight for South Africa are traitors. Why? Has the Holy Spirit become the property of the South African Government? Is the Holy Spirit trying to speak to us from Hammanskraal? Or does He speak to us from the Prime Minister's Office? I do not like to ask these questions. Is it not a further proof of the beauty and terror of human life that the Spirit which dwells upon the holy mountain where no one hurts or destroys is the same Spirit that can blow like a raging tempest through our churches and our parliaments and our traditional ways of life? Yet it is not strange; for it is written, 'I have long time holden my peace; I have been still and refrained myself; now will I cry like a travailing woman; I will destroy and devour at once.'

Let me conclude by saying something of our hope for our own country. All of us hope that our country, so race-corrupted, so fear-corrupted, will become – by peaceful means, we say, but I think the word 'peaceful' is too absolute – a more just, a more humane, a more Christian country. And many of us hope that this will happen soon, because we fear that if it does not happen soon, the day of the triumph of righteousness will be indefinitely postponed, and we shall have to live through a period of violence and desolation, and if we are white, our desolation will be the greater.

You all know that many people have rebelled against the other-world-liness and the future-worldliness of the Christian faith. They don't want pie-in-the-sky; they want pie-on-the-table. And what happens if they don't get pie-on-the-table? The logical thing – and a common thing – is to conclude that there's no pie at all; in other words, to give up faith and therefore hope.

Now suppose that you are a Christian and that your pie is the triumph of righteousness. And suppose that your particular South African right-eousness does not triumph. What are you to do? Are you to fall back on God's righteousness, which, St. Paul tells us, is not the same as our right-eousness? Are you in fact going to fall back on pie-in-the-sky?

To my mind there is only one resolution of this difficulty for me as a Christian. My dearest hope is for the triumph of righteousness, especially in my own country. But that is the holy mountain, that is the unattainable which determines what you may attain. And if righteousness did triumph, would you know, would you believe it? Or would you say as the parson said, when after a prayer the intransigent car engine suddenly started, 'Well I'll be damned!'?

Jesus said of the day of the triumph of righteousness, 'of that day and that hour knoweth no man, not even the Son, only the Father'. The date of the day of the triumph of righteousness is not our affair. Our task is to be the instruments of the Holy Spirit, knowing in full faith that His purpose also is the triumph of righteousness.

Do you remember those lines in Thomas Hardy's poem 'The Oxen'?

> Yet, I feel,
> If someone said on Christmas Eve,
> 'Come; see the oxen kneel,
>
> In the lonely barton by yonder coomb
> Our childhood used to know,'
> I should go with him in the gloom,
> Hoping it might be so.

I read the following passage of this address to a friend of mine: Is the Church of today the Church of the Holy Spirit? Or is it the Church of Christ crucified, resurrected, and then departed? Is it perhaps true to say that the Church of today is afraid of the Holy Spirit? Is it perhaps true to say that the South African Churches, the D.R.C.'s, the Romans, the Anglicans, the Methodists, the Congregationalists, the Presbyterians, are all afraid of the Holy Spirit? And my friend said, don't you think there are signs that the South African Churches are today listening to the Holy

Spirit? And I guessed that he was thinking of the Christian Institute and of SPROCAS, and perhaps of the new Archbishop of Cape Town and his enthronement sermon, and certainly of the SACC resolution at Hammans-kraal.

And of course I could have said to him, 'I'll go with you in the gloom, hoping it might be so.' But being a Christian, though a poor one, I said to him, 'Let us pray that it may be so.'

Glossary

Anerley: a village on the south coast of Natal

asseblief: (Afrikaans) please

baasskap: (Afrikaans) boss-ship, overlordship

banning order: a restriction imposed arbitrarily by the Government: normally a 'banned' person may not attend gatherings, may not leave a particular magisterial district, and may not be quoted

Bantu: African people: the word could be used without giving offence until it was appropriated by the Nationalist Government; now even the Government has begun to abandon it

Bavenda: an African people living in the north of South Africa

black consciousness: the view that fundamental political change can be brought about only by pressure from black people and that in order to exert this pressure blacks must become actively conscious of their corporate identity and of their potential power

Black Sash: a women's organisation dedicated to the promotion of 'peace and justice for all persons and peoples' in South Africa

blacks: all South Africans who are not 'white': the word has been used with increasing frequency in the last five years

Botha's Hill: a village situated between Durban and Pietermaritzburg

Buthelezi, Gatsha: Chief Minister of Kwa-Zulu

Butler, Guy: poet, playwright and university professor

Christian Institute: an ecumenical and non-racial body dedicated to the study and the implementation of the social aspects of the teachings of the Gospels

Christian-Nationalism: an amalgam fostered by a system of indoctrination known as Christian National Education

Coloured: of mixed black and white descent

Daar kom die Alabama: 'Here comes "The Alabama" ', an Afrikaans song popularly associated with the Coloured community

dagga: (Afrikaans) marijuana

die boeke: (Afrikaans) the books

Die Held: 'The Hero'

Die Stem van Suid-Afrika: 'The Voice of South Africa', the official national anthem

Diep River: suburb of Cape Town

Diepkloof Reformatory: (see p. 1)

Dominee: the title of a minister of religion

D.R.C.: Dutch Reformed Church

eenling: (Afrikaans) loner

Eensgevonden: (Dutch) once found

Groutville: a village in Natal

Hammanskraal: near Pretoria; the site of a seminary at which, in August 1974, a conference of the South African Council of Churches passed a resolution calling upon all Christians to consider seriously the question of conscientious objection

Hillcrest: a village situated between Durban and Pietermaritzburg

Hoernlé, Alfred: Professor of Philosophy at the University of the Witwatersrand from 1923 to 1943

Hofmeyr, Jan H.: eminent administrator and politician, for some years spokesman for the liberal cause in Parliament; Alan Paton's biography of him appeared in 1964 (1894–1948)

homelands: African 'reserves' (as they were previously called), comprising about 13 per cent of the total area of South Africa: they are now being given a certain amount of limited autonomy, and are destined, according to Nationalist policy, for complete political independence

Horwood, Owen: Nationalist cabinet minister

huistoe: (Afrikaans) go home

Ilange lase Natal: 'The Sun of Natal', a newspaper

Indians: South Africans of Indian origin

Ingwavuma: a river in northern KwaZulu

Institute of Race Relations: (see South African Institute of Race Relations)

Jabavu, John Tengo: newspaper editor and political leader (1859–1921)

Jacobson, Dan: South African writer now living in Britain

Jaycees: JCCs, Junior Chambers of Commerce, an organisation of men between the ages of 18 and 40 devoted partly to the furtherance of goodwill

Jones, Edith Rheinallt: (see pp. 239–40)

Kaapse: (Afrikaans) of the Cape

kaffirboom: (Afrikaans) African tree, an indigenous tree with bright red flowers kerkraad: (Afrikaans) church council

kind: (Afrikaans) child

King, Dick: the man who in 1842 rode on horseback from Port Natal to Grahamstown to carry the news of a Boer attack

kom binne: (Afrikaans) come in

Kommandodrift: (Dutch) commando ford

kragdadigheid: (Afrikaans) strength, rule by show of force

Krige, Uys: a writer in both Afrikaans and English, who has been an outspoken opponent of authoritarianism

KwaZulu: the 'homeland' of the Zulu nation

Liberal Party: a non-racial political party, which had as its policy the creation of a 'common society' in South Africa (see page 123)

Lions: an organisation devoted to the service of the community

locations: African areas on the edges of cities and towns; also known as townships

Luthuli, Albert: (see pp. 159, 250–2)

Maatland: the fictional name of an Afrikaans-speaking university

Malan, D. J.: Prime Minister of South Africa from 1948 to 1954

Malherbe, E. G.: former Principal of the University of Natal and an outspoken critic of the Nationalist Government

Marquard, Leo: founder of the National Union of South African Students, historian and eminent liberal (1897–1974)

meisiekind: (Afrikaans) small girl

Moedersgift: (Dutch) mother's gift

Na die Geliefde Land: (Afrikaans) 'To the Beloved Land'

Nationalist: belonging to the National Party, the party that has been in power since 1948

Native: an African person: the term was generally acceptable until the 1940s, but is today used only by elderly or unaware whites

natuurkind: (Afrikaans) nature child

Naudé, Beyers: founder and national director of the Christian Institute

Nederduits Gereformeerde Kerk: the largest of the three Dutch Reformed Churches in South Africa

non-European: (see 'non-White')

non-White: a word used to describe all South Africans who are not 'white': today the word is usually regarded as objectionable, as it defines by means of a negation

NUSAS: National Union of South African Students

Ons, die Afgod: (Afrikaans) 'We, the Idol'

Ons sal lewe, ons sal sterwe, ons vir jou, Suid-Afrika: (Afrikaans) 'We shall live, we shall die, we for you, South Africa', the last two lines of the national anthem

Orlando: an African township on the edge of Johannesburg

Parktown: a smart 'white' Johannesburg suburb

phelile: (Zulu) finished

pragtig: (Afrikaans) beautiful

pret: (Afrikaans) fun

Progressive Party: a political party which believes in the progressive extension of the franchise

referaat: (Afrikaans) report

Reisigers na Nêrens: (Afrikaans) 'Travellers to Nowhere'

reserves: parts of South Africa set aside for the exclusive occupation of African peoples: the reserves represent about 13 per cent of the total area of the country (see 'homelands')

Richard's Bay: a new port, about 150 kilometres north of Durban

Rietvlei: (Afrikaans) marshy valley with reeds

ring: (Afrikaans) circuit

SACC: South African Council of Churches

S.A.P.: South African Party, forerunner of the United Party

SASO: South African Students' Organisation, a black student body dedicated to the ideals of 'black consciousness'

Separate Development: the Nationalist Government's word for apartheid; sometimes a slightly more sophisticated version of apartheid

SPROCAS: Study Project on Christianity in Apartheid Society; it was sponsored by the Christian Institute and the South African Council of Churches

South African Institute of Race Relations: a body dedicated to the study of racial problems and the promotion of racial harmony

Suid-Afrikaanse Akademie: (Afrikaans) South African Academy

Sy Kom met die Sekelmaan: (Afrikaans) 'She Comes with the Sickle Moon'

townships: African areas on the edges of cities and towns; also known as locations

Transkei: the 'homeland' of the Xhosa nation

uhuru: (Swahili) freedom

Umtwalumi: a river in southern Natal; today usually spelt 'Mtwalume'

Union: Union of South Africa, created in 1910; South Africa became a republic in 1961

United Party: the official Opposition in the South African Parliament

Vendaland: an African area (now a 'homeland') in northern Transvaal

Verwoerd, H. F.: Prime Minister of South Africa from 1958 to 1966, and the chief architect of 'separate development'

volk: (Afrikaans) people

Volksrust: a town in northern Natal

Voortrekkers: Afrikaner pioneers who took 'white' culture and domination to the interior of the country

Vorster, J. B.: Prime Minister of South Africa since 1966

Vorster, J. D.: a very influential member of the Dutch Reformed Church; brother of the Prime Minister

vryheid: (Afrikaans) freedom

Wayfarers: 'a kind of Girl Guides for non-white children'